Permissible Dose

Permissible Dose

A History of Radiation Protection in the Twentieth Century

J. Samuel Walker

UNIVERSITY OF CALIFORNIA PRESS

Berkeley / Los Angeles / London

Published 2000 by the University of California Press
Berkeley and Los Angeles, California

University of California Press, Ltd.
London, England

Prepared by the Nuclear Regulatory Commission; work made for hire.

Library of Congress Cataloging-in-Publication Data

    Walker, J. Samuel.

  Permissible dose : a history of radiation protection in the twentieth
  century / J. Samuel Walker.

    p.   cm.

  Includes bibliographical references and index.

  ISBN 0-520-22328-4 (cloth : alk. paper)

    1. Radiation—Safety measures—History.   2. Nuclear energy—
Law and legislation—United States—history.   I. Title.

  TK9152.W35   2000

  363.17'996'0904—dc21   00-023398

Manufactured in the United States of America

09   08   07   06   05   04   03   02

10   9   8   7   6   5   4   3   2

Contents

Figures

Preface

This book is the third in a series of volumes on the history of nuclear regulation sponsored by the United States Nuclear Regulatory Commission (NRC). I am the coauthor, with George T. Mazuzan, of the first volume, *Controlling the Atom: The Beginnings of Nuclear Regulation, 1946–1962,* and the author of the second volume, *Containing the Atom: Nuclear Regulation in a Changing Environment, 1963–1971,* which were published by the University of California Press in 1984 and 1992 respectively. Each is a detailed history of major regulatory issues during the chronological period it covers. This book takes a somewhat different approach by examining the various facets of a single problem—radiation protection—over a period of about one hundred years.

Many years ago, when I was an employee of the National Archives, I met a senior scholar who was researching a book on a former president of the United States. He introduced himself to me and to others by saying that he was writing *the* biography of that president. My colleagues and I were amused and rather astonished by the pretentiousness of his claim, as we knew of several able scholars who had recently published or were working on books about the same subject. At the same time, however, we had to admit to a certain amount of grudging regard for a scholar with enough confidence to make such a claim without blushing. Now that I am quite a bit more senior, I remembered that experience when deciding on a title for this book. I thought that the subtitle "*The* History of Radiation Protection in the Twentieth Century" had a nice ring to it.

But then I blushed, because a subtitle suggesting that this book covers the entire subject of radiation protection since the discovery of x-rays would be misleading. In keeping with the institutional setting in which I write, the book focuses on the role of federal agencies in radiation safety and the evolution of radiation protection regulations. It traces how the principles and practices of radiation protection have changed over time in response to scientific and political developments. Much of the contentious debate over radiation has centered on the decisions and activities of the federal government, and this book attempts to explain and evaluate those controversies. Radiation protection is a complex and emotional topic that is difficult to sort out without a solid foundation in its historical background. My purpose is to contribute to that foundation by discussing the federal government's substantial and often predominant part in the history of efforts to provide adequate protection against the hazards of radiation to workers exposed in their jobs and to the general public.

There are several important aspects of the history of radiation protection that I do not treat at length. The history of radiation safety in nuclear weapons programs and the history of x-ray technology have been admirably covered by, in the former case, Barton C. Hacker, and, in the latter case, Bettyann Holtzman Kevles. I draw on their work as it relates to the development of radiation standards and public attitudes toward radiation hazards, but I do not retread the paths they have broken. I do not delve deeply into the activities and recommendations of scientific and professional groups or the role of the states in radiation protection, both of which need fuller discussion than I am able to provide here. And, despite my focus on federal activities, I do not deal with every element or nuance of federal regulations; to do so would run the risk of bogging down in excessive detail (the basic NRC regulation on radiation protection alone runs to more than one hundred printed pages). What I have attempted to do in this book is to show both continuity and change in the basic "permissible doses" for radiation protection over a period of several decades. That in itself was a challenging task, and now that it is completed, I hope to devote my energies to writing *the* history of Three Mile Island.

This book does not in any way represent an official position of the Nuclear Regulatory Commission on the issues it discusses. It is the product of my own professional training and judgment, and I bear full responsibility for its contents. The NRC placed no restrictions on me in the course of writing this book, and I had complete independence in deciding on its structure, approach, direction, and conclusions. The findings that I report and the conclusions that I reach in this book should be viewed as my own and not as a policy statement of the NRC.

I am grateful to many people who helped to make this book possible. I owe a large debt to Kathleen J. Nawyn and John G. Kinzie, historians with History Associates, Inc., who served as my research assistants on a part-time basis for a total of four years. Both demonstrated the skills that are absolutely essential for any good research historian—imagination in figuring out where to look for relevant documents and relentlessness in tracking them down. Those talents, along with another critical but more commonplace ability—deft speed on the copying machine—made the job of writing this book easier and, indeed, made it feasible. I also greatly appreciated having Ms. Nawyn and Mr. Kinzie around my office because they took so much interest in the subjects they researched. This gave me the rare pleasure of talking with other historians about the content of documents a quarter of a century old or the distinction between fencepost cows and real cows.

Archivists in the institutions in which I conducted research were enormously helpful. I am especially grateful for the assistance and expertise provided by Marjorie Ciarlante and Maryellen Trautman of the National Archives; Karen Holzhausen, Nancy Mirshah, William H. McNitt, and Jennifer Sternaman of the Gerald R. Ford Library; Martin Elzy of the Jimmy Carter Library; Daniel Barbiero of the National Academy of Sciences; Karyl Winn and Gary Lundell of Manuscripts and University Archives at the University of Washington; and Elizabeth Andrews of the Institute Archives at the Massachusetts Institute of Technology. I also benefited greatly from the assistance of colleagues in other federal historical offices, particularly Roger Anders and Betsy Scroger of the Department of Energy and John Swann and Donna Hamilton of the Food and Drug Administration.

Over a period of many years, I have been the beneficiary of strong support from the top levels of the NRC on down. The agency has provided me with the resources I need to conduct a historical program and required only that I seek to do it in a way that meets high professional standards. Of the many friends and colleagues at the NRC who assisted in the preparation of this book, I wish to acknowledge with special thanks those who read the entire manuscript in draft form and gave me very useful comments: Edward McGaffigan, Jr. (who offered much-appreciated encouragement), John H. Austin, Andrew L. Bates, Peter G. Crane, and John N. Sorensen. I am also indebted to Dr. Bates, Kathleen Ruhlman, Marsha Ward, and Elizabeth Yeates for easing and speeding the process of making nonpublic NRC documents cited in the notes of this volume available for research in the agency's Public Document Room. My colleagues in the Office of the Secretary have long provided moral support and valuable assistance for my historical projects, even when they were not as deeply concerned about subjects like real cows and fencepost cows as I was. I am very appreciative of the patronage and occasional advocacy that I have received from the Secretaries of the Commission under whom I have worked, Samuel J. Chilk, John C. Hoyle, and Annette Vietti-Cook.

I am also deeply grateful to Stanley Holwitz, assistant director of the University of California Press. Unlike most scholarly books, the manuscripts that I have written for the NRC have to go through the government's contract process before being evaluated by the press. Mr. Holwitz has been involved in the press's consideration and publication of the previous two volumes, but for the first time, perhaps to his regret, he was the point man for working through the government's contract procedures. I very much appreciate his willingness to take on that task, as well as the professionalism, courtesy, and commitment to excellence that he and his staff have demonstrated in the review, editing, and production process of three books.

J. Samuel Walker
Rockville, Maryland
June 1999

CHAPTER ONE

The Discovery
of Radiation and Its Hazards

During a period of several decades after the German physicist Wilhelm Konrad Roentgen discovered x-rays in 1895, radiation evolved from a source of public fascination and scientific acclaim to a source of widespread public fear and scientific controversy. Roentgen's discovery, highlighted by an image of the bones of his wife's left hand and her wedding ring, created a wave of excitement. Newspapers and magazines gave it headline treatment, dozens of books and hundreds of technical articles rapidly appeared, and department stores provided demonstrations to attract customers. The *Journal of the American Medical Association* reported in 1896 that "the surgeons of Vienna and Berlin believe that the Roentgen photograph is destined to render inestimable services to surgery."[1] By the latter part of the twentieth century, attitudes toward radiation had changed dramatically. In 1973 the economist and technology critic E. F. Schumacher, in his influential book, *Small Is Beautiful,* described radiation as "the most serious agent of pollution of the environment and the greatest threat to man's survival on earth." The sociologist Kai T. Erikson spoke for many informed observers when he

---

1. Bettyann Holtzmann Kevles, *Naked to the Bone: Medical Imaging in the Twentieth Century* (New Brunswick: Rutgers University Press, 1997), pp. 16–27; Joel D. Howell, *Technology in the Hospital: Transforming Patient Care in the Early Twentieth Century* (Baltimore: Johns Hopkins University Press, 1995), pp. 136–37; Catherine Caufield, *Multiple Exposures: Chronicles of the Radiation Age* (New York: Harper and Row, 1989), pp. 3–8; "Roentgen Photograph," *JAMA: The Journal of the American Medical Association* 26 (March 7, 1896): 491.

commented in 1991 that radiation "clearly has a special place in the human sense of terror."[2]

The transformation of public attitudes and scientific views over a period of a century reflected the gradual recognition and then growing fear of the hazards of radiation and the protracted scientific debate over the risks of low-level exposure. The debate centered on often conflicting assessments of whether the risks of using radiation sources outweighed the benefits they provided. There were no incontestable answers to the questions that were raised, partly because the scientific evidence remained inconclusive and partly because they were not strictly scientific matters. The result was the emergence of a sharp and sometimes bitter controversy that pitted scientists, public health professionals, and regulatory officials against one another and generated confusion, uncertainty, and fear among members of the public who had no reliable way to evaluate the competing positions.

Radiation Hazards and the Tolerance Dose

Despite the unreliability of the gas tubes used to produce x-rays and doubts among physicians about the medical value of the images they provided, x-rays were employed for a variety of purposes within a short time after their discovery. Some applications were beneficial, such as diagnosing injuries, locating bullet and shrapnel wounds, and solving crimes. Others were frivolous, such as removing unwanted body hair or observing parts of one's skeleton. At first there was little awareness, even among scientists and physicians, of the hazards of x-rays. E. P. Davis, editor of the *American Journal of Medical Sciences,* told the College of Physicians in 1896 that he had used x-rays "in obtaining a shadow picture of the fetal head" and suggested that they "might prove useful in the diagnosis of pregnancy."[3]

2. E. F. Schumacher, *Small Is Beautiful: Economics as if People Mattered* (New York: HarperCollins, [1973] 1989), p. 143; Kai T. Erikson, "Radiation's Lingering Dread," *Bulletin of the Atomic Scientists* 47 (March 1991): 34–39.

3. "The Roentgen Rays in Surgery," *JAMA* 26 (March 14, 1896): 548; John K. Sutherland, "The Discovery of Radiation," *Nuclear News* 40 (April 1997): 34–37; Robert G. Arns, "The High-Vacuum X-Ray Tube: Technological Change in Social Context," *Technology and Culture* 38 (October 1997): 852–90; Rebecca Herzig, "Removing Roots: 'North American Hiroshima Maidens' and the X Ray," *Technology and Culture* 40 (October 1999): 723–45; Kevles, *Naked to the Bone,* pp. 24–53; Howell, *Technology in the Hospital,* pp. 103–9.

It soon became apparent, however, that exposure to x-rays could cause serious bodily injury. Some physicians noticed inexplicable burns on the bodies of patients after lengthy exposure to x-rays. An Austrian doctor who treated a five-year-old girl for a mole on her back with heavy doses of x-rays in 1896, for example, reported that although the process helped with the mole, it also caused severe burns. Thomas A. Edison, the celebrated inventor and an early x-ray enthusiast, conducted a series of experiments that left him with sore eyes and skin rashes. He became thoroughly disillusioned with the technology when a scientist who worked in his laboratory, Clarence Dally, became seriously ill and in 1904 died a painful death from his acute exposure to x-rays. Others suffered similar fates; injuries, disease, and sometimes death were especially prevalent among technicians and physicians who received occupational x-ray exposure. Within two decades after Roentgen's discovery, scientists and physicians had concluded that exposure to x-rays could cause sterility, bone disease, cancer, and other harmful consequences. The hazards of x-rays were further underscored by the findings of the pioneering geneticist H. J. Muller, whose research with fruit flies during the 1920s indicated that reproductive cells were highly susceptible to damage from even small amounts of radiation.[4]

A similar pattern followed the discovery of the element radium; after an initial outpouring of public excitement and promiscuous misuse, the hazards of exposure gradually became apparent. Experiments with x-rays led to the discovery of natural radioactivity in 1896. The French physicist Henri Becquerel expanded on Roentgen's findings by conducting research on luminescent materials and found to his surprise that uranium salts produced weak penetrating rays. Although he misinterpreted aspects of the phenomenon he detected, he correctly concluded that the element uranium spontaneously gave off radiation. Becquerel's work was extended and refined by Marie and Pierre Curie, who in 1898 identified what were later confirmed to be the new elements polonium and radium. The Curies demonstrated that polonium and radium produced radiation of much greater intensity than that of uranium. They came up with a new word, "radioactive," to describe the spontaneous emissions that they observed. Largely on her own, Marie Curie undertook heroic efforts to iso-

4. Caufield, *Multiple Exposures,* pp. 8–9; Kevles, *Naked to the Bone,* pp. 33–48; Jack Schubert and Ralph E. Lapp, *Radiation: What It Is and How It Affects You* (New York: Viking, 1957), pp. 181–201; Isaac Asimov and Theodore Dobzhansky, *The Genetic Effects of Radiation* (Washington, D.C.: U.S. Atomic Energy Commission, 1966).

late tiny amounts of radium from tons of residue of uranium ore (called pitchblende).[5]

The announcement of the discovery of radium in late 1898, like the discovery of x-rays, commanded the attention of scientists and fascinated the public. Newspaper and magazine articles, books, and public lectures suggested that radium could be useful for purposes that included bicycle lights, fertilizer, and cures for blindness. Physicians quickly recognized that the element offered an important advance in treating cancer, though they were less certain about the best way to apply their new weapon. The legitimate medical benefits of radium were often overshadowed by many indiscriminate and ill-informed applications that exceeded even the abundant abuse of x-rays. Physicians prescribed radium solutions or injected radium intravenously to combat disorders ranging in severity from acne to heart disease, and hucksters sold radium water or salts as all-purpose health tonics. In perhaps the most notorious case of misuse, a wealthy socialite named Eben M. Byers died of radium poisoning in 1932 after drinking huge quantities of a popular elixir called Radithor, which he consumed over a period of several years for relief from minor afflictions.[6]

Even before Byers's highly publicized death from ingestion of radium, scientists and physicians had begun to recognize the hazards of the element. The dangers of exposure to radium were more insidious than those of x-rays and took longer to identify. Unlike x-rays, which posed a threat to the health of those exposed to their penetrating power from an external source, radium caused its greatest harm if it were taken into the body. Whereas at least some of the immediate consequences of exposure to heavy doses of x-rays were visible, the damaging effects of radium did not show up for an extended period of time. Some researchers sounded notes of caution about the possible health risks of radium soon after its discovery, but the hazards did not become an issue of major concern and investigation until the 1920s. This occurred as a result of growing evidence that young women who had worked in factories where they painted radium dials on watches and clocks had become gravely ill from

5. Lawrence Badash, *Radioactivity in America: Growth and Decay of a Science* (Baltimore: Johns Hopkins University Press, 1979), pp. 10–12; Susan Quinn, *Marie Curie: A Life* (Reading, Mass.: Addison-Wesley, 1995), pp. 145–55; Edward R. Landa, "The First Nuclear Industry," *Scientific American* 247 (November 1982): 180–93; Caufield, *Multiple Exposures,* 22–23.

6. Badash, *Radioactivity in America,* pp. 19–32; Caufield, *Multiple Exposures,* pp. 24–28; Schubert and Lapp, *Radiation,* pp. 108–16; Landa, "First Nuclear Industry," p. 189; Roger M. Macklis, "The Great Radium Scandal," *Scientific American* 269 (August 1993): 94–99.

their exposure. Prodded by officials of the New Jersey Consumers' League and the National Consumers' League who took up the cause of the "radium girls," researchers established a connection between occupational exposure to radium and the serious afflictions that some of the dial painters suffered.[7]

The investigator who was instrumental in providing evidence that the ingestion of radium could lead to serious illness and death was Harrison S. Martland, the medical examiner of Essex County, New Jersey. Martland conducted autopsies and clinical examinations of several young women who had painted radium dials; they had ingested large cumulative doses by licking their brushes to a point to facilitate the task. In 1925 Martland and two colleagues reported in the *Journal of the American Medical Association* that once radium or other "long lived radioactive substances" entered the body, they spontaneously and continuously irradiated the "blood-forming centers," in which over time they could cause severe anemia and other disorders. Further, the authors concluded that there was "no known way of eliminating, changing or neutralizing" internally deposited radiation. In this article and others he published later, Martland demonstrated the dangers of the "deadly . . . rays" that were introduced into the body. As a result of the clear evidence of the hazards of radium, the risks of accumulating radioactive elements inside the body joined the effects of x-rays from external sources as a strong incentive for protective measures against radiation hazards.[8]

By the time Martland published his articles, scientists had determined that the harmful consequences of radiation were produced by its ionizing effect on human cell structure. Researchers conducted many experiments that revealed important information about ionization in the first two decades of the twentieth century, but the pathological implications of their findings, at least in attempting to set an acceptable level of radiation exposure, were uncertain. Radiation causes ionization because of its high levels of energy, whether in the form of x-rays from machines or

7. Claudia Clark, *Radium Girls: Women and Industrial Health Reform, 1910–1935* (Chapel Hill: University of North Carolina Press, 1997), pp. 57–58, 88–111; William D. Sharpe, "The New Jersey Radium Dial Painters: A Classic in Occupational Carcinogenesis," *Bulletin of the History of Medicine* 52 (Winter 1978): 560–70; F. G. Gosling, "Dial Painters Project," *Labor's Heritage* 4 (Summer 1992): 64–77.

8. Harrison S. Martland, Philip Conlon, and Joseph P. Knef, "Some Unrecognized Dangers in the Use and Handling of Radioactive Substances," *JAMA* 85 (December 5, 1925): 1769–76; Harrison S. Martland, "Occupational Poisoning in Manufacture of Luminous Watch Dials," ibid., 92 (February 9, 1929, and February 16, 1929): 466–73, 552–59; Clark, *Radium Girls,* pp. 103–4; Sharpe, "New Jersey Radium Dial Painters," pp. 565–66, 569–70.

in the form of alpha particles, beta particles, or gamma rays, which are emitted as the atomic nuclei of radioactive elements undergo spontaneous disintegration. The products of this radioactive decay differ from one another in mass, electrical charge, and power of penetration. Gamma rays from natural radioactive decay and x-rays from machines—both energetic forms of light—can penetrate far inside the body from external sources. The more massive beta particles and the much heavier alpha particles, by contrast, do not penetrate deeply from outside. But if an element that emits alpha or beta particles is breathed or swallowed and lodges in internal organs, as occurred with the radium dial painters, it poses a serious biological risk.

When radiation passes through matter, it deposits energy and can alter the structure of atoms by stripping electrons from them. If this occurs, the total negative electrical charge of the electrons no longer balances the total positive charge of the protons in the atom's nucleus, and the atom is left with an electrical charge. Such charged atomic fragments are called ions. Those changes in the composition of the atom's nucleus can lead to mutations and ultimately to serious biological injury. Scientists recognized within a short time after the discovery of x-rays and radium that the damage caused by ionizing radiation depended on the dose received, and researchers later identified other variables that could affect the severity of injury, including the sensitivity of different body organs and the form of radiation absorbed.[9]

The growing evidence about the dangers of radiation in the early years of the twentieth century led to efforts to guard against needless or excessive exposure. As early as 1904, William H. Rollins, a Harvard-trained physician and a practicing dentist, reported that the hazards of x-rays could be reduced by using shielding methods to protect patients, physicians, and equipment manufacturers. He advised against the common practice of holding x-ray tubes against a patient's body and urged instead that the tubes be kept as far away as possible from those receiving treatment. Although the immediate impact of Rollins's recommendations was slight, professional groups gradually took steps to discourage improper or unwarranted use of radiation sources. In 1929 the American Medical Association passed a resolution condemning the use of x-rays to remove body

9. Merril Eisenbud, *Environmental Radioactivity* (New York: McGraw-Hill, 1963), pp. 11–29; Schubert and Lapp, *Radiation*, pp. 65–87, 98–136; Badash, *Radioactivity in America*, pp. 13, 43, 96–97, 217–23, 231–43; Martland, "Occupational Poisoning in Manufacture of Luminous Watch Dials," p. 552.

hair, and three years later it withdrew radium from its list of remedies approved for internal administration.[10]

Meanwhile, other organizations were attempting to encourage better safety practices for radiation workers. In 1913 the German Roentgen Society developed guidelines to shield x-ray operators from excessive exposure, and two years later the British Roentgen Society took similar action. In response to the significant increase in the use—and misuse—of x-rays during World War I, a group of British radiologists and physicians formed a radiation protection committee in 1921 and issued a series of more detailed recommendations for safeguarding workers from the harmful effects of x-rays and radium. During the 1920s growing recognition of the serious problems caused by overexposure to radium prompted professionals to devote even more attention to devising protective measures against radiation. In 1928 the Second International Congress of Radiology established the International X-Ray and Radium Protection Committee, and the following year several professional societies and x-ray equipment manufacturers formed an American counterpart, the Advisory Committee on X-Ray and Radium Protection. Both groups were made up of scientists and physicians who met periodically to discuss recent findings and offer guidance on radiation protection. They had no official standing or statutory authority, and they could only make recommendations that they hoped would increase awareness of the hazards of radiation and improve practices in dealing with it. Their advice was directed to physicians, x-ray technicians, and others frequently exposed to radiation sources in their work; it did not apply to patients receiving radiation for therapeutic purposes.[11]

The primary difficulty that faced radiation protection organizations was the lack of a standard for defining a level of exposure that did not cause observable injury. During the 1920s scientists who sought a solution to this problem worked on a standard drawn from the most immediate and visible effect of exposure to radiation from an external source, an inflam-

10. Barton C. Hacker, *The Dragon's Tail: Radiation Safety in the Manhattan Project, 1942–1946* (Berkeley and Los Angeles: University of California Press, 1987), p. 23; Schubert and Lapp, *Radiation*, p. 103; Kevles, *Naked to the Bone*, pp. 51–52; Caufield, *Multiple Exposures*, pp. 13–14.

11. Lauriston S. Taylor, *Organization for Radiation Protection: The Operations of the ICRP and NCRP, 1928–1974* (Springfield, Va.: National Technical Information Service, 1979), pp. 1-001 to 4-001; Lauriston S. Taylor, *Radiation Protection Standards* (Cleveland: CRC Press, 1971), pp. 9–20; Daniel Paul Serwer, "The Rise of Radiation Protection: Science, Medicine, and Technology in Society, 1896–1935" (Ph.D. diss., Princeton University, 1977), pp. viii–ix, 38–44, 68–70, 174–81; Schubert and Lapp, *Radiation*, p. 18.

mation of the skin known as an erythema. They realized that this was an imprecise method for measuring exposure and judging the level of hazard, but it was the best approach available. In 1934 both the American and the international radiation protection committees concluded that they had sufficient information to take the unprecedented step of recommending a quantitative "tolerance dose" of external radiation. The levels they proposed were based on experience with and research on calculating the amount of radiation it took to cause an erythema. Levels were measured by a unit that had recently gained wide acceptance among professionals, the roentgen, which indicated the quantity of x-rays that would produce a specified degree of ionization under prescribed conditions. The American committee agreed on a tolerance dose of 0.1 roentgen per day of exposure to the whole body and 5 roentgens per day for fingers. The international committee set a whole-body limit of 0.2 roentgen per day.[12]

Although the international committee's tolerance dose for x-rays was twice as permissive as that of the U.S. committee, the discrepancy resulted not from any fundamental disagreement but from differences in rounding off similar figures calculated from available data. Both groups based their recommendations on evidence that they acknowledged was incomplete, and neither claimed that its tolerance dose was definitive. They believed that available information made their proposals reasonable and provided adequate safety for persons in normal health working in average conditions. The radiation experts did not regard the exposure levels as inviolable rules; a person who absorbed more than the recommended limits would not necessarily suffer harm. Both committees recognized that exposure to radiation in any amount might be detrimental, but they considered levels below the tolerance dose to be generally safe and unlikely to cause permanent damage to the "average individual." Their recommendations represented a tentative effort to establish practical guidelines that would reduce injuries to radiation workers. Although the tolerance doses were based on imperfect knowledge and unproven assumptions, they were an important advance in the theory and practice of radiation protection.[13]

In May 1941 the American committee took another important step

12. Taylor, *Organization for Radiation Protection,* pp. 4-012 to 4-025; Taylor, *Radiation Protection Standards,* pp. 13–19; Robert S. Stone, "The Concept of a Maximum Permissible Exposure," *Radiology* 58 (May 1952): 639–58; Caufield, *Multiple Exposures,* pp. 16–21; Kevles, *Naked to the Bone,* pp. 88–91.

13. Taylor, *Organization for Radiation Protection,* pp. 4-012 to 4-021; Stone, "Concept of a Maximum Permissible Exposure," p. 642; Lauriston S. Taylor, "The Development of Radiation Protection Standards (1925–1940)," *Health Physics* 41 (August 1981): 227–32.

when it recommended tolerance doses for the principal sources of hazard from internally deposited radiation, radium and its decay product, the radioactive gas radon. The death of Eben Byers and the afflictions of the radium dial painters triggered scientific research on how to calculate the exposure from "internal emitters" that enter the body, which was considerably more difficult than measuring external radiation. Those tragedies also spurred efforts to determine an acceptable level of exposure. Radium was employed primarily for medical purposes, but it was also used in a variety of industrial applications, including not only the infamous watch dials but also aircraft instruments, roulette wheels, and rayon fabric. Although empirical evidence was sparse, a team of researchers, prodded by the U.S. Navy's desire for safety standards for producing instruments with radium dials, agreed on a "body burden" for radium and a maximum concentration of airborne radon in workplaces. While acknowledging that the standards for both external radiation and internal emitters were far from definitive, radiation experts believed that the recommended dose limits offered an ample margin of safety for the relatively small number of persons exposed to occupational radiation.[14]

The findings and recommendations of the U.S. Advisory Committee on X-Ray and Radium Protection provided the basis for the radiological health programs of the Manhattan Project during World War II. The effort to build an atomic bomb presented formidable challenges to the scientists who sought to ensure radiation safety for those employed on the project. They adopted the recommendations of the Advisory Committee on X-Ray and Radium Protection for those working with radioactive materials, but they encouraged the practice of preventing any exposure at all. The objective could not always be achieved; despite an impressive safety record, cases of overexposure inevitably occurred. The most serious took place after the war, when two separate accidents each claimed the life of a researcher who received acute exposure to radiation.[15]

14. Robley D. Evans, "Inception of Standards for Internal Emitters, Radon and Radium," *Health Physics* 41 (September 1981): 437–48; Taylor, *Radiation Protection Standards*, pp. 19–20.

15. Hacker, *Dragon's Tail*, pp. 10–83. Peter Bacon Hales argues that Manhattan Project officials were so indifferent to radiation hazards that they caused an "epidemic" of radiation injuries and disease. But he offers little epidemiological (or even anecdotal) evidence to support such a conclusion. Hales criticizes Manhattan Project scientists and physicians for failing to distinguish between "radiation emitters" and "radiation itself." He does not make clear what he means by those terms or what distinction he thinks could have been made. See Hales, *Atomic Spaces: Living on the Manhattan Project* (Urbana: University of Illinois Press, 1997), pp. 273–98.

A New Era for Radiation Safety

The opening of the atomic age in the aftermath of the bombings of Hiroshima and Nagasaki made radiation safety a vastly more complex task. One reason was that nuclear fission created many radioactive isotopes that did not exist in nature. Instead of dealing only with x-rays and radium, health physicists, as professionals in the field of radiation protection called themselves, had to consider the potential hazards of new radioactive substances about which even less was known. Further, the number of people exposed to radiation from the development of military and civilian uses of atomic energy was certain to grow dramatically. Radiation protection broadened from a medical and industrial issue of limited proportions to a public health question of, potentially at least, major dimensions.

In light of the radically different circumstances, both the American and the international radiation protection committees made organizational changes, modified their philosophy of radiological safety, and lowered their suggested exposure limits. Because its activities would inevitably extend beyond x-rays and radium, in 1946 the U.S. body adopted a new name, the National Committee on Radiation Protection (NCRP). It designated as its chairman Lauriston S. Taylor, who had served in that capacity since the establishment of the Advisory Committee on X-Ray and Radium Protection in 1929. Taylor, a Cornell-trained physicist who had conducted research on x-rays, was also the American representative on the International X-Ray and Radium Protection Committee. He remained a key figure in and prominent spokesman on radiation protection for more than sixty years. The NCRP also enlarged its membership and created several new subcommittees to study specific problems.[16]

Shortly after its reorganization in 1946, the NCRP reassessed its position on radiation exposure levels. Largely but not solely because of genetic considerations, it abandoned the concept "tolerance dose," which had suggested that exposure to radiation below the specified limits was generally harmless. The findings of H. J. Muller and other geneticists had indicated that reproductive cells were especially vulnerable to even small amounts of radiation and that mutant genes could be inherited from a parent with no obvious radiation-induced injuries. At least for genetic

16. Taylor, *Organization for Radiation Protection*, pp. 7-001 to 7-007; Taylor, *Radiation Protection Standards*, pp. 23–24.

effects, by the time World War II began most scientists had rejected the earlier consensus that exposure to radiation was biologically innocuous below a certain threshold.

The NCRP took action that reflected the newer view by replacing the term "tolerance dose" with "maximum permissible dose," which it thought better conveyed the idea that no quantity of radiation was certifiably safe. It defined the permissible dose as that which, "in the light of present knowledge, is not expected to cause appreciable bodily injury to a person at any time during his lifetime." It explicitly acknowledged the possibility of suffering harmful consequences from radiation in amounts below the permissible limits. But the NCRP emphasized that the permissible dose was based on the belief that "the probability of the occurrence of such injuries must be so low that the risk would be readily acceptable to the average individual."[17]

In response to the anticipated growth of atomic energy programs and a substantial increase in the number of individuals who would be subject to injuries from radiation, the NCRP revised its recommendations on radiation protection. It reduced the permissible dose for whole-body exposure from external sources to 50 percent of the 1934 level. It measured the new whole-body limit of 0.3 roentgen per six-day workweek by exposure of the "most critical" tissue in blood-forming organs, gonads, and lenses of the eyes; higher limits applied for less sensitive areas of the body. Although the committee did not formally publish its recommendations on permissible limits from external sources until 1954, it had agreed on its main conclusions by 1948.[18]

The NCRP also devoted careful attention to internal emitters. In the postwar world the major peril of internal emitters resulted not so much from misuse of radium as from the growing numbers of and expanded work with radioactive isotopes. Nearly every element has three or more isotopes, which have identical chemical properties but differ slightly in their nuclear composition. Only a few isotopes are naturally radioactive. Most radioactive isotopes are produced artificially in particle-accelerating machines or in nuclear reactions. After a four-year study by one of its subcommittees, in 1953 the NCRP published a handbook that cited max-

17. Stone, "Concept of a Maximum Permissible Exposure," pp. 642–44; Schubert and Lapp, *Radiation,* chap. 9; Taylor, *Radiation Protection Standards,* pp. 22, 35; National Committee on Radiation Protection, *Permissible Dose from External Sources of Ionizing Radiation,* Handbook 59 (Washington, D.C.: National Bureau of Standards, 1954), pp. 1–2, 17–19, 26–27.
18. Taylor, *Radiation Protection Standards,* pp. 24–25; NCRP, *Permissible Dose from External Sources,* pp. 61–73.

imum permissible "body burdens" and concentrations in air and water of a long list of radioactive isotopes. The committee based its recommendations on existing knowledge of x-ray, gamma ray, and radium injuries, comparison with the effects of naturally occurring radioactive isotopes, experiments with animals, and clinical experience with humans. To provide an adequate margin of safety, it proposed permissible levels as low as one-tenth of the numerical values derived from the sketchy data then available.[19]

The activities of the international committee, which was renamed the International Commission on Radiological Protection (ICRP), followed the example of the NCRP in the early postwar years. It too enlarged its membership, formed several subcommittees to examine specific problems, and abandoned the use of "tolerance dose" in favor of "maximum permissible dose." The ICRP also conformed with the NCRP in its recommendations for internal emitters and in lowering its suggested occupational whole-body exposure limits from external sources to 0.3 roentgen per week.

In its only major departure from the NCRP, the ICRP proposed a maximum permissible dose of one-tenth the occupational levels in case of exposure by persons other than radiation workers. In view of the genetic effects of radiation and the possibility that the general population, or at least a sizable segment of it, might be exposed in accidental or emergency situations, the ICRP agreed in 1953 on reducing the occupational level by a factor of ten. Although the NCRP had established the same limit for minors under the age of eighteen, it refused to do so for the entire population. It wished to avoid the appearance of a double standard of protection, one for radiation workers and one for the general public. Although the ICRP's recommendations on the issue were arbitrary and tentative, they represented the first formal effort to establish radiation protection guidelines for population groups outside the "controlled areas" where the permissible doses for radiation workers applied.[20]

While the NCRP and the ICRP were reorganizing and revising their recommendations on radiation protection, a new federal agency, the

19. Taylor, *Radiation Protection Standards*, pp. 28–30; Taylor, *Organization for Radiation Protection*, pp. 7-001, 7-123; Schubert and Lapp, *Radiation*, pp. 120–22; National Committee of Radiation Protection, *Maximum Permissible Amounts of Radioisotopes in the Human Body and Maximum Permissible Concentrations in Air and Water*, Handbook 52 (Washington, D.C.: National Bureau of Standards, 1953).

20. Taylor, *Organization for Radiation Protection*, pp. 7-087, 7-235; Taylor, *Radiation Protection Standards*, pp. 37–40; NCRP, *Permissible Dose from External Sources*, pp. 55–57.

United States Atomic Energy Commission (AEC) was established by the Atomic Energy Act of 1946 to manage the nation's atomic energy programs. Congress had agreed on atomic energy legislation only after a great deal of controversy over the role of the military in directing the activities of the AEC. The agency was headed by five commissioners appointed by the president for five-year terms and confirmed by the Senate. The 1946 law, passed as postwar disputes with the Soviet Union were intensifying into the cold war, emphasized the military applications of atomic energy. The principal functions that it assigned the AEC were the production of the "fissionable materials" that fueled nuclear bombs and the development and testing of new weapons. The 1946 act encouraged the AEC to investigate the civilian uses of nuclear technology, but this clearly was a secondary goal. The preoccupation with the military applications of the atom and the tight government monopoly of the technology ensured that progress in exploring the potential of peaceful nuclear energy would be, at best, sluggish.[21]

The exception to the bleak short-term prospects for civilian applications of atomic energy, and the example of the potential benefits of the technology that the AEC proudly proclaimed in its early years, was the widespread distribution of reactor-produced radioactive isotopes. Even before the AEC began operations in January 1947, the use of radioactive materials for civilian applications had received a great deal of attention. Under the auspices of the Manhattan Project, the first transfer of a "radioisotope" from a reactor occurred at Clinton Laboratories in Oak Ridge, Tennessee, on August 2, 1946, with considerable fanfare. E. V. Cowdrey, a physician from the Barnard Free Skin and Cancer Hospital of St. Louis, purchased a small amount of carbon 14 for use in cancer research as a crowd of one hundred fifty people watched and movie cameras rolled. The transaction was a front-page story in newspapers; the *Washington Post* reported that radioisotopes might lead to a cure for cancer within ten years. The isotopes program at Oak Ridge, one of the installations that the AEC inherited from the Manhattan Project, proved to be extremely popular. In August 1948 the AEC, hailing the program as "the first great contribution of the development of atomic energy to peacetime welfare," announced that isotopes from Oak Ridge were being used in more than one thousand projects in medicine, industry, agri-

21. Richard G. Hewlett and Oscar E. Anderson, Jr., *The New World, 1939/1946: Volume I of A History of the United States Atomic Energy Commission* (University Park: Pennsylvania State University Press, 1962), pp. 409–530.

Figure 1. E. V. Cowdrey (in light suit at right) speaks to reporters and other observers after the purchase of a reactor-produced radioisotope (in metal container) for medical research, August 2, 1946. (National Archives 434–OR–58–1870–5)

culture, and scientific research. The applications included measuring the thickness of materials, studying the wear qualities of engines, gears, and tires, and controlling weeds and insects. In the period from August 2, 1946, to May 31, 1954, the AEC shipped more than forty-seven thousand radioisotopes.[22]

The 1946 Atomic Energy Act assigned the AEC responsibility for protecting public health and safety from the hazards of radiation produced by nuclear fission. Its regulatory authority did not extend to radium, other naturally occurring sources of radiation, accelerator-produced isotopes, or x-rays. In its conduct of the isotopes program, the AEC was acutely

22. *Knoxville Journal,* August 3, 1946; *Washington Post,* August 3, 1946; United States Atomic Energy Commission, *Fourth Semiannual Report* (1948), pp. 5, 16; AEC, *Major Activities in the Atomic Energy Programs,* July 1954, p. 97; Henry N. Wagner, Jr., and Linda E. Ketchum, *Living with Radiation: The Risk, the Promise* (Baltimore: Johns Hopkins University Press, 1989), pp. 73–76.

mindful of the misuse of x-rays and radium that had led to tragedy for dial painters and others exposed to high doses. Drawing on the lessons of the not-too-distant past, it sought to enforce safe practices by imposing regulatory requirements for isotopes produced by reactors. It established licensing procedures for applicants to promote safe handling and use of radioactive materials under its jurisdiction.[23]

In its efforts to encourage radiation safety, the AEC drew on the recommendations of the NCRP. The AEC took a keen interest in the committee's activities because the NCRP's judgments affected its programs. The NCRP included among its membership officials from the AEC and other government agencies involved in radiation protection, but it was committed to maintaining the independence of its deliberations and conclusions. The relationship between the NCRP and the AEC was informal and generally cooperative, but at times it was uneasy. When the AEC learned that the NCRP was considering lowering permissible doses for radiation workers it pressed for information in advance of formal publication. Despite the reluctance of some members, the NCRP agreed to give the AEC preliminary guidance on what its new exposure levels were likely to be. The committee was less accommodating on another AEC request. In February 1947 the AEC asked to review an updated edition of an NCRP handbook on x-ray protection before its publication on the grounds that it might contain classified information. The request caused the NCRP "considerable concern." It replied that it would submit potentially sensitive material that the AEC was legally obliged to protect but found it unnecessary and undesirable to do so with publications on subjects outside the AEC's jurisdiction, such as the x-ray handbook. The AEC accepted this argument while reiterating its insistence that the NCRP guard against the inadvertent disclosure of classified information.[24]

While the AEC was promoting radiation safety in its programs, it was also seeking to gain more knowledge about the biological effects of radiation exposure. In June 1947 an AEC advisory panel, the Medical Board of Review, reported that the need for sponsoring research on radiation was "both urgent and extensive." This was especially true of the element plutonium, which fueled the atomic bomb that destroyed Nagasaki and the weapons that the AEC built after the war. It was apparent that the

23. Paul C. Aebersold, "Philosophy and Policies of the AEC Control of Radioisotopes Distribution," in *Radioisotopes in Medicine (ORO–125)*, ed. Gould A. Andrews, Marshall Brucer, and Elizabeth B. Anderson (Washington, D.C.: Government Printing Office, 1955), p. 1.

24. Taylor, *Organization for Radiation Protection*, pp. 7-008 to 7-010, 7-016, 7-032.

production of plutonium would subject many people to serious risks, and although experts recognized that plutonium was even more toxic than radium, there was much they did not know about the nature of its hazards. One approach to gaining a better understanding of the dangers of plutonium was to conduct experiments on hospital patients. The purpose of the experiments was to collect data on the amount of plutonium that remained in the body after exposure by measuring how much was excreted. The experiments furnished useful information on the movement of plutonium through the body that was unavailable from other sources and that provided a basis for calculating a permissible body burden for plutonium. But, then and later, they also raised sensitive ethical questions.

Between 1945 and 1947 eighteen patients received injections of plutonium as a part of the effort to calibrate body burdens. The experiments took place at the Oak Ridge Hospital (one patient), the University of Rochester (eleven patients), the University of Chicago (three patients), and the University of California (three patients) under the auspices of the Manhattan Project and the AEC. The researchers who conducted the tests were convinced that the doses they delivered were too small to produce any short-term consequences, and, from all indications, they were correct. The long-term risks were more problematic, however; in most cases, therefore, the injections were administered to patients who were not expected to live long enough to develop cancer or other delayed health effects from their exposures. The judgments about longevity sometimes proved to be mistaken; several of the patients lived for many years. Even though the investigators took precautions to protect the subjects of their experiments from injury, they were also careful not to disclose important information to them. In all cases but one, patients did not sign a form consenting to the tests; most did not know that radioactive materials were introduced into their bodies or even that they were the subjects of experiments. The researchers did not expect that the patients would receive any therapeutic benefits from the plutonium they received and made a deliberate effort to prevent them from learning about their unwitting participation in the experiments.[25]

The AEC sponsored other experiments that applied radioactive tracers to learn more about bodily functions, some of which used children as subjects. In 1946 and again between 1950 and 1953, for example, the AEC,

25. Advisory Committee on Human Radiation Experiments, *Final Report,* October 1995 (Washington, D.C.: Government Printing Office, 1995), pp. 28–30, 227–69.

along with the National Institutes of Health and the Quaker Oats Company, funded research carried out by scientists from the Massachusetts Institute of Technology that fed radioactive iron or calcium to students at the Walter E. Fernald School, an institution for mentally retarded children in Massachusetts. The tests sought to find how the body absorbed iron, calcium, and other minerals in food. The radiation doses in the tracers were very low and highly unlikely to cause harm to the children who received them. But, as in the case of the plutonium injections, the experiments were not designed or expected to provide any health benefits to the subjects. Although the school asked parents of the children who participated to sign a consent form, the information it offered was neither complete nor frank about the purpose or the possible risks of the tests. Instead, it misleadingly suggested that the experiments could improve the children's conditions.

The AEC did not sponsor or participate directly in most experiments that used radioactive substances on human subjects. It licensed the shipment of fission-produced radioactive isotopes to hospitals and physicians and issued broad regulatory guidelines for their use. In general, the human radiation experiments were consistent with medical practices at the time. The AEC took action to guard against unsafe exposures to human subjects. Many of the experiments provided valuable information on radiation safety and bodily functions that was not obtainable any other way.

Nevertheless, the experiments raised profound questions about informed consent that the AEC considered but did not resolve. In 1947 Carroll L. Wilson, the staff director of the agency, twice issued instructions that scientists working on AEC contracts should perform radiation research with humans only if (1) there was reason to hope for some therapeutic value for the subjects; and (2) those subjects were informed about the procedures and agreed to them. In a relatively small number of cases in which the need for information seemed unusually urgent, however, government officials placed the importance of the data that the tests offered ahead of concerns about the effects on subjects. The most prominent examples were the plutonium injections. All but one of those experiments took place under the auspices of the Manhattan Project, but for many years the AEC, for legal and public relations reasons, concealed their purpose and their very existence from their subjects. The plutonium injections were not the norm for radiation experiments in the postwar era. But they indicated that the AEC, like the Manhattan Project before it, would compromise its own guidelines and ethical sensibilities if it concluded that tests with human subjects served an essential purpose that could not be achieved by other means.[26]

The Fallout Controversy

At the same time that the AEC was attempting to learn more about radiation hazards from atomic fission, public awareness of and concern about the risks of exposure were growing. The initial public reactions to the bombings of Hiroshima and Nagasaki focused on the force of the blasts rather than on the effects of radiation. The radiation hazards of nuclear explosions received much more attention, however, in reports of the atomic tests conducted at the Bikini Atoll in the Marshall Islands in summer 1946. Articles in popular magazines such as *Reader's Digest* and *Life* emphasized the dangers of exposure to radiation. A best-selling book titled *No Place to Hide* by David Bradley, a physician who served in the Radiological Safety Section during the Bikini tests, vividly conveyed the same message when it was published in 1948. Bradley concluded that the "devastating influence of the Bomb and its unborn relatives may affect the land and its wealth—and therefore its people—for centuries through the persistence of radioactivity."[27]

Factual accounts of the effects of radiation were soon embellished in a wide variety of science fiction books and articles, comics, films, and other staples of popular culture. Almost invariably in those presentations, radioactive monsters, freaks, or mutants wreaked havoc on the physical and mental well-being of the population. In the film *The Thing* (1951), for example, a shadowy, slimy, radioactive humanoid from outer space killed defenseless earthlings with abandon. The hit movie *Them* (1954) featured gigantic radioactive ants that crawled away from the site of the first atomic bomb test to terrorize the citizens of New Mexico and other locations.[28]

26. Ibid., pp. 87–88, 283–365. On medical ethics and the use of human subjects in medical experiments, see David J. Rothman, *Strangers at the Bedside: A History of How Law and Bioethics Transformed Medical Decision Making* (New York: Basic Books, 1991); and Susan E. Lederer, *Subjected to Science: Human Experimentation in America before the Second World War* (Baltimore: Johns Hopkins University Press, 1995).

27. Paul Boyer, *By the Bomb's Early Light: American Thought and Culture at the Dawn of the Atomic Age* (New York: Pantheon Books, 1985), pp. 90–92; David Bradley, *No Place to Hide* (Boston: Little, Brown, 1948), p. 165.

28. Allan M. Winkler, *Life under a Cloud: American Anxiety about the Atom* (New York: Oxford University Press, 1993), pp. 96–99; Spencer R. Weart, *Nuclear Fear: A History of*

Within a short time after the ghoulish Thing, the colossal ants, and other diabolical creations alarmed moviegoers with fictional representations of the dangers of radiation, a scientific and public controversy over the actual effects of radioactive fallout from nuclear bomb testing gathered momentum. It arose largely as a result of atmospheric testing of hydrogen bombs by the United States, the Soviet Union, and Great Britain that produced radioactive fallout that spread to populated areas far from the sites of the explosions. This became a highly visible and divisive issue after a U.S. test explosion at Bikini in March 1954 produced so much fallout that it forced the evacuation of Marshallese from their island homes and accidentally showered a Japanese fishing vessel eighty to ninety miles away with radioactive ash. The crew of the fishing boat, the *Lucky Dragon,* suffered skin irritations and burns, nausea, loss of hair, and other effects of radiation. One of the men died within six months, either directly from his exposure or, more likely, indirectly from hepatitis caused by a blood transfusion administered to treat the symptoms of "atomic sickness." The Bikini bomb tests and the fate of the *Lucky Dragon* not only set off a panic in Japan over the threat of radioactive "ashes of death" but also generated a major debate in the United States over the hazards of low-level radiation from fallout and other sources. The risks of exposure from fallout that spread around the globe developed into a bitterly contested political question and remained a prominent policy issue until the Limited Test Ban Treaty of 1963 banned atmospheric nuclear weapons testing by its signatories. As low-level radiation moved from the rarified realms of scientific and medical discourse to a featured subject in newspaper reports, magazine stories, and political campaigns, it became for the first time a matter of sustained public concern.[29]

Scientists disagreed sharply about the seriousness of the risk of fallout.

Images (Cambridge, Mass.: Harvard University Press, 1988), pp. 191–95; Margot A. Henriksen, *Dr. Strangelove's America: Society and Culture in the Atomic Age* (Berkeley and Los Angeles: University of California Press, 1997), pp. 54–58; Joyce A. Evans, *Celluloid Mushroom Clouds: Hollywood and the Atomic Bomb* (Boulder, Colo.: Westview Press, 1998), pp. 93–113.

29. Robert A. Divine, *Blowing on the Wind: The Nuclear Test Ban Debate, 1954–1960* (New York: Oxford University Press, 1978), pp. 3–35; Richard G. Hewlett and Jack M. Holl, *Atoms for Peace and War: Eisenhower and the Atomic Energy Commission* (Berkeley and Los Angeles: University of California Press, 1989), pp. 172–77; Barton C. Hacker, *Elements of Controversy: The Atomic Energy Commission and Radiation Safety in Nuclear Weapons Testing, 1947–1974* (Berkeley and Los Angeles: University of California Press, 1994), pp. 140–52; J. Samuel Walker, "The Controversy over Radiation Safety: A Historical Overview," *JAMA* 262 (August 4, 1989): 664–68.

The AEC, which was responsible for conducting tests not only of hydrogen weapons in the Pacific but also of smaller atomic bombs at a recently developed site in Nevada, insisted that the levels of radioactivity were too low to significantly threaten public health and that the risks of testing were far less dangerous than falling behind the Soviets in the arms race. "The degree of risk must be balanced," an AEC report to the public declared in February 1955, "against the great importance of the test programs to the security of the nation."[30]

Critics of the AEC's position were not convinced; they contended that the agency underestimated the hazards of fallout. Ralph E. Lapp, a veteran of the Manhattan Project, a well-known physicist, and a freelance writer, accused the AEC of making "reckless or unsubstantiated statements." The AEC published a great deal of scientific data on fallout but undermined its own credibility by consistently placing the most benign interpretation on it. Opponents of testing used the same information to arrive at different conclusions. In response to the AEC's claims that an individual's chances of being harmed by fallout were statistically slight, for example, critics argued that the absolute number of people exposed to fallout, even if a small percentage of the population, represented an appreciable public health hazard. They further suggested that even low levels of continuous fallout could pollute food supplies and cause increased rates of birth defects, cancer, and other afflictions.

The central issue in the fallout debate was whether the national security benefits of nuclear bomb testing justified the hazards of radioactive fallout, which was, of course, fundamentally a political issue. The controversy not only highlighted the political judgments involved in radiation protection but also made clear that scientists did not know the answers to many important questions about the health effects of low-level exposure. The issue that attracted the most attention was whether there was a threshold for somatic radiation injury. Although experts agreed that there was no threshold for genetic consequences, some authorities maintained that because no short-term somatic effects of exposure to doses of less than 50 to 100 roentgens had been observed, there was a somatic threshold at some as yet undetermined level. The effects of acute exposure were clear; a dose in the range of 400 to 500 roentgens would be lethal to about half of those receiving it, and the percentage of deaths would increase at higher exposures. But even decades after issuing the first tolerance dose guidelines, sci-

---

30. "A Report by the United States Atomic Energy Commission on the Effects of High-Yield Nuclear Explosions," February 15, 1955, Fallout File, Lewis L. Strauss Papers, Herbert Hoover Library, West Branch, Iowa.

entists still lacked reliable information on the pathological consequences, if any, of exposures at levels that did not produce observable injury. They were also uncertain about other keys to understanding radiation hazards, such as the ability of both somatic and genetic cells to repair damage from exposure and about the impact of "dose rate," the amount of radiation absorbed per unit of time, on cell structure.[31]

In 1955, as the fallout controversy was intensifying, the National Academy of Sciences, a prestigious nongovernmental scientific body, undertook a major study of the effects of low-level radiation at the request of the AEC. The president of the National Academy, Detlev W. Bronk, appointed more than one hundred prominent scientists, most drawn from the academic world but some from government and industry, to six committees to examine various aspects of radiation: genetics, pathology, agriculture and food supplies, meteorology, oceanography, and radioactive waste disposal. Their report, released on June 12, 1956, received wide media attention and commentary. In some ways its findings were reassuring. It concluded that fallout from weapons tests up to that time did not represent a major health hazard, and it affirmed that "radiation problems, if they are met intelligently and vigilantly, need not stand in the way of the large-scale development of atomic energy."

In most respects, however, the National Academy's determinations were deeply disturbing, especially in their emphasis on the genetic effects of radiation. The report advised that exposure to radiation, even in small doses, could cause genetic consequences that would be tragic in individual cases and harmful over the long term for the entire population. Mutations that occurred from exposure to radiation would not show up immediately but would be added to the population's gene pool and increase the risks for future generations. The study acknowledged that its findings on genetics were based on limited evidence, but it was unequivocal in its basic recommendation: "We ought to keep all our expenditures of radiation as low as possible. From the point of view of genetics, they are all bad."

The National Academy's report also cited other existing and potential hazards of radiation. It warned that the levels of radioactive fallout should not be allowed to increase to "more serious levels." It called for careful control of radiation in the expanding uses of atomic energy for peaceful applications. And it urged that the administration of x-rays, which it found

31. U.S. Congress, Joint Committee on Atomic Energy, *Hearings on the Nature of Radioactive Fallout and Its Effects on Man,* 85th Cong., 1st sess., 1957, pp. 955–1008; "Radiation Exposure and Biological Effects," *Nucleonics* 21 (March 1963): 46–47; L. D. Hamilton, "Somatic Effects," *Nucleonics* (March 1963): 48–53.

to be excessive and at times indefensible, "be reduced as much as is consistent with medical necessity." X-rays were the source of highest average exposure to radiation by the population other than "natural background." The report estimated average annual exposure from background radiation, which is an unavoidable part of environmental exposure that comes from cosmic rays, radioactive elements in rocks and soil, and other natural sources, to be about 0.14 roentgen. Although the National Academy's survey was the most comprehensive and authoritative statement for the general public up to that time on the effects of radiation, it made no claim to being definitive. It called for further research on radiation, but it also pointed out that increased scientific data and technical knowledge were not enough in themselves to resolve controversies over the problems of radiation protection. The ethical, political, economic, and military questions about relative risks and benefits that the use of atomic energy raised could not be answered by scientific information alone.[32]

The fallout debate had an important and immediate impact on radiation protection in three ways. The first was to increase public awareness of and concern about the hazards of radiation exposure. This was apparent in public opinion polls. A survey taken in April 1955 revealed that only 17 percent of the respondents knew what was meant by fallout from a hydrogen bomb, but a poll taken in May 1957 showed that 52 percent of those questioned believed that fallout was a "real danger," compared to 28 percent who did not think so and 20 percent who did not know. More impressionistic evidence supported the same conclusion. A magazine article in a Sunday supplement in February 1958 cited the complaints of physicians that their patients were resisting legitimate x-ray treatment. It reported that "beyond any question, a good many of the 100 million people a year who get X-rays have been frightened."[33]

The second effect of the fallout controversy was to seriously damage the credibility of the AEC as a guardian of public health. The agency's responsibilities for both developing nuclear weapons and evaluating the hazards of fallout from bomb tests made its statements on radiation safety highly suspect. Representative Chet Holifield, who presided over exten-

32. *The Biological Effects of Radiation: A Report to the Public* (Washington, D.C.: National Academy of Sciences–National Research Council, 1956), pp. 2–6, 8, 14–20, 25–27, 30–32; *The Biological Effects of Radiation: Summary Reports* (Washington, D.C.: National Academy of Sciences–National Research Council, 1956), pp. 3–34, 60, 68–70, 101–8.

33. Hazel Gaudet Erskine, "The Polls: Atomic Weapons and Nuclear Energy," *Public Opinion Quarterly* 27 (Summer 1963): 163, 188; A. E. Hotchner, "The Truth about the X-ray Scare," *This Week,* February 23, 1958, pp. 8–9.

sive hearings on fallout in 1957 as chairman of the Special Subcommittee on Radiation of the AEC's congressional oversight committee, the Joint Committee on Atomic Energy, concluded that "the Atomic Energy Commission approach to the hazards from bomb-test fall-out seems to add up to a party line—'play it down.'" A farmer in Nevada was even more blunt: "You can't help feeling uneasy when you look up and see one of those clouds [from a bomb test]. You don't know what the hell it is all about—and as for the A.E.C.—I wouldn't believe them on a stack of Bibles." In 1959 President Dwight D. Eisenhower created the Federal Radiation Council (FRC) to advise the White House and federal agencies on radiological safety programs. He acted in part because of the recognition of his staff that the AEC's conflicting duties had undermined public confidence in the assessments of radiation hazards the government released. The president also strengthened the role of the Department of Health, Education, and Welfare in analyzing and interpreting data on radiation dangers in order to "reassure the public as to the objectivity of Government announcements."[34]

The third effect of the fallout controversy was to help to motivate the NCRP and the ICRP to tighten their permissible limits for radiation exposure. As public concern about radiation hazards increased, both organizations reduced the allowable doses for whole-body exposure to external radiation to one-third of the previous level. In their revised recommendations they employed units of measurement that had recently gained preference over the roentgen. One was the "rad," which indicated the amount of radiation delivered to human tissue by measuring the "absorbed dose" according to the degree of ionization it caused. Another unit, the "rem," applied to chronic low-level exposures and indicated the "relative biological effectiveness" of different kinds of radiation in producing biological injury. For x-ray and gamma radiation, one rem equaled one roentgen. The values of rems and rads were equivalent for x-rays and gamma rays but not for alpha and beta particles. Another unit of measure, the "curie," showed the rate of decay (or level of activity) of radioactive substances but did not indicate their biological effects.[35]

34. Chet Holifield, "Who Should Judge the Atom?" *Saturday Review,* August 3, 1957, pp. 34–37; *New York Times,* June 17, 1957; George T. Mazuzan and J. Samuel Walker, *Controlling the Atom: The Beginnings of Nuclear Regulation, 1946–1962* (Berkeley and Los Angeles: University of California Press, 1984), pp. 252–58.

35. Anthony V. Nero, *A Guidebook to Nuclear Reactors* (Berkeley and Los Angeles: University of California Press, 1979), pp. 32–39. These units were used throughout most of the period covered in this book. In the 1980s radiation protection organizations adopted new units that were gradually being phased in. They are the "gray," which equals 100 rads, the

The ICRP met in April 1956 and agreed to lower its suggested maximum occupational dose from external sources to 5 rems per year for whole-body exposure. The previous recommended level had been 0.3 roentgen per week or 15 per year. The ICRP adopted the adjusted limit to conform with the soon-to-be-published report of the National Academy of Sciences, which urged that radiation exposure be kept as low as possible. To provide further protection from genetic consequences by limiting exposure of younger individuals most likely to have children, the ICRP specified total permissible accumulated doses at various ages (50 rems to age thirty, 100 rems to age forty, and 200 rems to age sixty). It also tightened its recommendations for population exposure by corresponding proportions.

The NCRP set out similar guidelines in a preliminary statement published in January 1957 and, after some revisions, released in final form in April 1958. Like the ICRP, the American committee was influenced not only by scientific considerations, especially the findings of the National Academy of Sciences, but also by the "public clamor" that had arisen over radiation hazards. The NCRP recommended an average whole-body occupational exposure from external sources of 5 rems per year. In response to the concern of some members that a firm numerical level was too inflexible, it offered a formula to prorate the permissible limit by age. As long as a total accumulated lifetime dose was not exceeded, a worker could receive up to 12 rems in a given year (if the individual's exposure was below the 5-rem average limit in previous years). The formula was MPD [accumulated maximum permissible dose] = $5 (N - 18)$, where N was a person's age. The NCRP cautioned, however, that a dose of 12 rems in a single year was permissible only when adequate records of past exposure existed and even then "should be regarded as an allowable but not usual condition." The NCRP still refrained from explicitly setting a level for population exposure, although it went partway in that direction by recommending that persons living near sources of radiation but outside of controlled areas should be limited to one-tenth of the permissible levels that applied for radiation workers.[36]

"sievert," which equals 100 rems, and the "becquerel," which replaces the curie as a measure of the rate of radioactive decay. Richard Wolfson, *Nuclear Choices: A Citizen's Guide to Nuclear Technology* (Cambridge, Mass.: MIT Press, 1991), p. 46.

36. Joint Committee on Atomic Energy, *Hearings on Fallout*, pp. 805–19, 827–31, 852, and *Hearings on Employee Radiation Hazards and Workmen's Compensation*, 86th Cong.,1st sess., 1959, pp. 37–40; Taylor, *Radiation Protection Standards*, pp. 47–50; Taylor, *Organization for Radiation Protection*, p. 8-061.

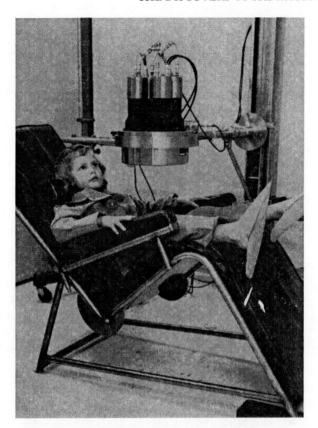

Figure 2. A whole-body counter used to measure levels of radiation. The child being measured participated in a study of the amount of radiation normally present in a person's body. The survey took whole-body counts of six thousand adults and children during the first half of the 1960s. (National Archives 434–SF–17–6)

Both the ICRP and the NCRP issued new recommendations on permissible body burdens and permissible concentrations in air and water of internal emitters in 1959. They calculated the allowable concentrations on the basis of what seemed likely to meet the 5-rem exposure limit if inhaled or ingested, according to the characteristics of different radioisotopes. A few months later the two organizations agreed on levels for population exposure, an issue that had generated some differences between them. They settled on recommending a limit of one-tenth of the occupational level for individuals (0.5 rem per year) and, to curtail genetic consequences, one-thirtieth of the occupational level as an average for the entire population (0.17 rem per year).[37]

The sharp reductions by both the ICRP and the NCRP in their suggested maximum permissible doses stirred some speculation that the previous levels had been dangerously high. Both groups denied such assertions. They pointed out that there was no indication that workers exposed to radiation had suffered harm under the older standards and that in most cases they had received less exposure than even the new levels allowed. The revised recommendations reflected the growing use of atomic energy and the scientific consensus that occupational and population exposure should be held to a minimum. Confident that their suggested limits provided a wide margin of safety, the ICRP and the NCRP sought to keep exposure to levels that seemed generally safe without being impractical. NCRP chairman Taylor expressed their philosophy in 1956: "Any radiation exposure received by man must be regarded as harmful. Therefore, the objective should be to keep man's exposure as low as possible and yet, at the same time, not discontinue the use of radiation altogether."[38]

From the time of its establishment in 1947, the AEC had adopted the NCRP's recommendations in its own installations and operations. Some critics charged that the NCRP operated in concert with the AEC, but there is no evidence that the agency exercised undue influence in the committee's deliberations over its exposure limits. The new Atomic Energy Act of 1954 made possible the widespread commercial application of atomic energy for the first time. The law eased the government monopoly on technical information and sought to encourage the use of atomic energy for peaceful purposes. It assigned the AEC the responsibility of both promoting and regulating the commercial nuclear industry. As a result the AEC issued radiation protection standards for the protection of its licensees' employees and the public. The AEC drew on the levels recommended by the NCRP for both external radiation and internal emitters and also imposed a limit of one-tenth of the occupational limit for members of the public potentially affected by the operations of its licensees. The first AEC regulations on radiation protection became effective in February 1957.

37. Mazuzan and Walker, *Controlling the Atom,* pp. 258–59, 333; J. Samuel Walker, *Containing the Atom: Nuclear Regulation in a Changing Environment, 1963–1971* (Berkeley and Los Angeles: University of California Press, 1992), p. 302.

38. Joint Committee on Atomic Energy, *Hearings on Fallout,* pp. 778–94, 807–10, 1062; and *Hearings on Employee Radiation Hazards,* p. 42; Taylor, *Radiation Protection Standards,* pp. 47–50; Taylor, *Organization for Radiation Protection,* pp. 8-068 to 8-072.

After the NCRP tightened its recommended doses, the AEC followed suit. In April 1959 the agency published for public comment revised regulations that incorporated the changes adopted by the NCRP the previous year. It limited occupational whole-body exposure from external sources to 5 rems per year. Where adequate records existed, the AEC allowed a dose of up to 12 rems in a single year if the 5-rem annual average was not exceeded. Like the NCRP, the AEC believed that the occupational exposure limits provided ample protection for most individuals, but it did not guarantee that its standards offered absolute safety for all radiation workers. It did not assume that its limits represented a threshold of safety for anyone who was exposed to radiation. The AEC's new regulations, like the previous ones, set limits for the population outside of controlled areas at one-tenth the occupational standards. After a public comment period, the AEC issued the revised standards in July 1960; they became effective on January 1, 1961.[39]

In a period of more than six decades after the discoveries of x-rays and natural radioactivity, scientists gradually increased their knowledge of radiation hazards. The ICRP and the NCRP drew on a growing body of evidence to propose exposure limits for radiation workers and the public. But the data remained fragmentary and inconclusive. As a result the recommendations on permissible doses were not absolute standards but imprecise estimates that reflected a conservative application of the best available information. Both the ICRP and the NCRP compensated for the uncertainties in knowledge about radiation by issuing recommendations that they believed erred on the side of caution. They worked on the assumption that exposure to radiation should be kept to a minimum but that the occupational limits should not be so low as to be practically unattainable. They tightened their permissible levels in the 1950s in response to the findings of scientific authorities, especially the National Academy of Sciences, the expanding uses of atomic energy, and the increasing public concern about radiation. The AEC, by adopting the NCRP's recommendations in its regulations for exposure limits in its areas of jurisdiction, accepted the judgment of acknowledged experts in the field of radiation protection on what constituted generally safe and achievable doses.

As radiation protection proceeded from a rather arcane scientific prob-

39. Mazuzan and Walker, *Controlling the Atom,* pp. 55–56, 333–35; Gilbert F. Whittemore, "The National Committee on Radiation Protection, 1928–1960: From Professional Guidelines to Government Regulation" (Ph.D. diss., Harvard University, 1986).

lem of safeguarding a relatively small number of workers to a public issue involving questions of national security and the health of millions of people and their unborn progeny, it inevitably created controversies. The most visible was the fallout debate, which highlighted differences among scientists about the severity of the risk from exposure to low-level radiation. Although they agreed that radiation exposure should be kept to a minimum, they expressed conflicting views on the likelihood that small amounts of radiation would lead to serious genetic and somatic consequences for the population. Even if the data had been more definitive, the fallout debate raised philosophical, moral, and political questions that scientific evidence alone could not resolve. At the same time that the use of atomic energy for civilian purposes became more common, public fear of exposure to radiation became more acute, largely as a result of the fallout controversy. Although the American people demonstrated no signs of panic over reports of rising fallout levels, they clearly showed increasing concern about the hazards of low-level radiation. A higher level of public awareness of and anxiety about radiation along with a diminished level of confidence in the AEC were legacies of the fallout controversy that played an important role in future debates over radiation protection.

CHAPTER TWO

The Debate over
Nuclear Power and Radiation

The fallout controversy of the 1950s and early 1960s largely disappeared as a prominent public policy issue after the Limited Test Ban Treaty of 1963. But many questions about the consequences of fallout remained unresolved, and the debate left a legacy of ongoing scientific inquiry and latent public anxiety about the health effects of low-level radiation. Those fears, and acrimonious scientific dissension, were rekindled in the late 1960s and early 1970s. This time the major issue was the hazards of radioactive effluents released from nuclear power plants. The Atomic Energy Commission, which the 1954 Atomic Energy Act had made responsible both for encouraging the development of nuclear power and for certifying its safety, stood at the center of the new debate over radiation risks. Critics emphasized the AEC's dual and inherently conflicting mandate to promote and to regulate nuclear power technology in their indictments of the agency's performance. By the end of the 1960s nuclear power was the focus of a growing national controversy over issues that came to include not only radiation dangers but also reactor safety, radioactive waste disposal, environmental protection, and terrorist threats to nuclear plants and materials. One result was the Energy Reorganization Act of 1974, which abolished the AEC and created a new agency, the Nuclear Regulatory Commission (NRC), to take over its regulatory functions. Like the AEC, the NRC was headed by five commissioners supported by a technical, legal, and administrative staff. The NRC staff provided expertise, information, and recommendations for policy decisions made by a majority vote of the commissioners. Unlike the AEC, the NRC's responsibilities applied only to regulatory matters.

The "Great Bandwagon Market"
and Radiation Protection

The efforts that the AEC undertook in response to its mandate to promote the commercial application of nuclear power achieved only limited success in the first decade after the 1954 Atomic Energy Act became law. This triggered sharp criticism from the Joint Committee on Atomic Energy, which charged that the AEC was not doing enough to encourage industrial participation in atomic energy programs. The halting pace of nuclear power development was largely due to utilities' reservations on technical, economic, and safety grounds. Beginning in the mid-1960s, however, a rapid growth in the nuclear power industry, described by one utility executive as the "great bandwagon market," took place. The reactor boom reached a peak in 1966 and 1967, exceeding, in the words of one industry authority, "even the most optimistic estimates." In 1966 utilities placed orders for twenty nuclear plants, representing 36 percent of the new generating capacity purchased that year, and in 1967 they bought thirty-one nuclear units, representing 49 percent of the total capacity purchased. The nuclear option suddenly became more popular for a number of reasons. Leading vendors offered to build nuclear plants for a fixed cost that was competitive with coal-fired units. Power pooling arrangements among utilities encouraged the construction of large generating stations, for which nuclear power was best suited, by easing fears of excess capacity. And growing public and political concern about air pollution made nuclear power an inviting alternative to coal.[1]

The bandwagon market was a source of pride and satisfaction to the AEC; after years of contention with the Joint Committee and doubt about the future of the technology, its approach to promoting the industry seemed to be vindicated. But the sudden expansion in nuclear orders also caused considerable uneasiness within the regulatory staff of

---

1. Joint Committee on Atomic Energy (JCAE), *Nuclear Power Economics—1962 through 1967,* 90th Cong., 2d sess., 1968, pp. 4–5, 11, 15, 32–33, and *Hearings on AEC Authorizing Legislation Fiscal Year 1970,* 91st Cong., 1st sess., 1969, pp. 975–1017; "The Harnessed Atom: It's a Business Now," *Newsweek,* April 18, 1966, p. 84; Tom O'Hanlon, "An Atomic Bomb in the Land of Coal," *Fortune* 74 (September 1966): 164–72; John F. Hogerton, "The Arrival of Nuclear Power," *Scientific American* 218 (February 1968): 21–31; Richard F. Hirsh, *Technology and Transformation in the American Electric Utility Industry* (New York: Cambridge University Press, 1989); J. Samuel Walker, *Containing the Atom: Nuclear Regulation in a Changing Environment, 1963–1971* (Berkeley and Los Angeles: University of California Press, 1992), pp. 18–36.

the agency because of the problems that the boom presented for protecting public health. One of several issues that concerned the regulatory staff was the possibility that public exposure to radiation from the normal operation of plants would increase to undesirable levels. The AEC's regulations governing releases from commercial nuclear power facilities were designed to protect plant workers from injury and the public from harm. But, given the ambiguities about radiation hazards, they were necessarily imprecise. The AEC attempted to compensate for the lack of definitive information by applying what was known in conservative ways.

The agency established limits for the amount of radiation a plant could release during routine operations to meet its standards for permissible exposure. Although most of the radiation produced by nuclear fission in a reactor is contained within the reactor core, small amounts of certain isotopes escape into the environment in gaseous or liquid discharges that are a normal part of plant operation. In determining the levels of external radiation that a member of the public could receive from such effluents, the AEC assumed that a person stood outdoors at the boundary of the plant 24 hours a day, 365 days a year. In a similar manner, it set the amount of internal radiation that a plant could add to cooling water at a level low enough that a person could drink it for a lifetime without exceeding the permissible limits. Operating experience in the late 1960s showed that nuclear plants were meeting the requirements easily. In 1968, for example, only one of the eleven power reactors then in operation exceeded 20 percent of the allowable limits for liquid effluents and only two exceeded 3.4 percent of the limits for gaseous effluents.[2]

"As Low as Practicable"

Despite the commendable performance of nuclear plants in limiting their radiation releases, the AEC's regulatory staff sought to tighten the standards for public exposure. In July 1968 Forrest Western, who was director of the Division of Radiation Protection Standards and

2. Clifford K. Beck to William T. England, July 25, 1969, Lester R. Rogers to Harold L. Price, May 12, 1969, Price to the Commission, April 22, 1970, Atomic Energy Commission Records (ORG-NRC History), Public Document Room, Nuclear Regulatory Commission, Washington, D.C. (hereafter cited as AEC/NRC).

well known among professionals in the field for his work with the NCRP and the ICRP, drafted a proposal for revising the regulations that he and other members of the regulatory staff had discussed for some time. The changes he suggested were largely matters of clarification and codification of existing practices. The most important was to specify that radiation releases from nuclear plants should be kept to a level "as low as practicable." The regulatory staff thought that adding this phrase might discourage licensees from assuming that approaching the permissible limits as a matter of course, rather than trying to reduce levels to a minimum, was acceptable. This seemed particularly vital in the light of expanding public exposure to radiation from a variety of sources, such as the rapidly growing use of color television and more frequent air travel as well as the increasing number of nuclear power plants. Western's proposals were modest in scope; they would not change the existing numerical limits. They were intended to provide an extra measure of protection to the public.[3]

While the regulatory staff was circulating its proposals internally, some observers outside the AEC were raising questions about the adequacy of the existing regulations. As concern about industrial pollution took on increasing urgency as a public policy issue in the 1960s, the environmental impact of nuclear power received more public scrutiny than ever before. A number of observers suggested that in light of the uncertainties about radiation effects, the AEC's regulations were insufficiently rigorous and should be substantially revised. This first emerged as a major controversy when the state of Minnesota, responding to questions raised by environmentalists, stipulated in May 1969 that the Monticello plant then under construction north of Minneapolis must restrict its radioactive effluents to a level of about 3 percent of that allowed by the AEC for an individual member of the public (500 millirems). The controversy in Minnesota attracted wide attention and generated much criticism of the AEC's radiation standards. An article in *Science* reported that Minnesota's challenge "cast doubt on the adequacy of existing AEC regulations to cope with radioactive effluent from the expected proliferation of new reactors."[4]

3. Saul Levine to the Files, March 31, 1966, Forrest Western to Harold L. Price, July 12, 1968, AEC/NRC; "Notes on a Conversation between D.D.C. [David D. Comey] and Dr. Peter Morris," January 7, 1969, Box 440 (SIPI—New York Chapter, Cayuga Lake), Barry Commoner Papers, Library of Congress, Washington, D.C.

4. Walker, *Containing the Atom*, pp. 309–17; Philip M. Boffey, "Radioactive Pollution: Minnesota Finds AEC Standards Too Lax," *Science* 163 (March 7, 1969): 1043–45.

The "proliferation of new reactors" continued to command the attention of the AEC's regulatory staff, which was still considering revisions of the existing regulations. The Monticello controversy gave the issue greater urgency and at the same time prompted the staff to suggest more drastic changes than those it had drafted in July 1968. In March 1969 Western prepared a new proposal calling for reducing permissible concentrations of radioactivity in liquid effluents to 1 percent of existing levels for individuals. A short time later he added a stipulation that concentrations in gaseous effluents be cut to 10 percent of existing levels. Together, the proposals would make the AEC's regulations even stricter than the limits that the state of Minnesota would soon impose on the Monticello plant. The AEC's regulatory staff believed that its recommendations would not place undue burdens on operating reactors and would avoid the "undesirable position" of allowing releases of radiation far larger than were necessary. It hoped that adoption of its new draft would help to ensure further protection of the public from unwarranted exposure and boost confidence in the AEC's commitment to safeguarding public health.[5]

The outcome of the regulatory staff's proposals depended on the support of the commissioners. The AEC devoted more of its attention and resources to its statutory responsibilities for developing nuclear weapons and promoting the commercial use of atomic energy than it did to regulation. The five commissioners, by a majority vote, were the final arbiters of the sometimes conflicting recommendations that they received from the different functional units of the agency's staff. The revisions that the regulatory staff proposed elicited strong objections from other staff offices in the AEC. Some high-level officials worried that the changes could not only discourage growth of the nuclear industry but also hinder their own programs. They submitted that even though the revised regulations would be imposed only on licensed nuclear power plants, "there would be strong pressure to apply any new limits to all nuclear operations." The Division of Production, for example, which was responsible for running the reactors that made plutonium and tritium for nuclear weapons, complained that tightening the standards would raise its costs "without any corresponding increase in safety." Other units within the AEC were equally adamant in opposing the regulatory staff's pro-

5. Lester R. Rogers to Harold L. Price, March 27, 1969, Forrest Western to Price, April 3, 1969, Price to the Commission, July 24, 1969, and Minutes of Regulatory Meeting 274, April 9, 1969, AEC/NRC.

posals. They insisted that there "was no valid health and safety reason for reducing the limits" and suggested that doing so would be, "in effect, an assertion that these limits are hazardous." In October 1969 the commissioners voted unanimously to reject the regulatory staff's recommendations for major revisions, though they approved adding the requirement that licensees keep the amount of radiation released from plants "as low as practicable."[6]

Despite the Commission's unequivocal rejection of the regulatory staff's appeal for a sharp reduction in the numerical limits for radiation releases, within a short time the proposals were revived in a somewhat altered form. One key to the sudden and highly unusual turnaround in the commissioners' views was that members of the AEC's Advisory Committee on Reactor Safeguards, a statutory committee of outside nuclear safety experts, questioned the soundness of the regulations. Acting committee chairman Joseph M. Hendrie thought that the existing limits were "too high to be justified." With those comments in mind, AEC chairman Glenn T. Seaborg changed his position on revising the regulations. The regulatory staff prepared a new set of proposals that offered a range of numerical values, rather than set figures, that licensees would be expected to meet under normal operating conditions. It also increased the flexibility of the numerical limits by making them "design objectives" rather than absolute requirements. Seaborg's efforts and the conviction that the AEC must respond affirmatively to growing criticism of its radiation standards led the commissioners to accept the regulatory staff's revised proposals. In February 1970 they voted to amend the regulations by adding design objectives that were a small percentage of the maximum permissible limits for an individual member of the public: 1 to 2 percent for liquid effluents and 3 to 6 percent for gaseous effluents.[7]

The regulatory staff's achievement in winning the support of a majority of commissioners despite the resistance of other AEC offices proved to be a short-lived success. It prevailed in the internal politics of the AEC only to fall victim to the vocal objections of the Joint Committee on

6. AEC 180/66 (October 24, 1969), AEC/NRC; *Journal of Glenn T. Seaborg*, 25 vols. (Berkeley: Lawrence Berkeley Laboratory PUB-625, 1989), 20:317, 349.

7. W. B. McCool to Harold L. Price, November 14, 1969, Theos J. Thompson to the Commission, November 4, 1969, Price to the Commission, February 19, 1970, with Draft Proposed Amendments to Parts 20 and 50, AEC/NRC; R. M. Ketchel to the File, February 9, 1970, Henry E. Bliss to Dennis Spurgeon, February 5, 1970, *Containing the Atom* File, History Division, Department of Energy, Germantown, Maryland (hereafter cited as AEC/DOE); *Seaborg Journal*, 20:463, 21:284, 322.

Atomic Energy. The views of the Joint Committee were of great importance, partly because of its traditional oversight and fiscal authority over the AEC and partly because it had strongly defended the agency from a growing chorus of nuclear critics. A short time after the commissioners voted in favor of revising the radiation regulations to include the new design objectives, Seaborg noted in his diary that he expected to "meet some opposition" from the Joint Committee. Seaborg's concerns understated the magnitude of the problem. The chairman of the Joint Committee, Chet Holifield, told Seaborg that the proposed revisions "would be letting the Joint Committee down after all the effort [it] had expended in defending the AEC and its standards." He added that if the AEC made the changes it was considering, it "would so undercut his effectiveness that he would no longer be [the agency's] supporter in Congress or any other matter that required his help." The hostility of Holifield and his colleagues killed the AEC's plan to tighten its radiation standards by cutting the permissible limits, even as design objectives.[8]

Unable to secure the endorsement of the Joint Committee for any numerical tightening of its radiation standards, the AEC elected simply to add an "as low as practicable" provision to the regulations and to require applicants to describe precisely how they would accomplish that goal. Although the changes were much more modest than those the AEC had originally planned to make, agency officials told a crowded press conference on March 27, 1970, that they were more than "just cosmetic." Director of regulation Harold L. Price explained that the new measures, which the AEC was publishing for public comment, would ensure that licensees installed the equipment needed to keep radiation releases as low as practicable. The AEC's critics were not impressed. The governor of Minnesota, Harold LeVander, suggested that the agency's proposals were a concession that the existing standards were too lax. He commented that "this appears an admission that the AEC regulations have not been realistic."[9]

8. Harold L. Price to the Commission, February 25, 1970, AEC/NRC; James B. Graham to Edward J. Bauser, February 23, 1970, Box 531 (Radiation Standards for Protection), Papers of the Joint Committee on Atomic Energy, Record Group 128 (Records of the Joint Committees of Congress), National Archives, Washington, D.C.; *Seaborg Journal,* 21:322, 349, 357, 362.

9. "AEC Acts to Strengthen Radioactive Discharge Standards," *Nuclear Industry* 17 (April 1970): 36–38; *Nucleonics Week,* April 2, 1970; *St. Paul Pioneer Press,* March 29, 1970; "Statement of Commissioner James T. Ramey," March 27, 1970, *Containing the Atom* File, AEC/DOE; *Seaborg Journal,* 21:432.

The Gofman-Tamplin Controversy

By the time the AEC announced the proposed revisions in its regulations, questions about and fears of radiation from nuclear power plants had reached major proportions. An extreme but not isolated example of the growing anxiety was a flyer distributed by an environmentalist group that named nuclear power the "greatest threat to the environment" of the northeastern United States because the "reckless promotion of the AEC and the electric utilities . . . threatens to increase cancer, leukemia, and defective births."[10]

Largely in response to the growth of the nuclear industry, protests against nuclear power gathered new strength and gained unprecedented national attention in 1969 and 1970. A critical element in the increasing impact of antinuclear arguments was popular concern about radiation effects, even the small releases from routine operation of nuclear plants. Two prominent books that appeared in 1969 reflected those fears and no doubt intensified them as well. Sheldon Novick's *The Careless Atom* warned that radiation from nuclear power "is in our surroundings, and will accumulate in living things until the point of severe damage is reached." Richard Curtis and Elizabeth Hogan's *Perils of the Peaceful Atom* described low-level radiation hazards in even more alarming terms: "We must realize that even if [reactor] accidents are averted, the slow, silent saturation of our environment with radioactive poisons will be raising the odds that you or your heirs will fall victim to any one of the horrors depicted here [cancer, shortening of life, genetic mutation], and possibly to some unexperienced in human history." By January 1970 Novick's book had gone into its fourth printing, and the publisher of the Curtis-Hogan volume reported that it had sold "quite well." Both books were issued in trade paperback editions a short time later.[11]

The reservations that nuclear power critics expressed about the expanding use of the technology were reinforced by an acrimonious debate over radiation hazards between the AEC and two scientists who worked at a national laboratory it supported. The origins of the dispute lay in the allegations of another scientist, Ernest J. Sternglass, about the health effects

10. Flyer of Anti-Pollution League, February 6, 1970, Series 2, Box 1 (Anti-Pollution League), Chesapeake Bay Foundation Papers, University of Maryland, College Park.

11. Sheldon Novick, *The Careless Atom* (Boston: Houghton Mifflin, 1969), p. 146; Richard Curtis and Elizabeth Hogan, *Perils of the Peaceful Atom* (Garden City, N.Y.: Doubleday, 1969), p. 44; *Nucleonics Week*, January 8, 1970.

of radioactive fallout from bomb testing. Sternglass attracted a great deal of attention from the news media in spring and summer 1969 by suggesting that fallout had caused 375,000 deaths of infants less than one year old and an untold number of fetal deaths between 1951 and 1966. He presented his findings in, among other places, a highly publicized article in *Esquire* magazine. Sternglass's methods, assumptions, and conclusions generated sharp and incredulous rejoinders from many scientific authorities—not only from the AEC and other government agencies but also from experts who were longtime critics of the AEC's weapons testing program.[12]

Among those who carefully evaluated Sternglass's thesis was Arthur R. Tamplin, a group leader in the biomedical division of Lawrence Livermore National Laboratory, a facility operated by the University of California under a contract funded by the AEC. Tamplin had joined the laboratory in 1963 to participate in a major project the AEC had established to investigate the health effects of fallout and other radiation releases. In April 1969 he prepared a paper assessing Sternglass's thesis for an informal seminar for Livermore employees. Like other critics, he charged Sternglass with misusing or manipulating data to suit his conclusions. Tamplin argued that the two most important influences on fetal and infant mortality were socioeconomic conditions and the introduction of antibiotics. He suggested that the best way to reduce the frequency of mortality among unborn and young children was to improve living standards for the poor. But he did not dismiss fallout as a contributing cause of fetal and infant death rates in the United States. He thought that Sternglass had overestimated the effect of fallout by a factor of at least one hundred. This meant that if Tamplin's calculations were correct, fallout could still be held accountable for perhaps as many as eight thousand fetal and four thousand infant mortalities.[13]

12. Ernest J. Sternglass, "Infant Mortality and Nuclear Tests," *Bulletin of the Atomic Scientists* 25 (April 1969): 18–20; Sternglass, "Can the Infants Survive?" ibid., 25 (June 1969): 26–27; "Infant Mortality Controversy: Sternglass and His Critics," ibid., 25 (October 1969): 26–33; Sternglass, "The Death of All Children: A Footnote to the A.B.M. Controversy," *Esquire*, September 1969, pp. 1a–1d; Philip M. Boffey, "Ernest J. Sternglass: Controversial Prophet of Doom," *Science* 166 (October 10, 1969): 195–200; Michael J. Friedlander and Joseph Klarmann, "How Many Children?" *Environment* 11 (December 1969): 3–8; Patricia J. Lindop and J. Rotblat, "Strontium-90 and Infant Mortality," *Nature* 224 (December 27, 1969): 1257–60; Alice Stewart, "The Pitfalls of Extrapolation," *New Scientist* 43 (July 24, 1969): 181; Chris A. Hansen to the Surgeon General, July 14, 1969, "Notes on Sternglass for Dr. Telles' Use," n.d., "Statement on the Assertions of E. J. Sternglass," n.d., File 183, U.S. Public Health Service Records, Division of Radiological Health, U.S. Public Health Service, Rockville, Maryland.

13. AEC 688/92 (September 10, 1969), Energy History Collection, AEC/DOE; Arthur R. Tamplin, Yvonne Ricker, and Marguerite F. Longmate, "A Criticism of the Sternglass

Tamplin planned to publish his findings in a quasi-popular journal such as *Environment* or the *Bulletin of the Atomic Scientists*. Officials in the AEC's Division of Biology and Medicine, however, worried that even though his conclusions were far less shocking than those of Sternglass, they were still alarming enough to fuel public concern about low-level radiation. John R. Totter, director of the division, expressed his reservations to Tamplin. He heartily approved of the publication of Tamplin's critique of Sternglass, but he objected to publication of Tamplin's estimates of fetal and infant mortality because they were unproven. He insisted that Tamplin made unwarranted assumptions about the causes of fetal and infant mortality and failed to account for experiments with mice and dogs that seemed to refute the magnitude of the mortality rates that he proposed. Totter suggested that Tamplin separate those sections from his paper and submit them to a technical journal read mostly by specialists. This led to a series of sharp exchanges; Tamplin conceded that his estimates were imprecise but argued that they were within the realm of possibility. Despite Totter's reservations, Tamplin published his article in the *Bulletin of the Atomic Scientists*.[14]

The disagreement with Totter did not prevent Tamplin from presenting his findings to a larger audience than the AEC preferred (and the agency made no further effort to prevent him from doing so). However, the dispute did breed considerable ill will between AEC officials and Tamplin. The rift widened when Tamplin turned his attention to the potential health effects of low-level radiation from nuclear power. In fall 1969 he began to suggest that the growth of nuclear power could cause the death of thousands of Americans from cancer every year. Tamplin was joined in airing his views about the hazards of nuclear power by John W. Gofman, his boss at Livermore. Gofman held both a doctorate in chemistry and a medical degree from the University of California. He had studied for his Ph.D. under Glenn Seaborg at Berkeley, where he co-discovered the artificially produced radioactive element uranium 233. When he was appointed to head the newly created biomedical division at Livermore in 1963, Seaborg called him one of his "most brilliant stu-

Article on Fetal and Infant Mortality," July 22, 1969, File 1583, Public Health Service Records; Pete Winslow, "Fallout from the 'Peaceful Atom,'" *Nation* 212 (May 3, 1971): 557–61.

14. AEC 688/92, Arthur R. Tamplin to Eugene Rabinowitch, July 29, 1969, Richard S. Lewis to Tamplin, August 15, 1969, Sheldon Novick to Tamplin, August 7, 1969, SECY 103 (July 16, 1970), Energy History Collection, John R. Totter to Tamplin, September 10, 1969, *Containing the Atom* File, AEC/DOE; Arthur R. Tamplin, "Fetal and Infant Mortality and the Environment," *Bulletin of the Atomic Scientists* 25 (December 1969): 23–29.

Figure 3. Officials of the AEC and Lawrence Livermore National Laboratory pose during a meeting on March 6, 1969, a few months before they clashed over radiation standards. Left to right: Michael M. May, director of Livermore Laboratory; John R. Totter, director of the AEC's Division of Biology and Medicine; John W. Gofman, associate director of Livermore Laboratory and director of its Biomedical Division; and Glenn T. Seaborg, chairman of the AEC. (Lawrence Livermore National Laboratory)

dents." Tamplin held a doctorate in biophysics from Berkeley, where he had studied under Gofman.[15]

In October 1969 Tamplin and Gofman delivered a paper at a symposium sponsored by the Institute of Electrical and Electronics Engineers in which they contended that if the entire population of the United States received the permissible population dose of 0.17 rad per year throughout their lifetimes, the result would be seventeen thousand additional cases of cancer annually. Basing their figure on extrapolations from the effects of high doses of radiation, they suggested that the risks of low-level exposure

15. AEC 859/12 (May 4, 1963), "Excerpt from Minutes of Commission Meeting 1929," May 6, 1963, *Containing the Atom* File, AEC/DOE; Leslie J. Freeman, *Nuclear Witnesses: Insiders Speak Out* (New York: W. W. Norton, 1981), pp. 81–89.

had been badly underestimated. Tamplin and Gofman admitted that the "population has not received anywhere near 0.17 Rads from atomic energy activities thus far," and they hoped that their calculations overstated the hazards of low-level radiation. But they insisted that in the absence of definitive knowledge about the consequences of exposure and the prospective growth of the nuclear industry, permissible levels should be made more conservative. They urged that the AEC and other federal agencies reduce their allowable doses by "at least a factor of ten." Gofman told a reporter that "to continue the present [exposure] guidelines is absolute folly."[16]

The AEC found Gofman and Tamplin's analysis unpersuasive on a number of grounds. One was their extrapolation from high doses of radiation to estimate the hazards of low-level exposure. This assumed that small doses delivered over a long period caused as much somatic damage as an acute dose. Although the evidence was not definitive, there were strong indications that low doses over an extended period were less harmful than heavy doses in a short time. In short, the dose rate was an important consideration in estimating radiation hazards. The AEC also noted that other experts had considered the same data as Gofman and Tamplin and judged the risks to be much lower. The Livermore scientists' conclusions were not derived from new findings or original research. The difference lay not in the "hard evidence" they claimed to have but in the interpretation of existing data. The AEC denied that Gofman and Tamplin had proven that their interpretation was more convincing than that of other radiation experts. It saw no way, for example, that the entire population of the country could be exposed to radiation in amounts close to the permissible limits, which by definition applied to continuous exposure at the boundaries of nuclear plants. Further, Gofman and Tamplin made some fundamental errors in discussing existing radiation standards, the most flagrant of which was insisting that the regulations assumed a threshold below which radiation exposure was safe.[17]

Despite the differences in the positions of the AEC and the Livermore scientists, Gofman and Tamplin's recommendations for reducing permissible limits were similar to the proposals that the AEC's regulatory staff was advancing behind the scenes in fall 1969. Indeed, the regulatory

16. John W. Gofman and Arthur R. Tamplin, "Low Dose Radiation, Chromosomes, and Cancer," October 29, 1969, printed in JCAE, *Hearings on Environmental Effects of Producing Electric Power,* 91st Cong., 1st sess., 1969, pp. 640–52; *San Francisco Chronicle,* October 30, 1969.

17. AEC 1318/27 (December 3, 1969), *Containing the Atom* File, AEC/DOE; JCAE, *Hearings on Environmental Effects of Producing Electric Power,* pp. 685–93.

staff supported revisions that were more drastic than those Gofman and Tamplin were calling for. At that point the staff's proposals had met strong opposition within the agency, and it was far from clear that they would receive the approval of the commissioners. Yet the irony remains that Gofman and Tamplin and the AEC's regulatory staff agreed that the regulations should be tightened to provide an extra measure of protection for the public. The regulatory staff's position was a matter internal to the agency; institutional restraints, the objections of other AEC divisions, and, finally, the hostility of the Joint Committee kept it from public view. Gofman and Tamplin faced fewer restrictions in making their opinions public. By the time the commissioners voted in favor of the regulatory staff's modified proposals, the questions raised by the Livermore dissenters had launched a bitter and highly visible dispute.

The breach between the AEC and Gofman and Tamplin gradually widened irreversibly. Although the commissioners considered restricting Gofman and Tamplin and other employees of AEC laboratories to publishing in scientific journals or requiring them to clear papers with the AEC, they rejected this approach to dealing with dissenting views. Nevertheless, when Tamplin prepared a paper for presentation at a meeting of the American Association for the Advancement of Science in December 1969, the associate director of Livermore, Roger E. Batzel, asked him to tone it down and make clear that he was not speaking in an official capacity. At the meeting Tamplin gave a modified version of the paper that strongly reiterated his warnings about low-level radiation hazards. The AEC, determined that those arguments should not go unchallenged, countered by passing out a staff critique of Gofman and Tamplin's position at the conference, a summary of which appeared in many newspapers. Batzel's and the AEC's actions further separated Gofman and Tamplin from their employing agencies and moved them toward the views and the rhetoric of antinuclear critics. When the Livermore scientists had first suggested the tightening of permissible radiation limits, they had used restrained language and affirmed their support for nuclear power. As they became increasingly alienated from the AEC and Livermore Laboratory, however, they became noticeably more strident in their rhetoric and inflexible in their arguments.[18]

18. Arthur R. Tamplin, "Nuclear Reactors and the Public Health and Safety," December 1969, James T. Ramey to Roger E. Batzel, January 5, 1970, John A. Harris to Edward J. Bloch, December 23, 1969, Glenn T. Seaborg to Edmund S. Muskie, December 24, 1969, Harris to the Commission, December 31, 1969, W. B. McCool to the File, January 6, 1969, *Containing the Atom* File, AEC/DOE.

Gofman and Tamplin's estrangement was most obvious in the rhetoric they used to attack those who disagreed with them. When NCRP chairman Lauriston Taylor told a congressional committee that Gofman and Tamplin had "presented no new data, new ideas, or new information" that "highly experienced" experts had not already considered, the two Livermore scientists denounced "this fraudulent, hypocritical, and incompetent document" and added: "Incompetence in the extreme is our only possible evaluation of Lauriston Taylor and his cohorts." Gofman, who soon emerged as the more outspoken of the dissenters, informed a special committee on environmental protection of the City Council of New York on March 4, 1970, that "the difference between us and the AEC is that we are not willing to play Russian roulette with human lives." The following day he predicted that the AEC would soon relax its radiation standards and that the result would be a 30 percent increase in cancer. "There is no morality," he said of agency officials, "and there is not a shred of honesty in any one of them." Gofman made this statement about a week after the AEC's behind-the-scenes effort to tighten its numerical limits for radiation exposure had been squelched by the Joint Committee.[19]

The Livermore scientists not only argued that the existing standards of the AEC and other radiation protection organizations were inadequate but also challenged the prevailing consensus that the benefits of nuclear power were worth the risks. Tamplin declared that it was "not obvious that the benefits of more electrical power outweigh the risks." Gofman was more vivid in his dissent; he insisted that in its radiation standards, "the AEC is stating that there is a risk and their hope that the benefits outweigh the number of deaths." He added: "This is legalized murder, the only question is how many murders."[20]

Gofman and Tamplin's conclusions were greeted skeptically by most scientists. A group of twenty-nine radiation authorities, most based at universities or national laboratories, advised the Joint Committee on Atomic Energy that a "tiny minority of experts" were creating unwarranted alarm. An editorial in *Physics Today* lamented that Gofman and Tamplin failed "to place their points of disagreement in proper perspective" or to compare

19. U.S. Congress, Senate, Committee on Public Works, Subcommittee on Air and Water Pollution, *Hearings on Underground Uses of Nuclear Energy,* 91st Cong., 1st sess., 1969, pp. 281–90; "Public Hearing of the Special Committee for Environmental Protection of the City Council of the City of New York," transcript, March 4, 1970, "Unedited Transcript of Remarks of Dr. John W. Gofman," March 5, 1970, Energy History Collection, AEC/DOE.

20. *Baltimore Sun,* December 8, 1970; Arthur R. Tamplin, "Issues in the Radiation Controversy," *Bulletin of the Atomic Scientists* 27 (September 1971): 25–27.

the risks of nuclear power with the hazards of air pollution from fossil fuel plants. An article in *Science* suggested that Gofman and Tamplin damaged their case "by indulging in verbal overkill that alienates their peers and undermines their credibility." In January 1971 the NCRP announced that after a ten-year study it had determined that its recommendations for basic exposure levels—0.5 rem (or 500 millirems) for individual members of the public and 0.17 rem (or 170 millirems) for population groups—were sound. Taylor told reporters that the NCRP had examined Gofman and Tamplin's arguments and found them unpersuasive.[21]

Gofman and Tamplin made a much greater impact in other circles. They were featured in articles in newspapers, magazines, and journals ranging from *Science* to the *National Enquirer*. They received prominent and sympathetic coverage on radio and television and were frequently cited by other critics of nuclear power and the AEC. In hearings that the Joint Committee held in January 1970, for example, Minnesota governor LeVander and Vermont attorney general James M. Jeffords used Gofman and Tamplin's arguments to support their own objections to nuclear power. *Nucleonics Week* observed in January 1970 that despite reservations among scientific authorities about Gofman and Tamplin's views, "no one doubts that they have scored verbal points."[22]

The effect of Gofman and Tamplin on the radiation safety issue was apparent in other ways. In January 1970 Secretary of Health, Education, and Welfare Robert H. Finch, acting in his capacity as chairman of the Federal Radiation Council (FRC), announced that the FRC would undertake a "careful review and evaluation" of the risks of low-level radioactivity. The FRC, which Eisenhower had set up in 1959 to advise the president and federal agencies on radiation protection, drew heavily on the recommendations of the NCRP in making its judgments. Finch declared, "We do not agree with all the premises, conditions, and extrapolations used by Gofman and Tamplin," but he suggested that it was ap-

21. Federal Radiation Council Information Paper, May 1, 1970, File 203, Public Health Service Records; Lauriston S. Taylor to Chet Holifield, February 5, 1971, Box 48 (National Committee on Radiation Protection), Chet Holifield Papers, University of Southern California, Los Angeles; Harold L. Davis, "Clean Air Misunderstanding," *Physics Today* 23 (May 1970): 104; Philip M. Boffey, "Gofman and Tamplin: Harassment Charges against AEC, Livermore," *Science* 169 (August 28, 1970): 838–43; *Washington Post*, January 27, 1971; *New York Times*, January 27, 1971; *Nucleonics Week*, January 28, 1971.

22. Transcripts, "Huntley-Brinkley Report," March 4, 1970, and "CBS Morning News," March 4, 1970, Energy History Collection, AEC/DOE; JCAE, *Hearings on Environmental Effects of Producing Electric Power*, pp. 1110–1420; *National Enquirer*, September 27, 1970; *Nucleonics Week*, January 8, 1970.

propriate for the FRC to examine developments in the decade since its establishment. The FRC promptly made arrangements with the National Academy of Sciences to reassess the scientific basis for radiation standards and to estimate the risks they presented to the public. Although one of Finch's aides insisted that the new study was "not intended to cast doubts or darkness on present standards," Gofman and Tamplin seized on it as a vindication of their position. "The A.E.C. says that our work has no merit," declared Tamplin, "but Robert Finch has overruled it and ordered a sweeping review of their standards."[23]

"As Low as Practicable" and Numerical Guidelines

The controversy over Gofman and Tamplin's views also played an important role in prodding the AEC to revise its radiation protection regulations again. In March 1970 it had published its proposal to require that licensees keep radioactive releases as low as practicable, and in light of the public comments it received and the continuing debate over radiation hazards, further changes seemed advisable. Most of the eighty comments sent to the regulatory staff supported tightening the regulations. A few environmental groups requested that the AEC reduce radioactive emissions to zero, but the most common complaint was that the meaning of "as low as practicable" was too vague. Twenty-five comments, including nineteen from nuclear utilities and vendors, urged the AEC to specify numerical limits as design objectives. They echoed the concerns expressed by the Westinghouse Corporation: "Interpretation difficulties due to the present vague wording will lead to uncertainties for the systems designer; major disagreements between applicants and regulatory personnel, hearing boards, and parties to hearings; increased intervention;

23. Robert H. Finch to Edmund S. Muskie, January 23, 1970, Federal Radiation Council, Minutes and Record of Actions, June 3, 1970, File 203, Public Health Service Records; Paul C. Tompkins, "Draft Action Staff Paper," March 20, 1970, Federal Radiation Council Action Paper, "Radiation Protection Policy," April 6, 1970, Box 3 (Council Meeting of May 8, 1970), Federal Radiation Council Papers, Record Group 412 (Records of the Environmental Protection Agency), National Archives, College Park, Maryland; *Nucleonics Week,* February 26, 1970; *Baltimore News American,* March 24, 1970.

The Gofman-Tamplin controversy is treated in more detail in Walker, *Containing the Atom,* pp. 338–62; and J. Samuel Walker, "The Atomic Energy Commission and the Politics of Radiation Protection, 1967–1971," *Isis* 85 (March 1994): 57–78.

lengthening of the licensing process; and uncertainties in reporting re-quirements." The agency had included quantitative design objectives in an earlier version of the revised regulations, only to remove them at the insistence of the Joint Committee. After the public comments offered such a clear message, the regulatory staff again suggested that it develop "definitive criteria on design objectives." The commissioners agreed; they made the proposed regulation effective January 2, 1971, with the provi-sion that the regulatory staff would immediately take action to define the "as low as practicable" requirement.[24]

On March 30, 1971, the regulatory staff sent a series of recommenda-tions to the Commission. It suggested that a licensee would meet design objectives if effluents from its plant were less than 5 percent of natural back-ground radiation. This was about 1 percent of the regulatory limit of a maximum exposure of 500 millirems by an individual member of the pub-lic, a level that remained in effect. Although the AEC's new numerical guidelines, if implemented, would not be inflexible requirements, the staff made clear that it would expect plants to comply with design objectives under normal operating conditions and would take enforcement action against those that did not.

As an alternative to the 5 percent of background exposure, the regula-tory staff proposed that a licensee would meet design objectives if it en-sured that an individual living at the boundary of a plant did not receive more than 5 millirems per year. And to provide additional protection for population groups, the staff introduced a new concept (though one that was widely used in Europe) for measuring exposure, the "man-rem." It submitted that a plant would conform with design objectives if the ex-posure of the population within a fifty-mile radius did not exceed 100 man-rems per year for each 1,000 megawatts of nuclear capacity. The man-rem, rather than assume a uniform dose for an entire population group (as the existing standard did), estimated the exposure to those who lived within different concentric areas from the plant. It was computed by multiply-ing the average dose received by members of a large group by the num-ber of people in that group. If one hundred thousand members of a pop-ulation group within an area that was a specified distance from a plant

24. SECY-R-52 (September 30, 1970), W. B. McCool to Lester R. Rogers, November 16, 1970, Harold L. Price to Chet Holifield, November 30, 1970, Minutes of Regulatory Meeting 288 (October 2, 1970), AEC/NRC; "Forum Committee Comments on AEC Pro-posed Radwaste Rule Changes," *Nuclear Industry* 17 (June 1970): 43–44; "AEC Receives Comments on Proposed New Ruling," *Nuclear News* 13 (August 1970): 57–59; *Nucleonics Week,* July 16, 1970, December 10, 1970.

were exposed to 5 millirems apiece, for example, the total dose would be 500 man-rems. This method of measurement not only provided additional assurance that population exposure would remain very low but also undercut Gofman and Tamplin's calculations, which were based on the assumption that every person in the United States received the allowable population exposure limit of 170 millirems.[25]

The commissioners promptly approved the regulatory staff's proposals. The Joint Committee, however, remained strongly opposed. Holifield had an "extremely adverse emotional reaction" and threatened, as he had done a year earlier when the AEC informed him of its plan to set numerical guidelines, to withdraw his support from the agency. Other committee members protested, though more mildly. Some utility representatives expressed keen disapproval of the proposal and complained that the AEC had "capitulated to the demands of Gofman and Tamplin." The agency made some revisions in its draft, the most important of which was to change the 100 man-rem limit to 400 man-rems. But, in contrast to its previous submission to Joint Committee pressure, it kept the basic proposals for numerical design objectives intact. It issued the proposed revisions for public comment in June 1971. "The force of the argument is so great," noted Seaborg, "that the Commission feels it simply must go ahead and make this improvement."[26]

Two major considerations made the "force of the argument" seem so great. One was the commitment of the AEC to provide a wide margin of safety from the radiation hazards of nuclear power plants. The objectives it prepared were intended to reduce the possibility of injury to the public without placing overly stringent requirements on the nuclear industry. The limits that the AEC proposed, despite some industry objections, were technically achievable and were generally being met by operating plants. Director of regulation Price told a press conference that there were two reasons for the AEC's new proposals: "We think it's right and we think it's technologically and economically feasible." The AEC was also influenced and motivated by its critics. Price denied that the AEC was acting in response to Gofman and Tamplin, but it is unlikely that the agency would have disregarded the opposition of the Joint Committee and leading industry officials if it had not felt pressed to demonstrate the adequacy of

25. Harold L. Price to the Commission, March 30, 1971, SECY-R-210 (April 8, 1971), AEC/NRC; *Nucleonics Week,* May 27, 1971.

26. *Seaborg Journal,* 24:512, 571, 582, 694, 25:23, 32, 294; James B. Graham to George F. Murphy, June 4, 1971, Box 48 (Staff Memoranda 1971), Holifield Papers; *Nucleonics Week,* May 27, 1971, June 10, 1971.

its regulations. The design objectives it published for public comment in June 1971 would effectively cut permissible limits for the public by a factor of one hundred, which was much more conservative than Gofman and Tamplin's original call for a reduction by a factor of ten. The AEC's credibility had suffered as a result of its dispute with Gofman and Tamplin, and it hoped to recover some lost ground by tightening its radiation regulations.[27] Thus the controversy over low-level radiation from nuclear plants in the early 1970s led to two major developments—a new study of radiation hazards for the general population conducted by the National Academy of Sciences and the AEC's publication of proposed numerical guidelines for public exposure to radiation from nuclear plant effluents.

The 1972 BEIR Report

The National Academy of Sciences undertook its review of existing radiation standards and the risks of low-level exposure in response to the request of the Federal Radiation Council, and it continued its study after the FRC's functions were transferred to the newly created Environmental Protection Agency (EPA) in December 1970. The National Academy's report, expected to take about two years to complete, was intended to consider new information and review the scientific bases for judging the risks to the U.S. population of exposure to low-level radiation. It would serve as an update of the influential assessment of radiation hazards issued by the National Academy in 1956. The National Academy named the panel of experts that it recruited to conduct the new study the Advisory Committee on the Biological Effects of Ionizing Radiations (BEIR). The BEIR committee divided its work among five subcommittees—general considerations, environmental effects, genetic effects, somatic effects, and effects on growth and development. While mindful of the arguments of critics of existing radiation standards, the BEIR panel resolved to address general issues concerning radiation protection rather than focus on the specific objections of dissenters.[28]

27. AEC Press Release, June 7, 1971, AEC/NRC; *New York Times,* June 8, 1971; *Nucleonics Week,* May 27, 1971; "Radiation Discharge Limits," *Nuclear Industry* 18 (June 1971): 17–19.

28. Minutes of Advisory Committee to the Federation Radiation Council, March 25, 1970, September 23, 1970, Advisory Committee—BEIR: Minutes 1969–1972, National Academy of Sciences Archives, Washington, D.C.

The National Academy submitted its report to the Environmental Protection Agency in early September 1972. After reviewing it and making some minor changes, EPA published the BEIR committee's findings on November 15, 1972, under the title "The Effects on Populations of Exposure to Low Levels of Ionizing Radiation." In important ways the BEIR study reaffirmed the conclusions of the National Academy's previous work on radiation hazards. It pointed out that the sources of greatest public exposure to radiation were natural background and medical uses. Diagnostic medical applications accounted for about 90 percent of the "total *man-made* radiation dose to which the U. S. population [was] exposed" and 35 percent of the total from all sources. Nuclear power, by contrast, contributed less than one-half of 1 percent from all sources of radiation, including natural background.

The BEIR report, like the 1956 study, urged that public exposure to radiation be kept to a minimum without sacrificing the benefits of medical uses of radiation, nuclear power, and other applications. Although it did not offer specific recommendations or numerical guidelines for levels of population exposure, it expressed strong support for the existing principle of maintaining a level that was as low as practicable, which EPA, the AEC, and other agencies followed. It reemphasized the National Academy's previous appeals to the medical profession to adopt procedures that would substantially reduce unnecessary public exposure to radiation.

In addition to reiterating some of the key findings of earlier studies, the BEIR report provided some new conclusions. Despite the small amount of radiation from nuclear power that affected the population, the BEIR study contended that nuclear plants generated concern because of their growth and "widespread distribution." It asserted that releases from nuclear power units should be held to a few millirems per year. Indeed, it concluded that the existing limit of 170 millirems per year for the entire population of the United States from all sources except natural background, which was the level recommended by the Federal Radiation Council before its functions were transferred to EPA, was "unnecessarily high."

There were a few other important new findings that the BEIR report presented. It placed greater emphasis than earlier studies on the somatic effects of radiation and somewhat less on the genetic effects. It pointed out that scientific knowledge and understanding of genetics had greatly expanded, and indeed had been "revolutionized," since the National Academy report of 1956. Although the genetic consequences of exposure to low-level radiation still could not be identified with precision, they appeared to be less harmful than earlier studies had indicated. Research performed since the 1956 report had shown that cells had a greater ability to repair radiation damage than previously recognized. Other research had demonstrated the importance of dose rate on radiation effects. It had established that, at least in mice, a dose of radiation delivered over an extended period produced less injury than the same dose delivered more rapidly.

The encouraging, though far from definitive, information about genetic effects was counterbalanced by the increased concern about somatic effects. The BEIR report affirmed that knowledge of the somatic risks of low-level radiation was still too limited to make conclusive judgments. And it recognized that existing evaluations were based largely on extrapolations from high doses and high dose rates, which were at best imprecise and at worst invalid. Nevertheless, the report contended that in the absence of better data there was no reasonable alternative to a "linear hypothesis," which assumed a straight-line correlation between dose and somatic damage and did not allow for a threshold below which no injury would occur. It projected that any amount of radiation would cause some harm to the population. Although the linear hypothesis might overestimate the risks by failing to account for the effects of dose rate and cell repair, the study submitted, it provided "the only workable approach to numerical estimation of the risk in a population."

The BEIR report found that the somatic risks of population exposure to low-level radiation were appreciable. It calculated that if everyone in the United States were exposed to the permissible population dose of 170 millirems per year, it might cause between 3,000 and 15,000 deaths annually from cancer, with the most likely number in the range of 5,000 to 7,000. The upper range of those estimates was close to the figures originally cited by Gofman and Tamplin. The BEIR report suggested, however, that Gofman and Tamplin overstated the risk and the number of deaths attributable to exposure to low-level radiation. It also acknowledged that it would be unimaginably difficult, if not "physically impossible," for the entire population of the United States to be exposed to 170 millirems annually. Thus, perhaps as a reflection of authorship by committee, the conclusions of the BEIR report on population risk showed a curious dichotomy: it offered an assessment of risk and estimate of death rates for circumstances that it found to be highly implausible.

Other new features of the BEIR study did not contain the same kind of internal contradictions, perhaps because they were less controversial. The report called for increased attention to the effects of radiation on the natural environment, even though it advanced the view that if standards were adequate to protect humans they were unlikely to cause harm to "other living organisms." It also strongly recommended that radiation standards be subjected to careful cost-benefit analysis. Although it admitted that this was a complex task that raised many difficult questions, it stressed the importance of permitting radiation exposure only with the "expectation of a commensurate benefit." At the same time, it warned against excessive protective measures that might substitute "a worse hazard for the radiation avoided." It pointed to the need to evaluate the risks of radiation from nuclear power *and* the less-known risks of effluents from fossil fuel plants. Moreover, the BEIR report cautioned that "it is becoming increasingly important that society not expend enormously large resources to reduce very small risks still further, at the expense of greater risks that go unattended."[29]

The BEIR report was a reasoned, balanced, and sober treatment of radiation hazards for the population. Its conclusions and recommendations were largely in keeping with existing practices. The regulations of the AEC and other government agencies and the recommendations of the NCRP and other expert groups accepted the linear hypothesis, assumed that no level of exposure to radiation was certifiably safe, and used the "as low as practicable" prescription. The NCRP's Lauriston Taylor hailed the report as "a whale of a job and highly objective." AEC chairman James R. Schlesinger agreed with the BEIR committee that further restricting public exposure to radiation might be a sound idea. "It is my belief that some tightening of standards may be required when radiation from all sources has been reviewed," he remarked. "We should deal with all sources with equal firmness."[30]

The most controversial feature of the BEIR report was the estimate of the number of deaths that could result if the entire population of the United States received the permissible annual dose of 170 millirems. News

---

29. National Academy of Sciences, Advisory Committee on the Biological Effects of Ionizing Radiations, *The Effects on Populations of Exposure to Low Levels of Ionizing Radiation,* November 1972, pp. 1–10, 18–19, 44–46, 58–60, 89–96, 183–88.

30. Robert Gillette, "Radiation Standards: The Last Word or at Least a Definitive One," *Science* 178 (December 1, 1972): 966–67; *Washington Post,* November 16, 1972.

A later report of the NCRP, of which Taylor was president, was obliquely critical of the BEIR report for suggesting that the existing standard of 170 millirems for population exposure was too high. It commented: "The 1972 NAS-BEIR Committee Report states in its Section on Summary and Recommendations, without developing the point in the body of the Report, that societal needs can be met with far lower average exposures and risks than permitted by the current Radiation Protection Guide of 170 millirems per year." National Council on Radiation Protection and Measurements, Report No. 43, *Review of the Current State of Radiation Protection Philosophy,* January 15, 1975, p. 3.

Figure 4. Scientists from the Hanford plutonium production complex in eastern Washington examine a white sturgeon in the Columbia River to check on
the amount of radiation it absorbed from the water used to cool the plant's
reactors. (National Archives 434–SF–51–79)

accounts focused on the conclusion that existing standards were "unnecessarily high" and the number of deaths that exposure to the permissible
levels conceivably could cause. Some observers viewed the estimates as
vindication for Gofman and Tamplin. Tamplin himself contended that the
report unambiguously supported his arguments, and Lester Rogers, the
AEC's director of regulatory standards, thought it "likely that the somatic
risk estimates in the Report will be interpreted as generally supporting
the original Gofman-Tamplin position." Others disputed the conclusion
that the BEIR study endorsed Gofman and Tamplin's judgments and
pointed out that it did not take a clear stand. As Robert Gillette observed
in an article in *Science,* the report "provided what might be read alterna-
tively as cold comfort for the critics of Gofman and Tamplin or as [a] measure of vindication for the two scientists."[31]

31. Lester Rogers to Chairman Schlesinger, October 25, 1972, Box 5127 (Regulatory
General), Office Files of James R. Schlesinger, AEC/DOE; Arthur R. Tamplin, "The BEIR

"As Low as Practicable" Hearings

While the BEIR committee was preparing its report, the AEC was holding a series of public hearings on its proposal to tighten its radiation standards through proposed "design objectives" for effluent releases. The design objectives provided numerical guidelines for the requirement that nuclear plants keep their releases as low as practicable. In November 1971 the AEC had decided to hold rulemaking hearings and invite public participation on two major issues—emergency core cooling systems for power reactors and the design objectives for effluent releases. The proceedings would follow the model of legislative hearings, the purpose of which was to compile a full record for Commission consideration in formulating final rules. The AEC hoped that by holding generic hearings on controversial, or potentially controversial, matters, it would resolve those issues and avoid the need to consider them repeatedly during licensing proceedings for individual plants.[32]

The hearings on numerical guidelines for plant effluents, which the AEC had issued for public comment in June 1971, began with opening statements by participants on January 20, 1972. In contrast to the hearings on emergency core cooling, which generated sharp acrimony and received a great deal of publicity, the radiation hearings produced little controversy and few headlines. Although representatives of the nuclear industry, including both vendors and utilities, and intervenors who were critical of the AEC expressed reservations about aspects of the proposed guidelines, they did not voice strong objections to the radiation levels that the AEC had proposed as design objectives. Rather, the concerns of both supporters and critics of nuclear power centered on how the new rules would be applied. The industry worried that the rules were not flexible enough; the intervenors complained that they were too flexible.

The design objectives that the AEC proposed were intended to limit the exposure of an individual at the boundary of a plant site to less than 5 percent of average natural background radiation. This generally worked out to an annual whole-body dose of less than 5 millirems. The design objec-

---

Report: A Focus on Issues," *Bulletin of the Atomic Scientists* 29 (May 1973): 19–20; "Radiation Protection Guide 'Unnecessarily High,'" *Nuclear Industry* 19 (October 1972): 46–47; *Washington Post,* November 16, 1972; *New York Times,* November 16, 1972; Gillette, "Radiation Standards," p. 967.

32. William O. Doub to the Commission, November 6, 1971, L–4–1 Part 50 (As Low as Practicable), AEC Press Release, November 29, 1971, AEC/NRC.

tives allowed a calculated dose of 5 millirems from liquid discharges and 10 millirems from noble gas emissions. Although the total dose a person might receive under the design objectives added up to 15 millirems, the AEC deemed it unlikely that an individual would be exposed to both liquid and gaseous effluents. It further reasoned that a person exposed to 10 millirems of airborne noble gases would not receive a *whole-body* dose exceeding 5 millirems. The basic guideline, then, was a total of 5 millirems from both gaseous and liquid effluents; by limiting emissions to that level, a licensee would comply with the "as low as practicable" goal. The AEC pointed out that the levels it proposed for nuclear plants were a small percentage of exposure from other sources and too low to be measured except by "calculational techniques." It suggested that conforming with the design objective would provide additional protection to the public.[33]

The numerical guidelines were not inviolable limits. The AEC explained that although it expected effluents from plants to remain within the guidelines under normal conditions, it also recognized that in some situations effluents might exceed those levels. The AEC did not want to shut down plants that experienced temporary problems that caused releases higher than the design objectives but still far below existing standards. Therefore, it provided for "operating flexibility" by allowing releases from plants to exceed the guidelines for a limited time. The AEC would take action against licensees if, over a period of three months, estimated annual releases seemed likely "to exceed a range of 4–8 times the design objectives."[34]

The intervenors in the "as low as practicable" hearings were wary of this provision. In a press release of March 6, 1972, the National Intervenors, a coalition of sixty environmental organizations that were participating in the hearings, announced that the proposed rules contained a loophole that would allow nuclear plants "to spew large amounts of radioactivity into the air and water." They charged that, in the absence of a specific prohibition against the release of radioactivity up to the regulatory limits of 500 millirems, the AEC could permit hazardous levels of radiation to reach the public in times of high demand for electricity under the guise of operating flexibility. They suggested that the AEC should apply stricter controls and exercise less discretion in allowing plants to operate if effluent levels exceeded the design objectives. They also raised questions during the course

33. SECY-R-210 (April 8, 1971), AEC Press Release, June 7, 1971, AEC/NRC; "Radiation Discharge Limits," *Nuclear Industry* 19 (June 1971): 17–19; Bernard I. Spinrad, "The New Emission Guidelines," *Bulletin of the Atomic Scientists* 27 (September 1971): 7.

34. AEC Press Release, June 7, 1971, AEC/NRC.

of the proceedings about whether reducing power levels in plants would curtail effluent releases, about the effectiveness of quality assurance checks on fuel rods, and about other issues relating to the AEC's priorities and intentions in enforcing the design objectives.[35]

Industry representatives, in contrast to the intervenors, faulted the AEC for insufficient flexibility in its proposed design objectives. This was highlighted most vividly in a dispute over the extent to which reactor manufacturers had to consider the dosage that a cow in a pasture might receive from an adjacent nuclear plant. The issue was important because grazing cows were the key to the "milk pathway" by which individuals were most likely to be exposed to dangerous levels of iodine 131. Airborne effluents escaping from the boundaries of a plant could deposit iodine 131 in pastureland, where it would be consumed by grazing milk cows. In that event, the iodine 131 could then be concentrated in the cows' milk and present an especially serious hazard to children who drank fresh milk. To guard against the hazards of iodine 131, the AEC imposed a "reduction factor" of one hundred thousand of the existing radiation standards for permissible levels of iodine 131 in gaseous effluents. This was intended to make certain that even after concentration of iodine 131 in the milk pathway, exposures of individual members of the public would not exceed 5 millirems.

The question that commanded attention in the "as low as practicable" hearings was whether the proposed limit of 5 millirems per year applied to the exposure of a hypothetical "fencepost cow," which remained at the boundary of a plant site 24 hours a day, 365 days a year, or whether it applied to the exposure of the "first real cow," which fed on the pastureland closest to the plant. The industry and the AEC had in the past based their calculations of potential iodine 131 exposure to humans on the location of the nearest dairy herd. But as the AEC's Joseph M. Hendrie, who had recently joined the regulatory staff as deputy director for technical review, told John F. O'Leary, director of licensing, in 1973, the regulatory staff reluctantly concluded that it should base the 5 millirem design objective on the fencepost cow. He cited the difficulties of trying to find the first real cow and of calculating or actually measuring the iodine content in her milk once she was located.

Hendrie pointed out that data for determining the best way to mea-

35. National Intervenors Press Release, March 6, 1972, Box 5111 (Environmental Matters), Schlesinger Office Files, AEC/DOE; *In the Matter of: Effluents from Light-Water Cooled Nuclear Power Reactors,* Transcript, April 10, 1972, pp. 1224–1335, Docket No. RM 50–2, AEC/NRC.

Figure 5. "Real cows" graze in a pasture at the National Reactor Testing Station in Idaho, where they were exposed to releases of iodine 131 to test the uptake of the radioactive isotope in their milk. (National Archives 434–SF–11–45)

sure iodine exposure were insufficient and unreliable. The data that were available indicated that iodine 131 did not appear in cow's milk, and, therefore, the likelihood that it would reach consumers was perhaps greatly overestimated. But in the absence of good data, the regulatory staff decided that it must use the fencepost cow as its standard for new plants. It recognized that this conclusion might put it "in the position of denying the use of otherwise acceptable plant sites by virtue of an incorrectly calculated, hypothetical infant iodine dose."[36]

36. Andrew P. Hull, "Reactor Effluents: As Low as Practicable or as Low as Reasonable?" *Nuclear News* 15 (November 1972): 53–59; Transcript, April 11, 1972, pp. 1465–84, Docket

Industry representatives took sharp exception to the AEC's position. They contended that a fencepost cow standard was unreasonably conservative. They argued that using the first real cow was already a conservative measure because of the reduction factors for concentration in the design objectives, the dilution that occurred when milk from the nearest herd was mixed with milk from other herds during processing, and the fact that cows did not graze year-round in most locations in the United States. They estimated that if the AEC insisted on the fencepost cow standard it would cost utilities $4 million to $12 million per plant for additional equipment, and they denied that the benefits justified the cost.

Industry officials suggested that the AEC's approach to the fencepost cow issue was symptomatic of its inflexible and ill-considered positions on applying the design objectives. George F. Trowbridge, attorney for Consolidated Utilities, twenty-eight companies that participated in the hearings, assailed the regulatory staff's proposals. He complained that the proposals suffered from failure to do the "homework essential" to evaluating their impact, from "almost complete inattention to the cost" of equipment required to carry them out, and from "a completely inadequate explanation of the assumption [to be used] for calculating releases of doses," among other serious deficiencies.[37]

The "as low as practicable" hearings were held intermittently for seventeen days between January 20 and May 6, 1972. After a suspension of eighteen months while the regulatory staff prepared an environmental impact statement on the design objectives, the hearings resumed for eight days and concluded on December 6, 1973. The transcript of the hearings ran to 4,172 pages, supplemented by thousands of pages of testimony and statements by the participating parties. The hearings and the documents assembled for them provided the raw material for the Commission's consideration of a final decision on numerical guidelines for the "as low as practicable" requirement.[38]

RM 50–2, Joseph M. Hendrie to John F. O'Leary, January 15, 1973, L–4–1 Part 50 (As Low as Practicable), AEC/NRC.

This issue was taken so seriously that the cows acquired their own abbreviations: FPC for the "fencepost cow" and FRC for the "first real cow." The abbreviations, however, were not widely used in discussions of the topic.

37. Transcript, October 1, 1973, pp. 2880–84, Docket RM 50–2, AEC/NRC; "Industry and AEC at Odds on Radioiodine Emission Control," *Nuclear Industry* 20 (March 1973): 39–39; Hull, "Reactor Effluents," p. 56.

38. "Concluding Statement of Position of the Regulatory Staff," February 20, 1974, p. 4, Docket RM 50–2, AEC/NRC.

The "ALARA" Rule

After weighing the arguments of the parties involved in the hearings, the regulatory staff issued its conclusions and recommendations to the Commission in February 1974. It attempted to satisfy the complaints of both the intervenors and the industry by making some modest revisions in the proposed design objectives. In response to the intervenors' objection that the design objectives as drafted could allow the release of "large amounts of radioactivity," the staff reduced the levels "above which the Commission will take appropriate action." Instead of allowing releases in a calendar quarter that projected to four to eight times the annual design objectives under unusual conditions, the new proposal stated that the AEC would take steps to curb releases if they exceeded twice the annual quantity cited in the design objectives in a single quarter or four times the annual quantity in a period of twelve consecutive months.[39]

The regulatory staff also sought to accommodate industry's concerns by revising its proposals. It retained the basic design objective of holding releases of both liquid and gaseous effluents to a level that would not deliver a whole-body dose of more than 5 millirems to an individual standing at the boundary of a plant site (the 5-millirem dose applied to a site, whether one plant or several were located on it). Although the basic design objective remained intact, the staff partially relaxed its original proposals. A plant would comply with the regulations if an individual received a dose of up to 15 millirems to the skin, a change the staff made because it found that limiting the skin dose to 5 millirems was "not practicable."[40]

The regulatory staff took a similar position on what it called "one of the most difficult issues in the proceeding," the design objective for iodine 131 releases. In light of the limited knowledge of the ways in which radioactive iodine escaped from a reactor and the effectiveness of equipment to prevent its release, the staff concluded that "it may not be practicable to meet a 5 millirems per year design objective." It substituted a thyroid dose of 15 millirems as a design objective for iodine 131. The staff also backed off the fencepost cow standard in favor of "the location of the nearest milk cows that are actually present at the time of design and construction of the reactor." It suggested that its position on iodine releases was still very conservative because the limited data available indicated that

39. Ibid., pp. 17–18, 70.
40. Ibid., pp. 13, 49.

the actual thyroid doses an individual received were less than the levels present in gaseous effluents. And the levels it proposed were far below the allowable doses recommended by professional organizations and embodied in the AEC's regulations. In keeping with the "as low as practicable" philosophy, the staff sought to strike a balance that considered the capabilities of technology and the costs of equipment while providing ample protection to the public.[41]

The staff's efforts to address the concerns of its critics received, at best, mixed reviews. The continuing objections of parties involved in the "as low as practicable" proceedings were made clear in a full-day hearing before the Commission on the staff's recommendations, held on June 6, 1974. On the whole the intervenors found less fault with the revised design objectives than did industry representatives. The National Intervenors were not present at the hearing; they had dropped out of the proceedings in October 1973, citing "extremely limited resources" and their "confidence in the ability of the Regulatory Staff to adequately protect the public interest."

Nevertheless, the environmentalist position did not go unrepresented in the hearings before the Commission. The state of Minnesota, which remained a party after the National Intervenors retired, criticized the revised proposals from an environmentalist point of view. Sandra Gardebring, special assistant to the attorney general of Minnesota, after suggesting that the AEC generally failed to protect the environment with sufficient zeal, objected to the provisions for operating flexibility in the revised proposals. Although she endorsed the tighter restrictions as an improvement, she contended that the design objectives should be "treated as maximum upper limits which are never to be exceeded."[42]

Industry complaints about the revised design objectives were more extensive and more vehement. Speaking for Consolidated Utilities, Trowbridge argued that the staff's assumptions for calculating the dose to exposed individuals were unduly conservative. He questioned its use of a worst-case linear hypothesis, especially in the case of iodine 131 hazards. The staff based its calculations on the assumption that an infant drank a liter of milk a day that was taken directly from the cow nearest to the plant boundary. Trowbridge and other industry spokesmen called for projections based on the "best estimate" of a situation that seemed likely to oc-

41. Ibid., pp. 14–15, 57–61.
42. Karin P. Sheldon to Algie A. Wells et. al., October 11, 1973, Vol. 17 [n.p.], Oral Argument, June 6, 1974, pp. 135–52, RM 50–2, AEC/NRC.

cur rather than on improbable and overly conservative assumptions. They also faulted the staff for setting limits on sites rather than individual reactors, which could sharply curtail plans for "nuclear parks" where several plants could be located.

Industry representatives maintained that the staff's approach distorted cost-benefit analyses by overstating the benefits of the new requirements and underestimating the costs. They objected to the staff's failure to consider carefully the cost of the improvements it expected plant owners to make in order to meet the design objectives. Trowbridge pointed out that the "as low as practicable" concept placed limitations on the imposition of requirements that would yield, at best, small dose reductions. He called for a reasonable ceiling, perhaps $1,000 per man-rem, on the cost of lowering population exposure to plant effluents. Industry officials supported the staff's decision to use the nearest cow rather than the fencepost cow in assessing iodine 131 hazards, but they still voiced concern about the possible costs of "backfitting" new equipment if land adjacent to a reactor was converted to a pasture after it began operating.[43]

The arguments that the industry presented carried considerable weight with the Commission, in part because they underscored reservations that the commissioners themselves held. They were not entirely satisfied that the "as low as practicable" hearings had provided a full record of salient issues. Indeed, for a time the commissioners considered reconvening the hearings to collect additional evidence. For one thing, they wanted more information on the impact of the proposed design objectives on the prospects for nuclear power parks that might serve as sites for as many as twenty individual plants.

The commissioners shared industry's concern that the regulatory staff based its proposals on excessively conservative assumptions rather than on best estimates of actual conditions. The staff explained that in most cases adequate data were not available to make best-estimate calculations, but the commissioners wanted more study of the issue, especially on iodine 131 hazards. Members of the Commission, particularly William A. Anders, wondered what purpose the "as low as practicable" requirement served when it was combined with numerical design objectives. Their concern was that use of "as low as practicable" would force further reductions in effluent releases in the future and impose costly backfitting. As a related matter, the Commission requested more information on how to

43. Oral Argument, pp. 51–134, RM 50–2, AEC/NRC; "AEC Commissioners Hear Final Arguments on 'Low as Practicable,'" *Nuclear Industry* 21 (June 1974): 32–34.

approach the issue of the costs of dose reduction and whether Consolidated Utilities' figure of $1,000 per man-rem was reasonable.

The commissioners, staff, and consultants evaluated and discussed those questions at considerable length over a period of six months between June and December 1974. But they did not settle on the provisions of a final rule. On December 31, 1974, less than three weeks before the AEC went out of existence, the Commission decided that, rather than make a decision, it would consign the issue to the Nuclear Regulatory Commission. Chairman Dixy Lee Ray commented that "there were still innumerable questions unanswered," and the Commission concluded that the "complexity and scope of the problem are such that the new NRC . . . should not be committed to a decision hastily reached by the AEC."[44]

Within a short time after the NRC began operations, industry representatives pressed for a final rule. They pointed out in March 1975 that the AEC had published the original design objectives nearly four years earlier but had never reached a final decision. They complained bitterly that in the absence of final action by the Commission, the regulatory staff had in some cases implemented the strictest version of the proposed design objectives and imposed requirements that the industry viewed as excessively conservative and costly. Richard Wilson, a professor of physics at Harvard, provided an example of how those enforcement practices adversely affected industry and consumers. He pointed out in April 1975 that Boston Edison's Pilgrim plant had been running at 80 percent power for months because of a small iodine leak. The AEC's regulatory staff had insisted that the company assume that the iodine was concentrated in the milk of a fencepost cow. Wilson commented: "There is no cow, so we in the Boston area are paying $60,000 per day for [replacement] oil *for nothing*." He added: "I believe that more iodine enters the biosphere from the drains of Massachusetts General Hospital (from the urine of its patients) than enters in an uncontrolled way from Pilgrim Station."[45]

Meanwhile, a group of four consultants from Oak Ridge and Argonne

44. SECY-A-74–128 (June 18, 1974), SECY-A-75–20 (August 30, 1974), Minutes, Adjudicatory Session 74–41 (June 11, 1974), Adj. Sess. 74–42 (June 21, 1974), Adj. Sess. 75–1 (July 2, 1974), Adj. Sess. 75–9 (September 30, 1974), Adj. Sess. 75–17 (December 31, 1974), AEC/NRC; "AEC Commissioners Hear Final Arguments on 'Low as Practicable,'" pp. 32–33.

45. Emphasis in original. George F. Trowbridge to the Commission, March 10, 1975, G. J. Stathakis to William A. Anders, March 21, 1975, Richard Wilson to Anders, April 2, 1975, Nuclear Regulatory Commission Records, NRC Public Document Room, Washington, D.C.

national laboratories was reviewing the transcripts of the "as low as practicable" hearings and other records. The consultants' task was to evaluate
the positions of the parties in the proceedings, including the regulatory
staff, and make recommendations to the Commission for a final rule. As
a result of their review and discussions with the commissioners, they recommended a few adjustments that made substantive revisions in the proposed rule. One was to reduce the dose that an individual could receive
from liquid effluents. Another was to apply the limits to each reactor at a
site rather than to all reactors at a site. This was done with the expectation
that the "dose commitment from multi-light-water-cooled reactor sites
should be less than the product of the numbers of reactors proposed for
a site." The consultants also suggested that the term "as low as practicable" be changed to "as low as reasonably achievable," a step that the ICRP
had recently taken. They argued that the new phrase more accurately described the intent of the rule, which was to weigh the advantages of lowering effluent releases in light of economic and social considerations.

The most delicate and divisive issue facing the consultants and the commissioners was placing a value on dose reductions. The industry insisted
that the NRC should observe a ceiling for requiring equipment that would
lower population exposure by only a minuscule or unmeasurable amount,
even if it were "practicable." The staff of the NRC, like the AEC regulatory staff before it, was reluctant to use dollar figures in cost-benefit analyses, not only because they were imprecise, but also because they gave the
impression that the agency was assigning a monetary value to human life.
The consultants, however, urged the Commission to adopt the limit of
$1,000 per man-rem reduction that the industry had advanced as accept-
able. A man-rem (as the unit was still commonly called) was computed
by multiplying the average dose received by members of a large group by
the number of people in that group. Thus if a population group of one
hundred thousand were exposed to 5 millirems in a year, the total whole-
body man-rem dose would be 500 man-rem. To reduce this figure to, say,
400 man-rems per year, using the proposed guideline of $1,000 per man-
rem, the NRC would have to show that the cost to a plant owner would
be less than $100,000 per year over the life of the plant.

The Commission accepted the recommendations of the consultants on
dose levels and on individual plant (rather than site) restrictions. The design objectives for annual population dose that the final regulation contained were: liquid effluents, 3 millirems per year whole body and 10 millirems for a single organ; gaseous effluents, 5 millirems per year whole
body and 15 millirems for skin; and iodine, 15 millirems. Those figures were

slightly more restrictive than the values that the AEC had considered. The change to measuring releases from individual plants rather than sites, in contrast, relaxed the previous proposals, at least potentially. It made the nuclear park concept, at that time an attractive prospect for the industry, more feasible.[46]

The commissioners were less certain about how to deal with the consultants' other recommendations. They directed the staff to prepare a proposed rule for public comment on the change in terminology from "as low as practicable" to "as low as reasonably achievable." The Commission also postponed final action on the question of assigning a $1,000 per man-rem value to cost-benefit evaluations. Although it agreed to use that figure on an interim basis, it decided not to adopt it formally without additional rulemaking proceedings. The NRC promised that the proceedings would begin at the earliest date "practicable" (reviving the word that it was considering replacing in another context). With those provisions, after four years of debate and deliberation, it issued the new rule on design objectives on May 5, 1975.[47]

The NRC staff took prompt action on the change in terminology that the Commission wished to consider. It issued a new rule for public comment in July 1975 that proposed to replace "as low as practicable" with "as low as reasonably achievable" (which soon became known by the acronym ALARA). It explained that the new term meant that licensees should keep radiation releases to a level as low as reasonably achievable "taking into account the state of technology, and the economics of improvements in relation to benefits to the public health and safety, and other societal and socioeconomic considerations, and in relation to the utilization of atomic energy in the public interest." After receiving only one comment on the proposed rule, the staff, to which the Commission had del-

---

46. SECY-A-75-10 (February 20, 1975), SECY-A-75-14 (March 3, 1975), SECY-A-75-20 (March 24, 1975), SECY-A-75-28 (April 16, 1975), John C. Hoyle, Memorandum for the Record, March 17, 1975, Samuel J. Chilk, Memorandum for the Record, April 9, 1976 [document is misdated March 9, 1976], "Opinion of the Commission," April 30, 1975, Docket RM 50-2, E. A. Mason, R. E. Cunningham, J. E. Ward, R. J. Mattson, R. D. Smith, and H. T. Peterson, Jr., "Regulatory Requirements for Radiation Protection," enclosure, Chilk to the Commission, March 30, 1977, NRC Records.

The four consultants used by the Commission to evaluate the record on "as low as practicable" were William Bibb, Warren Grimes, and Robert Bryan of Oak Ridge National Laboratory and Douglas Grahn of Argonne National Laboratory.

47. "Opinion of the Commission," April 30, 1975, Docket RM 50-2, SECY-75-343 (July 3, 1975), NRC Records; "NRC Defines Limits for 'As Low as Practicable,'" *Nuclear News* 18 (June 1975): 37.

egated responsibility on this matter, published the change in terminology to ALARA in December 1975.[48]

The other radiation issue on which the NRC undertook rulemaking action—the $1,000 per man-rem value for cost-benefit assessments—proved to be considerably more complicated. In response to the Commission's order to investigate the question, the staff pointed out that a series of issues relating to procedures, scope, and methodology had to be addressed. They included whether to conduct the rulemaking in collaboration with the Environmental Protection Agency, which was developing its own guidelines for population exposure; whether to include occupational radiation exposure; and how to weigh moral, societal, and human considerations in arriving at a dollar per man-rem reduction value. They were complex issues that required careful appraisal of advantages and disadvantages; in the case of "life value" questions, the staff was not certain that it had sufficient expertise to handle the range of specialized issues that would be raised.[49]

Over a period of nearly three years the staff, assisted by contractors, devoted considerable attention to determining reasonable dollar expenditures for man-rem reductions. They carefully examined issues relating to cost-benefit evaluations, risk perceptions, the hazards and economic penalties of radiation exposure, and other important but ethereal matters. In the end, they decided that the effort would not provide conclusive information and that it was probably unnecessary. In January 1978 the staff recommended that the Commission discontinue the rulemaking proceedings. It cited two reasons for doing so. The first was that EPA had issued its own standards for population exposure to radiation. Although they did not directly deal with the questions that the NRC had been addressing, they seemed to largely supersede them by providing generic standards that applied to populations surrounding any nuclear facility.

The staff also argued that defining an appropriate dollar figure for reducing population exposure was unnecessary because the individual doses that were a part of the ALARA rule provided more protection to the public. Experience with implementing the rule indicated that complying with the individual dose limits was more restrictive than using a

48. SECY-75-343 (July 3, 1975), SECY-75-674 (November 20, 1975), Samuel J. Chilk to the Office of the Federal Register, December 16, 1975, NRC Records.

49. Roger J. Mattson to Kenneth R. Chapman and others, September 4, 1975, SECY-74-524 (September 15, 1975), SECY-75-679 (November 24, 1975), SECY-75-715 (December 15, 1975), Peter Strauss and Ben Huberman to the Commission, January 28, 1976, NRC Records.

cost-benefit analysis based on dollars per man-rem. Despite a strong dissent from the Office of the General Counsel, which argued that EPA's rule was not an adequate substitute for a dollar per man-rem rule, the Commission agreed with the staff. It voted 4–0 in February 1978 to suspend the rulemaking.[50]

By the time the NRC decided on design objectives for plant effluents, the controversy over radiation standards had lost much of its intensity. As early as 1972 the charges of Gofman and Tamplin and others that the AEC was inattentive or indifferent to the severity of radiation hazards from nuclear power had, as an article in *Science* noted, "largely faded from public view." In December 1973 White House officials concluded that the issues that Gofman and Tamplin raised had "ceased to be a major public concern." When the NRC issued its "as low as practicable" rule in 1975, Commissioner Edward A. Mason lamented the lack of media interest in the subject. The diminished level of public interest and debate was partly attributable to the AEC's and the NRC's tightening of the regulations on plant emissions. By the end of the "as low as practicable" hearings, the critics who had once found the standards too lax had largely stopped objecting. The radiation controversy was also defused by the BEIR report. It was an authoritative and independent survey of the risks of exposure that called for some changes but did not detect a public health crisis of the magnitude that Gofman and Tamplin and their supporters claimed. And although the controversy over nuclear power as a major source of energy continued to grow in the early 1970s, the focus moved away from radiation protection to other issues that the expanding use of the technology raised.[51]

Nevertheless, the radiation controversy, like the fallout debate a decade earlier, left its mark on public attitudes. Although it is impossible to measure the impact of Gofman and Tamplin's allegations, they received a great deal of attention in the popular media. Their critique of the AEC sounded persuasive to many observers for a number of reasons. Both Gofman and

50. SECY-75–679A (March 18, 1976), SECY-79–679B (June 3, 1976), SECY-78–63 (January 31, 1978), James L. Kelley to the Commission, February 15, 1978, Ken Pederson to the Commission, February 15, 1978, Memorandum for the Record re. SECY-78–63, February 16, 1978, NRC Records.

51. "A Curious Lack of Interest," *Nuclear News* 18 (July 1975): 27; Gillette, "Radiation Standards," p. 966; Richard Fairbanks and John Sawhill to Roy L. Ash, December 5, 1973, Box 6 (AEC-EPA Jurisdiction), Glenn Schleede Subject Files, Staff Member Office Files, White House Central Files, Richard M. Nixon Papers, Nixon Presidential Materials Project, National Archives, College Park.

Tamplin had excellent professional qualifications, and their status as AEC insiders gave them additional credibility. The AEC and others who took issue with Gofman and Tamplin occasionally pointed out that they did not base their views on original research, but this did little to undermine their position, particularly with those who harbored their own doubts about the adequacy of existing radiation standards. Further, Gofman and Tamplin were articulate, confident, and impressive in outlining their opinions in public appearances.

The attention and regard that Gofman and Tamplin commanded were products of more than just their personal and professional attributes. Their arguments on low-level radiation hazards were tailor-made headline material; their general assertions were easy to understand and certain to arouse public interest. They were also difficult to refute, partly because the precise effects of low-level exposure were still an open scientific question and partly because there was no simple way to explain the bases for existing radiation standards. The AEC, NCRP, and other organizations insisted that their standards were extremely conservative and provided more than adequate protection, but their explanations were usually too technical and always less dramatic than Gofman and Tamplin's allegations.

The political atmosphere of the times worked to the advantage of Gofman and Tamplin and to the disadvantage of the AEC and other agencies. Gofman and Tamplin's rise to prominence came at about the same time that public concern over environmental protection and public health was reaching new heights, especially in the wake of alarming reports about oil spills, insecticides, food additives, and other perils. As this occurred, the credibility of the statements and the performance of federal agencies in general and the AEC in particular was declining. The AEC's policies and pronouncements on environmental issues were suspect, in part because it had acted grudgingly to fulfill the mandate of the National Environmental Policy Act of 1970 and slowly to combat the problem of thermal pollution from nuclear plants. When Gofman and Tamplin launched a frontal assault on the established assumption that the benefits of nuclear power were worth the risks, they won a respectful hearing from growing numbers of state and local government officials, environmentalists, and other citizens who worried that the hazards of low-level radiation were greater than they had been led to believe.

The AEC rejected the conclusions that Gofman and Tamplin drew about the severity of public risks from low-level radiation, but it agreed with their basic contention that emissions from nuclear plants should be reduced. It took action that eventually produced a substantial tightening of the regulations on radioactive effluents. For a time, questions about the hazards of low-level radiation moved from the headlines of daily newspapers back to professional journals and meetings. But the hiatus was short-lived, and the legacy of the doubts that Gofman and Tamplin and other critics raised about the soundness of radiation standards and the commitment of federal agencies to ensuring adequate protection from radiation hazards helped to fuel new controversies.

CHAPTER THREE

The Role of Federal Agencies in Radiation Protection

While the AEC and, after its abolition, the NRC were trying to decide on a "practicable" and then a "reasonably achievable" level of radiation emissions from nuclear power plants, they were also engaged in a bureaucratic battle with the Environmental Protection Agency over jurisdictional boundaries on radiation safety. The roles of the AEC/NRC and EPA in protecting the public from the radiation hazards of nuclear power generated sometimes sharp differences. The importance of the issue was magnified by the energy crisis of the mid-1970s, which made increasing energy supplies a major national goal that often conflicted with the objective of preserving and improving the environment. The interagency debate over regulating radiation from nuclear power did not deal with what remained by far the greatest source of public exposure other than natural background—medical applications. This was an area in which federal agencies had only limited responsibilities, but their participation was still substantial enough to cause considerable controversy.

The AEC/NRC and EPA

Differences between the AEC and EPA surfaced within a short time after President Richard M. Nixon's Reorganization Plan No. 3 established EPA in December 1970. The creation of EPA consolidated federal pollution control programs from fifteen agencies or parts of agencies into the largest single regulatory body in the government. It began its existence with a staff of six thousand and a budget of $455 million. From the beginning EPA faced the difficult problems of trying to integrate the functions and personnel of so many agencies into a cohesive unit and trying to balance the demands of competing interests. As Nixon's first appointee as EPA administrator, William D. Ruckelshaus, later remarked, the agency was caught "between two irresistible forces." On one side stood environmental groups, "pushing very hard to get emissions down no matter what they were—air, water, no matter what—almost regardless of the seriousness of the emissions." On the other side stood industry advocates, "pushing just as hard in the other direction, . . . again almost regardless of the seriousness of the problem."[1]

The radiation controversies of the 1950s and 1960s had focused on the AEC's programs, and the AEC had played, sometimes involuntarily, the most visible role among federal agencies involved in radiation safety. The creation of EPA, however, gave the AEC a potentially strong rival. The new agency took over the duties of the Federal Radiation Council, and its functions included the protection of the population from environmental radioactivity. The scope of EPA's regulatory mandate under Nixon's reorganization plan extended, potentially at least, to all sources of radiation. Despite the breadth of its mandate, however, radiation protection was not a priority issue for EPA. In the years following the establishment of the agency, its Office of Radiation Programs suffered substantial cuts in personnel and budget allocations. A U.S. General Accounting Office (GAO) investigation published in January 1978 concluded that "radiation protection is the least funded program in EPA." It reported that "morale in the Agency's radiation program is low and most people interviewed said that there is not adequate staff, data, laboratory support, or research to do an effective job."[2]

Despite the radiation office's lack of clout and the low priority its programs received, its functions were of considerable importance to EPA. They were, symbolically at least, a measure of the agency's commitment to and effectiveness in carrying out its environmental responsibilities. EPA

1. Kirkpatrick Sale, *The Green Revolution: The American Environmental Movement, 1962–1992* (New York: Hill and Wang, 1993), p. 36; Philip Shabecoff, *A Fierce Green Fire: The American Environmental Movement* (New York: Hill and Wang, 1993), pp. 130–31.

2. Edward F. Tuerk to John R. Quarles, Jr., January 31, 1977, Box 10 (Air and Waste Management), Intra-Agency Memorandums 1977–1983, Tuerk to Walter C. Barber, Jr., May 15, 1981, Box 408, General Correspondence, Office of the Administrator, Record Group 412 (Records of the Environmental Protection Agency), National Archives, College Park, Maryland; U.S. General Accounting Office, "The Environmental Protection Agency Needs Congressional Guidance and Support to Guard the Public in a Period of Radiation Proliferation" (CED-78-27), January 20, 1978, pp. 8, 21.

officials were troubled in March 1976 by sharp criticism of its radiation protection efforts by the Environmental Policy Center. The environmental group accused EPA of gutting its radiation programs and allowing the AEC's successors, the Energy Research and Development Administration and the NRC, to "pick up the slack." William D. Rowe, EPA's deputy assistant administrator for radiation programs, promptly told one of his staff members to contact the author of the report to correct its "numerous inaccuracies, misinterpretations, and misleading statements."[3]

The importance of radiation safety to EPA and the ambiguity of its role under Reorganization Plan No. 3 soon led to contention with other agencies. The Department of Health, Education, and Welfare, for example, disputed EPA's claim that its responsibilities included medical uses of radiation. Differences also quickly arose between EPA and the AEC over their respective roles in radiation protection. Nixon's order made EPA responsible for radiation standards outside the boundaries of nuclear plants, while the AEC continued to regulate occupational exposure in and effluents from individual plants. A small number of staff members from the AEC who had worked on population exposure limits shifted to EPA. The dividing line between the two agencies was clear enough in theory: EPA would regulate population exposure outside plant boundaries, and the AEC would regulate the radiation safety programs of its licensees within the boundaries of their plants. But the line was much less clear in practice, and the precise allocation of responsibilities for the AEC and EPA remained ill-defined.

The differing perspectives of the AEC and EPA became evident in spring 1971 as the AEC prepared to announce its proposed design objectives for the "as low as practicable" regulation. AEC chairman Seaborg and EPA administrator Ruckelshaus each contended that his own agency should issue guidelines for plant emissions. Seaborg argued that the AEC had been working on the effluent limits before EPA had been created; Ruckelshaus countered that EPA "should do it first in order to establish credibility with the public." This issue was settled with compromise wording, and the AEC announced the proposed design objectives in June 1971. But it was a harbinger of future differences between the AEC and EPA, often rooted more in questions of agency stature, jurisdiction, and image than in substantive disputes over radiation standards.[4]

3. W. D. Rowe to Mr. Train, March 11, 1976, with attached "public information article" from the Environmental Policy Center, February 18, 1976, Box 166 (Office of Air and Waste Management), General Correspondence, Office of the Administrator, EPA Records.

4. General Accounting Office, "Environmental Protection Agency Needs Congressional Guidance," pp. 17–19; J. Samuel Walker, *Containing the Atom: Nuclear Regulation*

Within a short time after Seaborg and Ruckelshaus resolved their disagreement, other issues generated sharp discord between the AEC and EPA. One major source of dispute was a proposal by EPA to independently monitor the operations of AEC-licensed plants. EPA maintained that it should conduct its own inspections of nuclear facilities in order to assess their environmental impact and make certain that they were complying with radiation standards for population exposure. It also suggested that its inspections would help "establish the credibility of EPA as an independent agency." The AEC strongly objected on the grounds that EPA's programs would duplicate the AEC's responsibilities, undercut its authority, exact high costs, and confuse the public while providing little, if any, benefit. Clifford K. Beck, a veteran regulatory staff official whose responsibilities included liaison with EPA, told director of regulation L. Manning Muntzing in February 1972 that EPA's claims "could grow into serious areas of conflict, needless expenditure of money and manpower and confusion in the licensing process."[5]

Despite a sincere effort on the part of both the AEC and EPA to settle their differences, the question of their respective roles in monitoring the operations of nuclear power plants remained unresolved for nearly two years. The AEC acknowledged EPA's authority to set general environmental standards for radiation protection, but it continued to resist EPA's claims for inspecting the operations of its licensees. It did not want to be placed in the awkward position of merely serving as the enforcement arm of the EPA rather than monitoring compliance with its own regulations. The AEC had far greater expertise in reactor design, operations, and safety issues, and it resented the implication that it could not be trusted to enforce radiation standards without EPA overseeing its performance.

This issue was finally resolved in August 1973 with a memorandum of understanding between the two agencies. It affirmed the primary role of the AEC to "take appropriate action" to ensure that its licensees complied with EPA's environmental standards. At the same time, it allowed EPA

in a Changing Environment, 1963–1971 (Berkeley and Los Angeles: University of California Press, 1992), pp. 367–68.

5. Clifford K. Beck to Chairman Schlesinger, December 14, 1971, Box 5132 (AEC-EPA Relations), Office Files of James R. Schlesinger, Atomic Energy Commission Records, Department of Energy, Germantown, Maryland; Beck to L. Manning Muntzing, February 9, 1972, SECY-R-484 (June 23, 1972), Atomic Energy Commission Records (ORG-NRC History), Public Document Room, Nuclear Regulatory Commission, Washington, D.C. (hereafter cited as AEC/NRC).

to accompany AEC inspectors on occasion at the discretion of EPA. This agreement proved a satisfactory approach to the inspection issue, but it did not prevent other differences between the AEC and EPA from creating debate and mutual irritation.[6]

Conflicts between the two agencies were exacerbated by a report that EPA published in February 1974 on the possible long-term hazards of radioactivity from nuclear power plants. The study projected the potential health effects of long-lived radioisotopes released to the environment from the normal operation of nuclear power plants during the next fifty years. EPA acknowledged that its estimates were imprecise and "subject to considerable uncertainty." But it insisted that finding ways to predict the health consequences of "dose commitments," defined as the "sum of all doses to individuals over the entire time period the material persists in the environment," was essential for informed policy making. It concluded that the cost of radiation releases from nuclear power in the years between 1970 and 2020 could be as high as twenty-four thousand deaths (including a period of one hundred years after the releases took place). It also suggested that the number of deaths over the same period could be as low as twenty-four.[7]

The AEC took sharp exception to EPA's findings. Chairman Dixy Lee Ray told a press conference that EPA had employed a "totally misleading yardstick." Lester Rogers, the director of regulatory standards, complained that EPA's estimates were based on "completely unrealistic projections" and worried that the "large number of [worst-case] health effects projected will cause considerable public concern." The AEC issued a statement declaring that "the measures it already has taken, and those which will be taken in the future, . . . will assure that the effects will be well within the lowest projections in the EPA report." As Rogers had feared, however, other reactions were less optimistic. To the dismay of the nuclear industry, headlines featured the report's worst-case projections along the lines of "A-Plants May Kill 24,000: EPA." The AEC's protests failed to make as much impact as the report or the headlines, which was clear when the

6. SECY-R-650 (March 9, 1973), SECY-R-671 (April 12, 1973), Lester Rogers to Edward J. Bauser, August 31, 1973, Rogers to Commissioner Doub, April 20, 1973, L. Manning Muntzing to Mr. Rogers and Dr. Beck, May 14, 1973, William O. Doub to the Commission, May 21, 1973, AEC/NRC; "EPA Prepares for Increasing Role in Environmental Radiation Protection," *Nuclear Industry* 20 (June 1973): 33–35.

7. U.S. Environmental Protection Agency, "Environmental Radiation Dose Commitment: An Application to the Nuclear Power Industry" (February 1974), EPA Press Release, February 19, 1974, AEC/NRC.

commissioners were probed about EPA's estimates of cancer deaths in congressional hearings.[8]

Agency differences also arose over an issue of even more fundamental importance to the AEC—radiation standards for effluent releases during normal nuclear plant operation. Once again the line between EPA's responsibility for regulating population exposure beyond plant sites and AEC's authority for regulating emissions within plant boundaries was vague enough to generate debate between the two agencies. Initially EPA expressed support for the AEC's design objectives for implementing the "as low as practicable" rule. At the direction of Ruckelshaus, who saw no reason to issue standards that were similar to those the AEC was considering, EPA announced in early 1972 that it would not publish its own regulations on permissible population exposure to radiation from nuclear power.[9]

Under new leadership, however, EPA decided to issue standards for permissible levels of environmental radiation that applied to releases from facilities in the entire uranium fuel cycle, which included not only nuclear power production but also fuel fabrication, fuel reprocessing, and other processes. In August 1973 EPA published for public comment its own standards for population exposure to radiation outside the boundaries of nuclear fuel cycle plants. The numerical limits in EPA's proposal conformed with the design objectives that the AEC was still considering. In other respects, however, they departed from the AEC's proposals and aroused objections from AEC officials. The AEC was concerned that EPA's method of developing environmental standards would inevitably draw heavily on the AEC's resources or overlap its responsibilities. EPA planned to use risk-benefit analyses to prepare its population exposure limits, which required thorough knowledge of the characteristics, capabilities, and costs of reactor systems and designs. Thus EPA would have to either depend on the AEC's expertise to enforce its standards or expand its own competence in nuclear engineering. The first alternative seemed undesirable and the second unnecessary to the AEC.

8. Lester Rogers to H. D. Bruner and others, February 15, 1974, John A. Harris to the Commission, February 20, 1974, AEC/NRC; U.S. Congress, Senate, Committee on Government Operations, Subcommittee on Reorganization, Research, and International Organizations, *Hearings on S. 2135 and S. 2744,* 93d Cong., 2d sess., 1974, pp. 325–26; "EPA Report on Plutonium Radiation Effects Stirs Controversy," *Nuclear Industry* 21 (March 1974): 39–40; "Nuclear News Briefs," *Nuclear News* 17 (March 1974): 25–26; *New York Times,* February 24, 1974.

9. "EPA Decides Not to Issue Its Own Radioactive Effluent Standards," *Nuclear Industry* 19 (February 1972): 51–52.

The AEC also objected to EPA's proposal for radiation standards because it was less flexible than the AEC's approach. The AEC's design objectives allowed licensees to exceed the levels on occasion, but EPA viewed its permissible levels as upper limits except in emergencies. EPA's position was closer to that taken by environmental groups in the "as low as practicable" hearings, and the AEC found it unduly rigid and technologically problematic. To make matters worse in the AEC's view, EPA's requirements would place emissions limits on individual facilities licensed by the AEC rather than set generally applicable ambient standards. This seemed to represent "an unauthorized extension of EPA jurisdiction."[10]

Efforts by both the AEC and EPA to resolve, or at least smooth over, their differences on relative responsibilities for radiation standards proved fruitless. After a series of meetings, letters, and telephone calls failed to provide a solution, the AEC concluded that it should ask the Office of Management and Budget (OMB) to mediate the dispute. By that time the AEC had grown increasingly exasperated with EPA. As early as May 1973 Commissioner William O. Doub had told his colleagues that he thought it "unlikely that the two agencies will be able to reconcile their differences." The Commission took the same view and asked for OMB mediation after its efforts to modify EPA's stance on radiation standards foundered. The ill will created by the standoff was compounded when William Rowe, head of EPA's radiation programs, was quoted in the Charlottesville, Virginia, *Daily Progress* as raising questions about the adequacy of the AEC's safety programs and adding: "We need to see proof of the safety they claim." Three weeks after the article appeared, Rowe told the AEC that he had been badly misquoted, but the statement attributed to him left a residue of suspicion and resentment.[11]

The differences between the AEC and EPA were, if not irreconcilable, almost certainly inevitable. They arose partly from the legacy that EPA inherited. Most of its radiation protection programs had formerly been carried out by the U.S. Public Health Service's Bureau of Radiological Health, which had clashed with the AEC over the role of the states in nu-

10. SECY-R-671 (April 12, 1973), Lester R. Rogers to William O. Doub, April 20, 1973, Clifford K. Beck to L.M.M., June 21, 1973, A. Giambusso to Rogers, August 22, 1973, L. Manning Muntzing to the Commission, August 28, 1973, "Memorandum for the Record," September 4, 1973, Doub to John Quarles, September 5, 1973, Marcus A. Rowden to Melvin Price, October 9, 1973, AEC/NRC; "EPA Prepares for Increasing Role," pp. 33–34.

11. William O. Doub to the Commission, May 21, 1973, "Memorandum for the Record," June 7, 1973, John A. Harris to the Commission, October 4, 1973, Marcus A. Rowden to Melvin Price, October 9, 1973, W. D. Rowe to Dixy Lee Ray, October 23, 1973, AEC/NRC.

clear regulation and claimed a larger role in monitoring the operations of nuclear power plants. Further, EPA was concerned with establishing its credibility as a strong and effective regulator. One way to do this was to take a tougher position on radiation protection than that of the AEC. Although EPA followed the same basic guidelines, it was less inclined to apply them in a flexible way. Rowe insisted in an interview published in June 1973 that EPA was "going to bite the bullet and [require that] the numbers will be upper limits."[12]

EPA's constituency was quite different from, and in many ways quite opposed to, that of the AEC. By 1973 the AEC was the object of sharp and relentless attacks by environmental groups and other critics who charged it with failure to protect the public from the hazards of nuclear power and radiation. Those same groups were an important part of the constituency of EPA; in his June 1973 interview Rowe explained that his agency was "saying that the [radiation] levels will be low enough . . . to satisfy the environmentalists." Radiation protection was but a small part of EPA's responsibilities, but it remained an important signpost for establishing its credibility. This made disputes with the AEC unavoidable. EPA was not indifferent to the positions of the nuclear industry, and the AEC was not indifferent to environmental protection. The two agencies agreed on the basic limits for population exposure to radiation. But they departed on how the regulatory limits should be enforced. The issues on which they disagreed were, in themselves, subject to compromise settlements. The stakes involved, however, went beyond relatively narrow issues to larger matters of the credibility of and public confidence in both the AEC and EPA. This made resolution of their differences much more difficult.

As a result, it fell to the Office of Management and Budget, a part of the Executive Office of the President, to resolve the question of the roles of the AEC and EPA in setting emission standards for nuclear power plants. Both agencies submitted their positions on radiation protection to OMB in October 1973. Even this seemingly straightforward procedure fueled animosity, because EPA waited to see the AEC's paper and then submitted a rebuttal, after which the AEC filed a strongly worded rejoinder to EPA's arguments. After the procedural jockeying ended, members of the White House staff carefully weighed the competing positions. They recognized that the "bitter issue" to be resolved was the jurisdictional one. In terms of protecting the public from radiation hazards, OMB

12. Beck to Schlesinger, December 14, 1971, AEC Records, Department of Energy; "EPA Prepares for Increasing Role," p. 33.

associate director John Sawhill and Domestic Council assistant director Richard Fairbanks told OMB director Roy L. Ash, "a decision in either agency's favor will have *little if any significant effect upon the amount of radiation released to the environment,* since both agencies are striving for standards as low as practicable" (emphasis in original).[13]

But the AEC-EPA dispute threatened to have an important impact on the energy crisis, which became a major national concern in fall 1973 as the White House staff was conducting its review. As early as 1971 Nixon had publicly expressed concern about the long-range energy needs of the United States, and in June 1973 he issued another statement on energy in which he declared that "America faces a serious energy problem." A short time later a war between Israel and its Arab neighbors led to an oil embargo by the Organization of Petroleum Exporting Countries, which gave much greater urgency to Nixon's efforts to increase the nation's energy supplies. In a television speech on November 7, 1973, he called for a program he named Project Independence, so that "by the end of this decade we will have developed the potential to meet our own energy needs without depending on any foreign energy sources." A key component of Project Independence was a major expansion in the use of nuclear power.[14]

Sawhill and Fairbanks told Ash that deciding in favor of EPA in its conflict with the AEC "could mean higher costs and technological hurdles for nuclear power, since EPA is now proposing standards that AEC believes are neither necessary nor technologically feasible." A judgment in favor of the AEC, on the other hand, would "tend to encourage the use of nuclear power and increase its contribution towards meeting the energy crisis." While recognizing that supporting the AEC would antagonize the environmental community, they recommended that EPA be instructed to restrict its activities to an ambient standard for the total amount of radiation in the environment from fuel cycle facilities. Ash accepted their views, and on December 7, 1973, he announced his decision. He con-

13. SECY-R-74–58 (October 24, 1973), SECY-R-74–62 (October 29, 1973), Dixy Lee Ray to Richard M. Fairbanks, November 9, 1973, AEC/NRC; William J. Dircks to Glenn Schleede, November 1, 1973, Richard Fairbanks and John Sawhill to Roy L. Ash, December 5, 1973, Box 6 (AEC-EPA Jurisdiction), Glenn Schleede Subject Files, Staff Member Office Files, White House Central Files, Richard M. Nixon Papers, Nixon Presidential Materials Project, National Archives, College Park.

14. White House Press Release, "Statement by the President," June 29, 1973, Staff Member Office Files, Energy Policy Office, Nixon Papers; "The Energy Emergency," November 7, 1973, *Presidential Documents: Richard Nixon, 1973,* Vol. 9, No. 45, pp. 1312–18; David E. Nye, *Consuming Power: A Social History of American Energies* (Cambridge, Mass.: MIT Press, 1998), pp. 217–19.

cluded that EPA had "construed too broadly its responsibilities" and ordered it to "discontinue its preparations for issuing, now or in the future, any standards" for individual fuel cycle facilities. He instructed EPA to set "an ambient standard which would have to reflect AEC's findings as to the practicality of emission controls."[15]

In light of the importance that the Nixon administration placed on nuclear power to deal with the energy crisis, especially during the Arab oil embargo, Ash's decision was not surprising. Nevertheless, it was not accepted without complaint or criticism. Some observers interpreted OMB's action as a power grab by the AEC that compromised public safety and environmental protection. Ash's decision did not produce a prompt settlement of the differences between EPA and the AEC. EPA's Rowe commented that he was "disturbed" by the ruling and suggested that his agency might not be able to set useful overall standards in accordance with Ash's instructions. Another high-level EPA official recommended to administrator Russell E. Train that the agency circumvent Ash's judgment and continue to make plans to set radiation standards for fuel cycle facilities. He urged that EPA *make a decision now to do further work toward the possible setting of these standards but to withhold any indication to the rest of the Executive Branch or to the public about what our intentions are* (emphasis in original). The AEC soon obtained a copy of the EPA memo. AEC officials were troubled by EPA's reaction, as were members of the White House staff. Glenn Schleede of the White House Domestic Council reported disapprovingly that "EPA is now considering new ways of impacting radiation standards and AEC programs."[16]

EPA's Fuel Cycle Standards

Despite EPA's complaints about Ash's decision and the AEC's concerns with how EPA would respond to it, the two agencies

15. Roy L. Ash to Administrator Train and Chairman Ray, December 7, 1973, AEC/NRC; Fairbanks and Sawhill to Ash, December 5, 1973, Nixon Papers.

16. Tom Wesselmann to President R. Nixon, December 15, 1973, Clark H. Woolley to Nixon, December 26, 1973, Charles L. Elkins to the Administrator, January 10, 1974, attached to A. Giambusso to L. Manning Muntzing, February 5, 1974, AEC/NRC; Glenn Schleede to Ken Cole, July 5, 1974, Domestic Council—Glenn R. Schleede Files (Domestic Policy Review of Environmental Protection Agency, 1974), Gerald R. Ford Papers, Gerald R. Ford Library, Ann Arbor, Michigan; "AEC Supported over EPA on Fuel Cycle Radiation Standards," *Nuclear Industry* 20 (December 1973): 26–27; *New York Times,* December 13, 1973.

worked together to draw up radiation protection standards that reflected their respective roles. In April 1974, after consultation with the AEC, EPA issued an advance notice of proposed rulemaking that announced its intention to develop ambient standards for environmental radiation. The AEC was satisfied that EPA was acting in accordance with Ash's dictates, and it sought to make certain that its "as low as practicable" guidelines, then under consideration, and EPA's rulemaking would be compatible.[17]

In December 1974, as the AEC's existence was coming to a close, EPA completed a draft of proposed rules on environmental radiation standards. It set a basic annual limit of 25 millirems of whole-body exposure to a member of the public from uranium fuel cycle operations. The response to the proposals was, in the words of Allan C. B. Richardson of EPA's Office of Radiation Programs, "quite predictable." He reported that "environmental groups criticize the standards as being too high," and one individual "accuses us of being in the employ of the industry." The nuclear industry also expressed opposition to EPA's draft rules. "We did not expect to receive a warm endorsement of new requirements for effluent control," Richardson commented, "and have not been disappointed."[18]

The AEC and later the NRC found EPA's proposed standard to be generally consistent with the "as low as practicable" design objectives, but they raised questions about whether the proposed rules were entirely "practicable." The NRC expressed doubt that EPA's proposals were cost-effective; in some cases they might require expensive emission control equipment that would offer little benefit to public health. The NRC also sought a better definition from EPA of how its standards would be implemented and clarification of other matters that potentially caused discrepancies between EPA and NRC regulations. Above all, it argued that EPA's proposed regulations were unnecessary because existing NRC requirements provided adequate protection against radiation hazards. It suggested that EPA, rather than consider new restrictions on nuclear fuel cycle plants, could more profitably allocate its resources and energies to "control of more significant environmental problems."[19]

17. SECY-R-74-169 (April 16, 1974), AEC/NRC.

18. Allan C. B. Richardson, speech, "The Development and Impact of EPA Radiation Standards," September 1975, Box 130 (EPA), Lauriston S. Taylor Papers, Francis A. Countway Library of Medicine, Boston, Massachusetts.

19. SECY-R-75-202 (January 7, 1975), SECY-75-35 (February 11, 1975), SECY-75-46 (February 19, 1975), SECY-75-408 (August 1, 1975), Lee V. Gossick to Russell E. Train, February 25, 1975, Gossick to Train, September 15, 1975, Darrell Eisenhut to R. J. Mattson, July 8, 1975,

Over a period of several months in 1975 exchanges between EPA and the NRC narrowed their differences on the proposed regulations, and the deputy administrator of EPA, John R. Quarles, Jr., instructed his staff to find ways to resolve the agency's debates with the NRC. EPA revised the text of its proposal to alleviate NRC concerns about the costs and difficulties of implementing the regulations and adopted a more flexible approach on variances to the rules. EPA determined that the NRC's "as low as reasonably achievable" design objectives would in most cases provide an acceptable basis for implementing its environmental radiation standards. When EPA issued the final regulations in January 1977, the NRC was generally satisfied with them (though it still described them in June 1978 as "an unnecessary and costly overlay" to NRC programs). On this issue the two agencies found ways to settle their differences and to formulate regulations that were compatible. The EPA regulations also gave the NRC a way to close out the complicated question of a dollar per man-rem reduction value after three years of study.[20]

In the first decade after its creation, EPA's relations with the AEC/ NRC were always uneasy and sometimes tense. The two agencies managed to resolve their differences on the issue of standards for environmental radiation. But more often jurisdictional disputes and constituent demands produced divisions. The inherent bureaucratic discord between the two agencies was heightened by divergent views on nuclear power among their top officials. AEC and NRC officials were keenly aware of the hazards of nuclear power, but most tended to regard the technology as an important, if not essential, part of the nation's energy future, especially over the long term. This position was consistent with the energy policies of Presidents Nixon and Gerald R. Ford. At least some leading EPA officials were not convinced that nuclear power should play a leading role in ensuring energy sufficiency. Russell Train, who served as EPA administrator under both Nixon and Ford, was particularly outspoken in his views. Although he did not favor the immediate shutdown of nuclear plants, he declared a short time after leaving EPA in January 1977, "We need to develop a very firm commitment to

---

Richard E. Cunningham to Daniel R. Muller, July 16, 1975, Don Davis to Mattson, July 29, 1975, Nuclear Regulatory Commission Records, NRC Public Document Room, Washington, D.C.

20. John R. Quarles to Roger Strelow, July 30, 1976, Box 215 (Chronological File), General Correspondence, Office of the Administrator, EPA Records; SECY-76-492A (November 16, 1976), Carlton Kammerer to the Commission, June 14, 1978, NRC Records; "EPA Limits Dose to Public Releases from Fuel Cycle," *Nuclear News* 20 (February 1977): 30–31.

the elimination of nuclear power as a source of energy on the earth."
William Rowe, who headed EPA's radiation office, was more ambivalent. He defended nuclear power when he found the charges of critics
to be overstated or misleading. But he also expressed skepticism, though
in less categorical terms than Train, about the long-term prospects for
nuclear power.[21]

Differences between the agencies over radiation protection were not
a conflict of an "antinuclear" EPA versus a "pronuclear" AEC/NRC. Both
agencies used similar assumptions in deciding on radiation protection regulations. They relied heavily on the judgments of radiation experts as set
forth in the reports of the ICRP, the NCRP, the National Academy of
Sciences, and others. They adopted a linear model for estimating the effects
of exposure to low-level radiation, even though they acknowledged the
uncertainties of extrapolating from experience with high-level exposure.
They attempted to develop radiation regulations that offered an ample
margin of safety without guaranteeing absolute safety. They sought to provide adequate protection without disregarding the social and economic
benefits of radiation sources. The differences between the AEC/NRC and
EPA were largely triggered by questions of agency jurisdiction, stature,
and priorities rather than of ideological commitments. But the views
of EPA authorities on nuclear power doubtlessly contributed to their
agency's strained relationship with the AEC and the NRC. President
Jimmy Carter's selection for EPA administrator, Douglas M. Costle,
sought to enhance public support for his agency by shifting its focus from
pollution control and ecological balance to health and safety issues, particularly the prevention of cancer. This increased the likelihood that EPA
and the NRC would continue to disagree over protecting against the risks
of low-level radiation exposure, especially when radiation reemerged as
a prominent source of public concern.[22]

21. William D. Rowe to Daniel Ford, March 24, 1977, Box 33 (Environmental Protection Agency), Union of Concerned Scientists Papers, Institute Archives, Massachusetts Institute of Technology, Cambridge; "What Is EPA's Role in Radiation?" *EPA Journal* 2 (February 1976): 12–14; "Russell Train Gives Views on the Environment," *Conservation Foundation
Newsletter,* January 1977, pp. 1–8 (quotation on p. 3); "Campaigning for an Embattled Cause,"
Time, March 21, 1977, p. 73; Robert L. Cohen and S. Robert Lichter, "Nuclear Power: The
Decision Makers Speak," *Regulation* 7 (March–April 1983): 32–37.

22. U.S. Environmental Protection Agency, Office of Radiation Programs, "Policy State-
ment: Relationship between Radiation Dose and Effect," March 3, 1975, Box 130 (EPA),
Taylor Papers; Marc K. Landy, Marc J. Roberts, and Stephen R. Thomas, *The Environmental
Protection Agency: Asking the Wrong Questions, from Nixon to Clinton* (New York: Oxford
University Press, 1994), pp. 40–42.

Regulating the Medical Uses of Radiation

The differences that commanded considerable attention from officials in EPA and the AEC/NRC arose over the issue of radiation hazards from nuclear power. But public exposure from the nuclear fuel cycle was but a tiny percentage of the radiation exposure that the population received from medical sources. Medical exposure accounted for approximately 90 percent of the total radiation other than natural background received by the population of the United States in the 1970s. The medical applications of radiation continued to trouble experts, who found a disturbing number of examples in which x-rays and other radiation sources were employed in ways that were inappropriate, excessive, or unduly risky for patients and practitioners. The BEIR study of 1972 echoed the recommendations of the National Academy of Sciences report of 1956 by concluding that "medical radiation exposure can and should be reduced considerably" without sacrificing the benefits it provided. Karl Z. Morgan, a pioneer in the field of radiation protection and a longtime chairman of ICRP and NCRP committees on internal dose, told a group of colleagues that some physicians required pelvic x-rays before they would accept new patients who were or might be pregnant. "There are some fairly large communities in our country," he observed in 1971, "where your wife would not be able to get a doctor to take her pregnancy case unless she were x-rayed."[23]

Leonard A. Sagan, a physician at the Palo Alto Medical Clinic in California, warned his colleagues in an editorial in the *Journal of the American Medical Association* in 1971 that they should pay greater heed to the dangers of radiation exposure. "It seems likely that public attention, now focused on the very small exposures from reactors," he wrote, "will not for long ignore the much larger doses from medical sources." The alternative to improved practices might be new regulatory laws that could "cre-

23. Leonard A. Sagan, "Medical Uses of Radiation," *JAMA: The Journal of the American Medical Association* 215 (March 22, 1971): 1977–78; National Academy of Sciences, Advisory Committee on the Biological Effects of Ionizing Radiation, *The Effects on Populations of Exposure to Low Levels of Ionizing Radiation,* November 1972, pp. 3, 13–15; Karl Z. Morgan, "Excessive Medical Diagnostic Exposure," May 1971, printed in U.S. Congress, Senate, Committee on Governmental Affairs, Subcommittee on Energy, Nuclear Proliferation, and Federal Services, *Hearings on Radiation Protection,* Part 1, 96th Cong., 1st sess., 1979, p. 163. For a brief historical overview of the medical applications of radiation, see Allen Brodsky, Ronald L. Kathren, and Charles A. Willis, "History of the Medical Uses of Radiation: Regulatory and Voluntary Standards of Protection," *Health Physics* 69 (November 1995): 783–823.

ate disadvantages for both doctor and patient." Sagan pointed out that the existing permissible doses for population exposure (170 millirems) excluded medical sources "as being best determined on a benefit-risk basis for each patient by his personal physician." But he suggested that if the medical profession failed to police itself it would increase the likelihood of facing regulatory requirements imposed by the government.[24]

The most common source of medical exposure continued to be x-rays, and critics of existing practices pointed out weaknesses that needed correction. One problem was that physicians received little formal instruction in medical school about x-ray hazards and radiation protection. This deficiency was compounded by technicians who were ill-informed about radiation dangers or poorly supervised. Only a few states required licenses or special training for operators of x-ray machines. At times the machines were defective, which created hazards for both technicians and patients. Although x-rays in hospitals were generally administered by professional radiologists, most x-rays were taken in the offices of nonspecialists who might or might not be well acquainted with suitable procedures. In addition to exposure from x-rays, patients also received radiation in much smaller doses from diagnostic radiopharmaceuticals, the use of which expanded rapidly in the 1960s. The use of radiation for therapeutic purposes, especially as a treatment for cancer, required much heavier doses than diagnostic examinations. Permissible dose restrictions did not apply to patients receiving treatment, but radiation therapy still required proper procedures and equipment to protect technicians from excessive exposure and patients from "misadministrations" that delivered too much or too little radiation.[25]

The primary responsibility for radiation safety in medical procedures rested with state governments. State health departments controlled the licensing and use of x-ray machines, radiopharmaceuticals, and radioactive materials that were naturally occurring or produced by accelerators. In addition, professional societies, including the Society of Nuclear Medicine, the American Board of Nuclear Medicine, the American College of Radiology, the American College of Nuclear Medicine, the American College of Nuclear Physicians, the American Board of Health Physics, and the Health Physics Society, provided information, certification, and

24. Sagan, "Medical Uses of Radiation," pp. 1977–78.
25. Ibid., p. 1978; National Academy of Sciences, BEIR Committee, *Effects . . . of Exposure to Low Levels of Ionizing Radiation*, p. 14; "Growing Debate over Dangers of Radiation," *U.S. News and World Report*, May 14, 1979, pp. 25–26; *New York Times*, July 4, 1979.

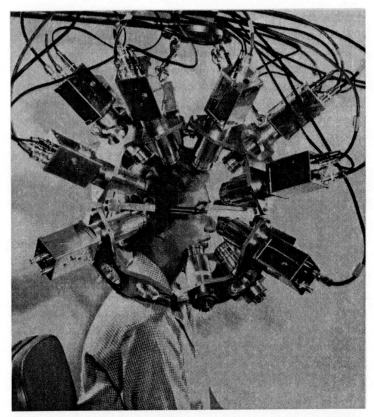

Figure 6. A "multi-detector positron scanner" used for locating tumors in conjunction with radioisotopes that was under development in the early 1960s. (National Archives 434–SF–54–44)

other peer group services. Federal agencies exercised only limited authority over the medical applications of radiation. Several of them performed regulatory functions that were considerably more peripheral than the role of the states. The Environmental Protection Agency, through its responsibilities for ambient radiation standards, could indirectly regulate medical uses of radiation that resulted in releases to drinking water or the atmosphere. The Occupational Safety and Health Administration, under the Department of Labor, had jurisdiction over worker safety and could claim a role in limiting occupational radiation exposure, though its statutory mandate did not extend to radiation produced by nuclear fission. The Social Security Administration could exert a measure of control over nuclear medicine through its regulation of Medicare and Medicaid providers.[26]

The federal agencies with the largest role in regulating the medical uses of radiation by the mid-1970s were the Food and Drug Administration (FDA), under the Department of Health, Education and Welfare, and the AEC/NRC. FDA's authority covered the manufacture of drugs, including those containing radioactive substances, but not their use. It also issued performance standards for x-ray machines manufactured after 1974. As with drugs, it had no jurisdiction over the use of x-ray machines that met its manufacturing standards, though it offered recommendations and education for those who operated the equipment. The AEC and, after 1975, the NRC regulated reactor-produced radioactive materials that were used both for diagnostic and therapeutic purposes. Until 1974 the FDA exempted radioactive drugs from its jurisdiction and the AEC regulated them. When the FDA terminated the exemption, the AEC and then the NRC remained responsible for regulating certain radioactive devices, such as pacemakers that contained plutonium, and radioactive substances that were applied externally and internally to treat cancer and other diseases or that were administered as diagnostic tracers. The AEC and the NRC granted licenses to qualified manufacturers, pharmacies, medical institutions, and individual physicians for the use of those materials.[27]

26. SECY-76-529 (October 29, 1976), NRC Records; "Report of the Interagency Task Force on Ionizing Radiation on Institutional Arrangements," draft, April 17, 1979, printed in Senate Subcommittee on Energy, Nuclear Proliferation, and Federal Services, *Hearings on Radiation Protection,* Part 2, pp. 209–14; Brodsky, Kathren, and Willis, "History of the Medical Uses of Radiation," p. 809.

27. SECY-76-529, NRC Records; "Report of the Interagency Task Force on Ionizing Radiation," pp. 214–15; Senate Subcommittee on Energy, Nuclear Proliferation, and Federal Services, *Hearings on Radiation Protection,* Part 1, pp. 455–59.

The FDA's authority to regulate the manufacture of x-ray machines was a part of its responsibilities under the Radiation Control for Health and Safety Act of 1968. This law came about largely in response to growing concern over radiation from color television sets. In 1967 the General Electric Company announced a recall of one hundred thousand color sets because they provided inadequate shielding against the emission of x-rays. The vacuum tube in most television receivers was a potential source of x-rays, and the more powerful tubes in color sets presented more serious hazards than black-and-white models. Color televisions came into widespread use in the United States for the first time in the mid-1960s. Further investigation showed that televisions manufactured by other firms had similar flaws. The radiation control act instructed the Department of Health, Education, and Welfare to set limits for radiation emissions from televisions and other electronic products, which included x-ray machines. Edward W. Lawless, *Technology and Social Shock* (New Brunswick: Rutgers University Press, 1977), pp. 199–207, and telephone conversation with former FDA official Donald Hamilton, May 27, 1998.

Controversy over
Regulating Medical Radiation

The regulation of the medical uses of radiation did not create jurisdictional disputes such as those between EPA and the AEC/NRC over effluents from nuclear power plants. It did, however, generate debate and sometimes sharp exchanges over the extent of the federal government's role in medical procedures. This was apparent, for example, in the efforts of the AEC and the NRC to strike a balance between the promotion of safety in the medical programs they regulated and the reluctance to interfere unduly in the practices of their medical licensees.

In August 1972 the General Accounting Office, as a part of a general review of the AEC's regulatory programs, recommended that the agency revise its regulations to, among other things, improve its oversight of the medical uses of radioactive materials. It urged the AEC to (1) define the activities that physicians could delegate to technicians in the use of radiation sources; (2) stipulate that physicians make certain that technicians were properly trained in the use of radioactive materials; and (3) require that medical licensees report all misadministrations to the AEC. The GAO report cited a case of a patient who had died in 1968 after receiving a dose of radioactive material a thousand times greater than prescribed, and it strongly suggested that the AEC strengthen its inspection, enforcement, and reporting requirements.[28]

The AEC agreed with the GAO's first two recommendations and took prompt action to amend its regulations to include them. It was initially less certain about imposing a reporting requirement for misadministrations because of its implications for violating physician-patient confidence. Further, the AEC was not convinced that misadministration of radioactive materials in medical practice was a major problem. It found that only twelve cases of misadministrations involving twenty patients had been brought to the AEC's attention between 1961 and 1972, though it acknowledged that it had no way of establishing the exact number of misadministrations that had occurred. After consulting with its Advisory Committee on the Medical Uses of Isotopes, a group of outside experts, the AEC decided to accept the GAO's advice and propose to require that licensees report all misadministrations. It went even further than the GAO

28. "GAO Review Finds Laxity in AEC Materials License Inspection and Compliance," *Nuclear Industry* 19 (September 1972): 28–32.

by also proposing to require that a physician tell the patient or a responsible relative if a misadministration occurred, unless the physician believed that notification would be "contrary to the best interests of the patient."[29]

In 1973 the AEC published for public comment proposed revisions to its regulations that included all three requirements. The proposed reporting requirement received a great deal of criticism from physicians and professional medical organizations. They objected on the grounds that it might amount to "self-incrimination" by those responsible for misadministrations, that it invited government intrusion into the physician-patient relationship, that it might violate the privacy of patients, and that there were no comparable requirements for other medical treatments or drugs. Several comments suggested that the AEC should limit reports of misadministrations to therapy procedures and large radiopharmaceutical doses; the diagnostic use of radioisotopes did not seem sufficiently hazardous to justify notification of the AEC or the patient. The AEC did not take any action on the 1973 proposal, and questions related to the regulation of radiation medicine, for a time, again faded into the background.[30]

The issue reemerged as a major concern in 1976 after errors in the operation of a cobalt 60 teletherapy unit at a Columbus, Ohio, hospital caused the overexposure of scores of patients ("teletherapy," or therapy from a distance, refers to treatment from outside the body). In April 1976 the licensee, Riverside Methodist Hospital, announced that excessive exposures had occurred between March 1, 1975, and January 30, 1976, but it was slow to inform the affected patients or the Nuclear Regulatory Commission. The NRC, which first learned of the problem from an official of the FDA, immediately launched an investigation. It revealed that, as a result of improper calibration of the cobalt 60 source, 393 patients received overexposures of 10 percent or more above the prescribed amounts. Some overdoses were as high as 41 percent above the prescribed levels. This happened because the responsible staff member at the hospital had miscalculated the output of the cobalt 60 machine and had failed to periodically calibrate it. At the time the NRC received information that at least two patients died as a direct result of the overdoses; much later it learned that ten patients might have died from severe radiation injury.[31]

29. SECY-R-460 (May 16, 1972), SECY-R-462 (May 17, 1972), SECY-R-621 (January 11, 1973), AEC/NRC.

30. SECY-77–194 (April 8, 1977), NRC Records.

31. Linda Stern Rubin, "The Riverside Radiation Tragedy," *Columbus Monthly*, n.d., and Appendix A, "Incident at Riverside Methodist Hospital," enclosures to James M. Taylor to the Commission, January 8, 1993; Myron Pollycove to John E. Glenn, January 13, 1993, en-

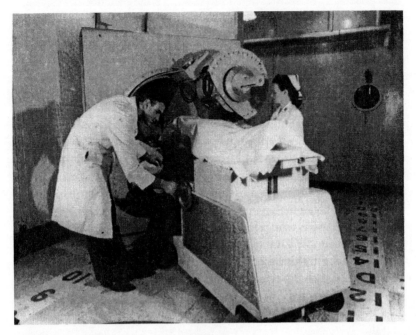

Figure 7. A teletherapy unit for treating patients by using radioactive cobalt 60, ca. 1972. (National Archives 434–SF–53–28)

The NRC acted promptly to prevent recurrence of the specific errors that had led to the Riverside tragedy. In July 1976 it modified Riverside's license to require full calibrations of teletherapy machines at least annually, spot checks every month, and record keeping of all such procedures. In May 1977 it issued a proposed rule that would place the same basic requirements on all teletherapy licensees. The NRC pointed out that it had found that in some cases teletherapy machines had not been calibrated for as long as five years. A final rule governing proper and periodic calibration became effective on July 9, 1979.[32]

While the NRC was revising its regulations to address the specific problems that the Riverside overdoses revealed, it was also considering broader questions relating to the regulation of radiation medicine. In light of the

closure to Taylor to Slade Gordon, May 11, 1993; "Summary: Riverside Methodist Hospital—Teletherapy Unit Calibration," enclosure to Marcus Rowden to Edward I. Koch, September 29, 1976, all in NRC records.

32. Appendix A of Taylor to the Commission, January 8, 1993, SECY-76–574 (December 6, 1976), NRC Press Release, May 19, 1977, NRC Records.

Riverside accident, the basic question was, in the words of a staff paper of October 1976, "how far does the NRC want to go in regulating nuclear medicine?" The NRC needed to consider not only the potential harm to patients but also the attitudes of physicians and medical institutions toward government regulation. In late 1976 the Commission asked the staff to proceed with plans for a public meeting to discuss the subject of NRC involvement in radiation medicine and to provide information on the issues to be raised and alternatives available. When the staff failed to act promptly, the Commission ordered it to give the matter "higher priority" in February 1977. The commissioners complained that "many months have passed since the Riverside incident focused concern on this area, [and] we still have only the outlines of a program."[33]

The staff conducted a meeting on May 6, 1977, to address questions pertaining to the role of the NRC in regulating radiation medicine. It invited representatives of medical organizations, professional societies, public interest groups, federal agencies, and state governments. More than ninety people attended the meeting. Members of the medical community wanted to keep the NRC's role to a minimum and to discourage any agency involvement in issues relating to medical judgment. State representatives, however, tended to favor greater NRC participation in guarding against overexposure of patients.[34]

Based on the ambivalent guidance it received, the NRC staff drew up a draft policy statement. It sought to achieve an appropriate and generally acceptable balance between the extremes of overly zealous or excessively cautious regulation. In February 1978 the staff proposed that the Commission adopt a policy statement with three basic provisions: (1) in accordance with its statutory mandate, the NRC would continue to regulate the medical uses of radiation to protect workers and the general public; (2) the NRC would regulate the safety of patients from radiation hazards in cases in which it was justified by the risk to patients and in which voluntary standards, or compliance with standards, were inadequate; and (3) the NRC would minimize intrusion into medical judgments affecting patients and into other areas traditionally considered to be a part of the practice of medicine. The NRC issued a final policy statement incorporating those three guidelines in February 1979.[35]

33. SECY-76–529, Samuel J. Chilk to Lee V. Gossick, December 8, 1976, February 10, 1977, NRC Records.

34. SECY-78–68 (February 1, 1978), NRC Records.

35. Ibid., SECY-78–614 (November 22, 1978), Samuel J. Chilk to Lee V. Gossick and others, January 22, 1979, NRC Press Release, February 9, 1979, NRC Records.

The policy statement made the NRC's intentions clear, but the ways in which the agency would carry out its principles remained an open question. After considering approaches to the NRC's role in regulating radiation medicine, the staff recommended two major changes in existing requirements. The first would reduce the NRC's involvement in the medical uses of radiation by withdrawing restrictions on the freedom of physicians to select diagnostic radiopharmaceuticals. This seemed sensible, because diagnostic procedures posed hazards that were generally lower than those of therapy procedures by several orders of magnitude. After a public comment period and Commission approval, this change became effective in March 1979.[36]

The other, much more controversial revision that the staff recommended would increase the NRC's role in radiation medicine. It revived in altered form the 1973 proposal to require medical licensees to report misadministrations. The proposal stirred dissent not only from physicians and other outside groups but also within the NRC. In the wake of the Riverside hospital overdoses, general counsel Peter L. Strauss urged that the rule on calibration then under review should direct licensees to report misadministrations exceeding a specified amount. When the Commission agreed to consider a requirement for reporting misadministrations to the NRC and to the referring physician, some staff officials demurred. Kenneth R. Chapman, director of the Office of Nuclear Material Safety and Safeguards, suggested that in light of the "sensitivity of misadministration in the medical community," the NRC should delay a decision until it consulted with its Advisory Committee on the Medical Uses of Isotopes. Strauss took sharp exception. "I do not see how even the narrowest conception of NRC's regulatory mission," he told the commissioners, "can justify the repeatedly expressed concern for the 'sensitivity' of the medical community without any expression of concern for the patients."[37]

By early 1978 the NRC staff had largely accepted Strauss's position. The Office of Standards Development recommended in February that the NRC require reporting of all misadministrations occurring during therapy procedures. To reduce the number of reports, it further advised that diagnostic misadministrations be required only in cases that could cause a "clinically detectable adverse effect." Finally, the staff suggested that "po-

36. SECY-78-69 (February 1, 1978), SECY-78-615 (November 22, 1978), Samuel J. Chilk to Lee V. Gossick and others, January 22, 1979, NRC Records.

37. Peter L. Strauss to the Commission, August 5, 1976, December 16, 1976, April 22, 1977, SECY-77-194 (April 8, 1977), SECY-78-70 (February 1, 1978), NRC Records.

tentially dangerous" misadministrations be reported to the NRC and the referring physician but not directly to the patient. It noted that physicians had objected to the 1973 proposal for directly informing patients about misadministrations on the grounds that it was "an intrusion into the physician-patient relationship."[38]

The staff proposals set off a new exchange of differing views on the question of whether patients should be advised of misadministrations. The Office of the General Counsel suggested that the Commission consider a "stronger method for providing misadministration information to the patient." Agency lawyers denied that this would be an intrusion into the physician-patient relationship and argued that "there [were] sound administrative and policy reasons for imposing such a requirement." Other staff offices disagreed, contending that a rule stipulating that patients or responsible relatives must be informed of misadministrations was "excessive." As a result of the exchanges within the NRC, the Office of the General Counsel changed its thinking dramatically. Acting general counsel Stephen F. Eilperin cited legal barriers to informing patients and asserted that such a requirement "would insert the NRC into the physician-patient relationship without a demonstrated benefit."[39]

Howard K. Shapar, who headed a separate legal office within the NRC staff, forcefully denied that informing patients about misadministrations represented a violation of the physician-patient relationship. "The objective of this [proposed] policy is to protect the patient—not to protect the physician," he wrote. "The proposed rule would in no way interfere with the delivery of care to the patient or result in harm to the patient." After considering Shapar's opinion, the Office of the General Counsel again shifted its position to support his recommendations. In June 1978 the Commission voted to publish for public comment a proposed rule by which licensees would report misadministrations to the NRC, the referring physician, and the patient or responsible relative. The Commission added a condition similar to that in the 1973 proposed rule by stipulating that the patient need not be informed if "the referring physician shall personally inform the licensee that in his medical judgment telling the patient or the patient's responsible relatives would be harmful to one or the other." It invited commenters to examine closely the reporting require-

38. SECY-78–70, NRC Records.
39. James L. Kelley to the Commission, February 9, 1978, Ken Pederson to the Commission, May 11, 1978, Stephen F. Eilperin to the Commission, May 12, 1978, SECY-78–244 (May 5, 1978), NRC Records.

ment because "the Commission has expressed concern about the possibility about undue intrusion into the physician-patient relationship."[40]

The medical community responded to the NRC's invitation by expressing strong, nearly unanimous opposition to the proposed rule. Ninety percent of the one hundred fifty commenters objected to it, largely on the basis of the requirement to report misadministrations to the NRC and to the patient. They complained that the proposed rule was a serious and unjustified intrusion into medical practice and claimed that it would lead to "unwarranted malpractice suits" and to "undue alarm" on the part of patients.

The NRC staff did not find the objections convincing; it advised the Commission to issue a final rule with the reporting requirement intact. It recommended that all diagnostic and therapy misadministrations be reported to the NRC (thus dropping the ambiguous "clinically detectable" threshold for diagnostic misadministrations). It suggested that therapy misadministrations also be reported to the referring physician and, unless the referring physician objected, to the patient or responsible relative. On April 2, 1980, the Commission unanimously approved the final rule that the staff recommended. Its action marked an important milestone on an issue that had simmered for years, but this did not end the controversy over the agency's role in regulating the medical uses of radiation sources. The issue continued to stir debate within the agency, and proposals to expand the NRC's requirements inevitably drew strong protests from the medical community.[41]

Although the role of the NRC in the safety of radiation medicine was a matter of importance to the medical community, it was not in itself an issue that grabbed headlines or commanded the attention of the public. But the medical use of radiation, which continued to increase after the BEIR study of 1972, remained a source of wide interest and concern. The *New York Times* reported in July 1979 that the "extent of risk in the use of X-rays is subject to considerable debate." It found that "there are growing expressions of concern . . . about the long-term hazards of [diagnostic] X-rays."[42] Such "expressions of concern" were nothing new, of course, but they were accorded front-page treatment as a part of a renewed and highly visible public debate about the hazards of low-level radiation.

40. Howard K. Shapar to the Commission, June 1, 1978, James L. Kelley to the Commission, June 16, 1978, Samuel J. Chilk to Lee V. Gossick and others, June 22, 1978, NRC Records.

41. SECY-80-26 (January 16, 1980), Excerpt from SRM of Affirmation Session 80-14, April 2, 1980, NRC Records.

42. *New York Times*, July 4, 1979.

CHAPTER FOUR

New Controversies, New Standards

During the late 1970s and early 1980s the publication of several studies on the effects of low-level radiation, increasing fears about the long-term consequences of exposure to fallout from nuclear bomb testing, a serious accident at the Three Mile Island nuclear power plant in Pennsylvania, and a new BEIR report rekindled scientific debate and public concern about radiation. As always, the evidence was too fragmentary to be conclusive, and scientists disagreed sharply about its meaning. In an atmosphere of continuing controversy and unavoidable uncertainty, both EPA and the NRC undertook major revisions of their regulations on radiation protection. Both incorporated new findings and approaches, but neither escaped criticism for policies that were in some minds overly lax and in others unduly stringent.

Renewed Controversy over Radiation Hazards

After a brief respite, by the late 1970s the hazards of low-level radiation became, once again, a highly visible and fiercely debated issue. *Nuclear Industry* magazine observed in July 1978, "Last year radiation was the subject of quiet, ongoing scientific and medical research. This year, likely as not, it is the subject of another three-minute spot on the network evening news." A few months later Senator John Glenn described the debate over the effects of low-level radiation as a "raging controversy." And in July 1979 the *New York Times* reported, "From New York to Washington State, from Texas to Montana, people are edgy, if not outright angry, over radiation."[1]

The revival of acrimonious public debate over low-level radiation was triggered by complaints of "atomic soldiers" who had been exposed to radiation while witnessing nuclear weapons tests during the 1950s and by a series of studies that raised new concerns about the hazards of small doses. The atomic soldiers issue became a source of controversy and concern in early 1977 after the Veterans Administration rejected the claims of a retired army sergeant named Paul Cooper for a service-related disability. Cooper was suffering from leukemia, which he linked to his experience of observing atomic bomb tests and conducting maneuvers in a contaminated area. After the Veterans Administration denied his claim, his plight received a great deal of attention on television and in newspapers. One member of Congress, Tim Lee Carter of Kentucky, took a special interest in Cooper's story because his own son had died of leukemia. Carter was the ranking minority member of the Subcommittee on Health and the Environment of the House Committee on Interstate and Foreign Commerce, and he convinced the subcommittee chairman, Paul G. Rogers of Florida, to hold hearings on the health hazards of radiation.[2]

Meanwhile, three highly publicized studies intensified the scientific debate and public concern over low-level radiation. Irwin D. J. Bross, director of biostatistics at the Roswell Park Memorial Institute in Buffalo, published a report that he said proved that the hazards of exposure to levels as low as one rad of radioactivity were "far worse than anyone expected." He contended that persons exposed to diagnostic radiation ran a much higher risk of leukemia and other diseases, and because of genetic damage, so did children of parents exposed to low doses of radiation. He told the Rogers subcommittee in February 1978 that "as a direct consequence of [the] lie that low-level radiation is harmless, millions of Americans have been needlessly exposed to unnecessary and useless radiation that has produced, is producing, or will produce, tens of thousands of cases of leukemia and other serious diseases."

1. John O'Neill, "Low-Level Radiation Limits Command Top Level Attention," *Nuclear Industry* 25 (July 1978): 24–29; John O'Neill, "Low-Level Radiation: How Risky?" *Nuclear Industry* 26 (June 1979): 3–6; *Nucleonics Week*, January 5, 1978; Constance Holden, "Low-Level Radiation: A High-Level Concern," *Science* 204 (April 13, 1979): 155–58; *New York Times*, July 1, 1979.
2. Barton C. Hacker, *Elements of Controversy: The Atomic Energy Commission and Radiation Safety in Nuclear Weapons Testing, 1947–1974* (Berkeley and Los Angeles: University of California Press, 1994), pp. 7–9; Barton C. Hacker, "Radiation Safety, the AEC, and Nuclear Weapons Testing," *Public Historian* 14 (Winter 1992): 31–53.

Bross based his views on a mathematical model he developed and used to analyze data collected by other researchers in an extensive survey of leukemia victims in New York, Maryland, and Minnesota between 1959 and 1962. To evaluate Bross's claims, the NRC asked Kenneth J. Rothman, a professor at the Harvard School of Public Health, to review his findings from the perspective of a professional epidemiologist. When Rothman protested that he was not an expert on radiation and had not been involved in the controversies over low-level exposure, NRC officials made clear that they wanted someone without a "public stance to defend." After Rothman accepted the assignment to conduct an independent assessment, he concluded that Bross's methodology was deficient and his arguments unpersuasive. In April 1978 he reported that although Bross's work should not "be totally disregarded," he did not believe "that his findings warrant any revision in our thinking about the health consequences of radiation exposure."[3]

At about the same time that Bross's thesis was commanding attention, Thomas Najarian, a physician and fellow in hematology at the Veterans Administration Hospital in Boston, reported that employees of the Portsmouth, New Hampshire, naval shipyard who worked on nuclear submarines were much more likely to die of leukemia or cancer than the general population. Najarian examined death certificates of shipyard workers, and while admitting that his sources did not provide definitive information, he concluded that compared to the population of the United States or workers at Portsmouth not exposed to occupational radiation, leukemia deaths for nuclear workers were 450 percent higher. He further suggested that the radiation exposures of nuclear workers at the shipyard were well within permissible limits. The results of Najarian's investigation were prominently featured in the *Boston Globe* in February 1977 and in other reports.[4]

3. U.S. Congress, Senate, Committee on Commerce, Science, and Transportation, *Hearings on Radiation Health and Safety*, 95th Cong., 1st sess., 1977, pp. 171–91; U.S. Congress, House, Committee on Interstate and Foreign Commerce, Subcommittee on Health and the Environment, *Hearings on Effect of Radiation on Human Health, Volume 1, Health Effects of Ionizing Radiation*, 95th Cong., 2d sess., 1978, pp. 905–1019; Irwin D. J. Bross and N. Natarajan, "Genetic Damage from Diagnostic Radiation," *JAMA: The Journal of the American Medical Association* 237 (May 30, 1977): 2399–2401; Irwin D. J. Bross, "Hazards to Persons Exposed to Ionizing Radiation (and to Their Children) from Dosages Currently Permitted by the Nuclear Regulatory Commission," [April 1978], Kenneth J. Rothman, "Review of Dr. Irwin Bross' Presentation on Radiation Exposure and Cancer Risk," April 7, 1978, Nuclear Regulatory Commission Records, NRC Public Document Room, Washington, D.C.

4. House Subcommittee on Health and the Environment, *Hearings on Effect of Radiation on Human Health*, pp. 1207–66; Ralph E. Lapp, *The Radiation Controversy* (Greenwich, Conn.: Reddy Communications, 1979), pp. 7–16.

Najarian's general findings were supported by the most visible and controversial of the three reports that appeared virtually simultaneously on the dangers of exposure to low-level radiation. Thomas F. Mancuso of the University of Pittsburgh, in collaboration with Alice Stewart and George Kneale of the University of Birmingham (England), published in November 1977 a long-awaited study on the health effects of radiation at the Hanford installation in eastern Washington, where plutonium had been produced and chemically separated since the later stages of World War II. Mancuso had been working on a study of the effects of occupational exposure under a contract originally issued by the AEC in 1964. After analyzing records on the deaths of Hanford workers, Mancuso, Stewart, and Kneale concluded that the incidence of fatal cancer among them was significantly higher than among the general population, even when their exposures had not exceeded permissible limits. The *Los Angeles Times* observed that Mancuso's results brought "environmental groups and the government into renewed conflict over the adequacy of federal and international radiation safety standards that apply both to the nuclear industry and the general public."[5]

The findings of the Bross, Najarian, and Mancuso reports captured a great deal of sympathetic attention in the popular media and in congressional hearings. They raised doubts about the soundness of existing radiation standards and new concerns about the dangers of low-level radiation. All three studies were sharply contested by many radiation experts, who questioned their data, methodology, and conclusions and denied that, contrary to presentations in some popular publications, their findings were definitive. In addition to the questions raised about Bross's methodology, respected authorities pointed out, for example, that Najarian's sampling was too small to draw firm conclusions and that Mancuso had not considered other possible causes of cancer at Hanford. Conflicting views of the meaning of the Bross, Najarian, and Mancuso research were exchanged in journals, newspaper columns, and congressional hearings.[6]

The disputes focused not only on the scientific validity of the studies

5. House Subcommittee on Health and the Environment, *Hearings on Effect of Radiation on Human Health*, pp. 523–633; Thomas F. Mancuso, Alice Stewart, and George Kneale, "Radiation Exposures of Hanford Workers Dying from Cancer and Other Causes," *Health Physics* 33 (November 1977): 369–85; *Los Angeles Times*, December 1, 1977.

6. Jean L. Marx, "Low-Level Radiation: Just How Bad Is It?" *Science* 204 (April 13, 1979): 160–64; *New York Times*, October 25, 1976; House Subcommittee on Health and the Environment, *Hearings on Effect of Radiation on Human Health*, pp. 640–77, 869–904; Lapp, *Radiation Controversy*, pp. 95–106; Hacker, *Elements of Controversy*, pp. 260–61.

but also on suggestions that the results they reported had been suppressed by uncooperative or hostile government agencies. Columnists Jack Anderson and Les Whitten claimed, "In a deadly attempt at censorship, the federal government has systematically suppressed disagreeable news about the danger of radiation." Bross made the same allegation in testimony before the Rogers subcommittee; he protested that "big science Federal agencies such as the AEC" exercised "control of the peer review mechanism to suppress, vilify, or cut off the funding of the little scientists who told the truth, or thought they were telling the truth." The charges of government interference were most prominent in the case of Mancuso, who received a great deal of attention in the media by insisting that the government muzzled him. He accused the Energy Research and Development Administration (which inherited the AEC's nonregulatory functions and in 1977 became a part of the newly created Department of Energy) of terminating his contract to study mortality among Hanford workers because it did not like his findings. Those allegations were found to be groundless in a lengthy report by the Inspector General of the Department of Energy, but its investigation did not settle the controversy. Congressmen Rogers and Carter, contending that the Inspector General's review was so seriously flawed that it "may only fuel the charges of 'coverup' already voiced," asked the GAO to carry out its own study of Mancuso's treatment. The GAO investigation reached the same conclusions as the Inspector General of the Department of Energy about Mancuso's complaints. Nevertheless, the Mancuso affair continued to stoke the debate over low-level radiation hazards.[7]

The Libassi Task Force

In an atmosphere of pointed and sometimes bitter debate, President Jimmy Carter ordered a new study of federal radiation pro-

7. *Washington Post,* December 3, 1977; John F. O'Leary to Dale Myers, July 25, 1978, with enclosed Department of Energy Office of Inspector General Report, May 13, 1978, Box 4 (Mancuso Controversy), Herbert Parker Papers, University of Washington, Seattle; Paul G. Rogers and Tim Lee Carter to James R. Schlesinger, August 2, 1978, Box 15 (IG Report and Additional Information), Records Relating to the Study of Health and Mortality among Atomic Energy Workers — "Mancuso Study," Record Group 434 (General Records of the Department of Energy), National Archives, College Park, Maryland; John O'Neill, "DOE Cleared in Firing Mancuso," *Nuclear Industry* 26 (March 1979): 29–31; Holden, "Low-Level Radiation," 155–58; House Subcommittee on Health and the Envi-

tection programs. The White House staff had followed the growing controversy, and in April 1978 Stuart Eizenstat, special assistant to the president for domestic affairs, urged Carter to "develop a coordinated approach to answering the scientific questions" raised by the Rogers hearings, particularly the evidence of increased cancer rates among naval shipyard workers. He proposed that an interagency group headed by Secretary of Health, Education, and Welfare Joseph Califano study the effects of radiation exposure on participants in nuclear weapons tests and workers in nuclear facilities. Carter approved Eizenstat's recommendation, and the White House established a task force that included Secretary of Defense Harold Brown, Secretary of Energy James Schlesinger, and Administrator of Veterans Affairs Max Cleland as well as Califano in May 1978. Within a short time the NRC, EPA, and the Department of Labor also joined the investigation. Califano appointed the general counsel of his agency, F. Peter Libassi, to chair the task force.[8]

Drawing on the expertise of high-level officials from the seven participating agencies and advice from scientists, environmental groups, nuclear industry representatives, medical practitioners, labor unions, veterans' organizations, and members of Congress and their staffs, the Libassi task force published a draft of its survey in April 1979 and a slightly revised final version two months later. The report was mostly a straightforward description of the sources and hazards of radiation exposure and of federal programs for protecting against their risks. In the sections in which it drew conclusions about the effectiveness of existing radiation standards, it offered little support for the Mancuso, Bross, or Najarian studies. "While these studies are suggestive," the report declared, "none of them is sufficiently extensive, complete, or free from methodologic complications to provide conclusive information at present on the effects of radiation at low doses." It also affirmed that the risks from exposure to low levels of radiation, which it defined as 5 rems

ronment, *Hearings on Effect of Radiation on Human Health*, p. 912. For stories on the suppression of the Mancuso report, see, for example, *Chicago Sun-Times*, November 13, 1977; *Pittsburgh Post-Gazette*, November 17, 1977; *Washington Post*, January 16, 1978; *Washington Star*, January 19, 1978.

8. Kitty Schirmer to John Ahearne, November 16, 1977, Box 10 (Vol. 27), Records of the Mancuso Study, DOE Records, National Archives; Stu Eizenstat and Frank Raines to the President, April 28, 1978, Eizenstat and Zbigniew Brzezinski to the Secretary of Defense and others, May 9, 1978, Subject File—Health (HE 8), White House Central File, Jimmy Carter Papers, Jimmy Carter Library, Atlanta, Georgia; U.S. Congress, House, Committee on Government Operations, Subcommittee on Environment, Energy, and Natural Resources, *Hearings on Radiation Protection*, 95th Cong., 2d sess., 1978, pp. 411–39.

or less, were "thought to be very low." The Libassi task force reiterated the counsel that standards-setting organizations and regulatory agencies had advanced for years: any unnecessary exposure to radiation should be avoided and the risks of exposure should be balanced against the benefits.

The conclusions of the task force were not, however, simply an endorsement of the status quo. It focused on the problems of institutional arrangements within the federal government, which it found to be confusing, overlapping, and sometimes contradictory. As a result, it recommended that an interagency unit be established that would perform the same functions as the Federal Radiation Council, which had become a part of EPA in 1970. Responding to concerns that EPA had not devoted adequate attention or resources to carrying out the responsibilities it had inherited from the FRC, the Libassi task force called for a new council that would provide broad guidance on radiation protection policies and coordinate the activities of federal agencies. President Carter responded by establishing the Radiation Policy Council in February 1980. The council was short-lived; it ceased to exist in 1981 when the Office of Management and Budget under President Ronald W. Reagan refused to fund it. The functions of the radiation council and another unit that Carter created, the Interagency Radiation Research Committee, were combined in the Committee on Interagency Radiation Research and Policy Coordination that Reagan established in 1984.[9]

The Libassi report was greeted with relief and satisfaction by most radiation protection professionals, both inside and outside of the federal government. They viewed it, quite correctly, as a general, if not an unqualified, endorsement of their assumptions, principles, and practices. Critics of existing standards and programs, by contrast, attacked the findings of the Libassi study. Bross, for example, told a Senate subcommittee chaired by John Glenn that it was another in a series of "useless, incompetent, and false reports" on radiation. The efforts of the Libassi task

9. Report of the Interagency Task Force on the Health Effects of Ionizing Radiation, June 1979, Peter Libassi to All Radiation Task Force Members, May 22, 1979, Joseph J. Fouchard to the Commission, October 25, 1979, NRC Records; Stu Eizenstat and Frank Press to the President, October 19, 1979, Staff Offices: Counsel-Cutler, Box 81 (Ionizing Radiation), Eizenstat and Press to the President, February 20, 1980, Carter to the Secretary of Defense and Others, February 21, 1980, Subject File—Health (HE 8), White House Central File, Carter Papers; U.S. Congress, Senate, Committee on Governmental Affairs, Subcommittee on Energy, Nuclear Proliferation, and Federal Services, *Hearings on Radiation Protection*, 96th Cong., 1st sess., 1979, Part 2, pp. 173–241; *Inside N.R.C.*, June 15, 1981; Hacker, *Elements of Controversy*, p. 263.

Figure 8. In response to the Three Mile Island accident, demonstrators rally against nuclear power in Harrisburg, Pennsylvania, April 9, 1979. (National Archives NWDNS–220–TMI–2812–25)

force, then, did not end the controversy over low-level radiation and in some ways contributed to it.[10]

As the Libassi task force completed its review, other developments magnified the intensity of the debate over radiation. A series of congressional hearings and news stories in 1978 and 1979 suggested that Americans who lived downwind from the Nevada weapons testing site were suffering unusually high rates of cancer from their exposure to radioactive fallout. An article by the epidemiologist Joseph L. Lyon and colleagues fueled such fears when it was published in the *New England Journal of Medicine* in early 1979. The Lyon study indicated a dramatic increase in childhood leukemia among residents of Utah exposed to fallout from atmospheric nuclear testing. Those findings did not go unchallenged. Critics questioned Lyon's results because of the small size of the population on which they were based and the fact that other types of childhood cancer decreased in the same areas in which Lyon found a sharply elevated incidence of leukemia.[11]

10. John O'Neill, "HEW Report and Witnesses Put Radiation in Perspective," *Nuclear Industry* 26 (April 1979): 3–7; Senate Subcommittee on Energy, Nuclear Proliferation, and Federal Services, *Hearings on Radiation Protection*, Part 1, p. 306.

11. Hacker, *Elements of Controversy*, pp. 261–64; Howard Ball, *Justice Downwind: America's Atomic Testing Program in the 1950s* (New York: Oxford University Press, 1986), pp. 109–16.

The debate over the effects of fallout on "downwinders" was over-shadowed by the enormous publicity generated by the accident at the Three Mile Island nuclear power plant near Harrisburg, Pennsylvania, in March 1979. Shortly after the plant suffered a severe loss-of-coolant accident that melted a large portion of its nuclear core, monitoring teams detected only small amounts of radiation that had escaped to the environment from the crippled reactor. Nevertheless, uncertainties about conditions at the plant, garbled communications, and a recommendation from the NRC and Pennsylvania governor Richard Thornburgh that pregnant women and pre-school-age children evacuate the area triggered alarms about the threat of radiation exposure. The Three Mile Island accident raised awareness of and concerns about radiation hazards to unprecedented levels. Federal and state radiation protection officials, meeting at the National Conference on Radiation Control in May 1979, asserted that the public's attitude toward low-level radiation had changed from "total indifference" before the Three Mile Island accident to "an obsession with total safety" after it.[12]

The 1980 BEIR Report

A new BEIR report further extended the debate over the hazards of low-level radiation. In 1976 the Environmental Protection Agency asked the National Academy of Sciences to update its 1972 report on the effects of radiation and to determine whether the earlier conclusions were still applicable in light of new data. The National Academy signed an agreement with EPA to undertake the new review on September 30, 1976. It recruited twenty-two scientists, most of whom were affiliated with universities or national laboratories, to serve on the committee. After considerable internal debate and contention, the committee released its preliminary findings in May 1979.[13]

The draft report reaffirmed the major conclusions of the 1972 BEIR study, even after considering the information available from new animal studies and improved methods for predicting and evaluating cancer risks.

12. *Washington Post,* March 29, 1979; *New York Times,* May 11, 1979; Philip L. Cantelon and Robert C. Williams, *Crisis Contained: The Department of Energy at Three Mile Island* (Carbondale: Southern Illinois University Press, 1981), pp. 30, 41–45, 54–55.

13. National Academy of Sciences, Committee on the Biological Effects of Ionizing Radiations, *The Effects on Populations of Exposure to Low Levels of Ionizing Radiation: 1980* (Washington, D.C.: National Academy Press, 1980), pp. v–10 (hereafter cited as BEIR-III).

But it also provided some different perspectives. One important departure from the 1972 review was that the new study refrained from offering a single range of estimates of the number of deaths that could occur if the entire population of the United States were exposed to the permissible radiation dose for population groups. Instead, it furnished estimates of the incidence of and mortality from cancer per million people exposed to a single dose of 10 rads or a dose of 1 rad per year continuously over a lifetime.

The report, while contending that doses at those levels were "areas of concern," acknowledged that they did "not reflect any circumstances that would normally occur." The values it used produced somewhat higher estimates of cancer deaths than the totals cited in the 1972 study if applied to the entire population. If read correctly, however, the calculations in the new report avoided the implication that the entire population of the country could be exposed to the permissible dose. But the figures cited could still be extrapolated to ominously large numbers in aggregate. The *New York Times* reported in a front-page story that exposure to low-level radiation from all sources, including natural background and medical uses, "would lead to the development of 220,000 cases of cancer in the lifetime of today's population."

The new BEIR report, like the 1972 version, emphasized the paucity of data to support firm estimates on the health effects of exposure to low levels of radiation. The committee cautioned that its risk estimates "should in no way be interpreted as precise numerical expectations" because they were "based on incomplete data and involve a large degree of uncertainty." It was, however, much more categorical in assessing the validity of the Mancuso, Bross, and Najarian studies that suggested a higher risk of cancer from exposure to low-level radiation. The BEIR draft concluded that all three reports were seriously flawed.[14]

The debate that took place within the BEIR committee arose from sharply conflicting views about the methods for estimating the risks of low-level radiation. The draft update of the BEIR report, like the 1972 study, used a linear hypothesis to estimate risks. This was a straight-line

14. SECY-79-322 (May 10, 1979), NRC Records; David G. Hawkins to the Administrator, [May 1979], Box 41 (OANR), Intra-Agency Memorandums, 1977–1983, Office of the Administrator, Record Group 412 (Records of the Environmental Protection Agency), National Archives, College Park; Eliot Marshall, "NAS Study on Radiation Takes the Middle Road," *Science* 204 (May 18, 1979), 711–14; *New York Times,* April 30, 1979; *Nucleonics Week,* May 3, 1979; O'Neill, "Low-Level Radiation," pp. 3–6.

extrapolation from fatality rates from exposure to high doses of radiation, for which the evidence was more definitive. The linear model suggested that deaths from exposure to low levels would occur at a rate proportional to those at higher levels. Edward P. Radford of the University of Pittsburgh, the chairman of the BEIR committee, was a strong proponent of using the linear model. Based on its projections, he urged that existing radiation standards be tightened by a factor of ten.

Other members of the committee took a different position. They argued that the linear hypothesis was not appropriate and that a "quadratic model" would more accurately reflect low-level radiation risks. It suggested that adverse health effects increased very gradually at low doses and followed a linear model only at much higher levels. This would mean that the risks of exposure to low-level radiation were considerably less than the linear model indicated. When the draft BEIR report was released, five members of the committee announced their disagreement, apparently to the surprise of many of their colleagues and the National Academy. The dissenters contended that the 1972 survey had overestimated the risks by as much as a factor of ten. If the overstated risk was not corrected, they complained, the new report could encourage "excessive and potentially detrimental apprehension over radiation hazards."

In response to those objections, the National Academy stopped distribution of the draft report, which it had expected to release in final form within a short time. The BEIR committee reconsidered its preliminary conclusions in light of the methodological dispute over the linear and quadratic models. Eventually, after more contention, it settled on a compromise. Most members of the committee endorsed a "linear-quadratic model" that split the difference between the two approaches. They agreed that the linear model showed the upper limits of risk and the quadratic model the lower limits. The linear-quadratic line fell between the two extremes.

The final report was issued in July 1980. It was identified as BEIR-III to distinguish it from the 1972 study, which gained a Roman numeral and became known as BEIR-I (BEIR-II was a 1977 report on methods of evaluating benefits and costs of the uses of radiation). The final BEIR-III report differed from the 1972 survey principally by projecting cancer rates from exposure to low-level radiation that were about one-half as great. All but two members of the BEIR committee accepted the final report as "a fair and balanced statement of the state of knowledge." The two dissenters represented the opposite ends of the spectrum of opinion among the membership. Radford continued to promote the linear model as the most reasonable approach. Harald H. Rossi of Columbia University took sharp exception to Radford's position and claimed that the quadratic model was vastly preferable.[15]

Despite their animated differences on methodological issues, Radford and Rossi agreed that the public was overly fearful of low-level radiation. Radford commented, "I don't think the alarm about radiation is justified. At low doses the risks are very small." Rossi offered a similar view: "The public is incredibly overconcerned about radiation to the point of superstition." One anonymous source familiar with the committee's deliberations described the arguments between members as disagreements over "whether the effects are negligible or less than negligible."[16]

EPA's Revised Occupational Standards

The new scientific evaluations of radiation hazards and the publicity they attracted focused on the risks to the general population. Although the Mancuso and Najarian studies had examined dangers to radiation workers, the implications of those and other reports for the health of the general public obscured the fact that EPA's and the NRC's radiation standards applied primarily to occupational exposure. The population standards, which the ICRP and the NCRP had first recommended in the 1950s, were a rather arbitrary function—a reduction of a factor of ten—of the basic occupational limits. During the 1970s both EPA and the NRC decided to review and possibly revise their occupational radiation standards in the light of new information and new issues. In both cases the process turned out to be lengthy, complicated, and, perhaps inevitably, controversial.

The Environmental Protection Agency initiated action on occupational standards in September 1974, before radiation hazards had reemerged as

15. BEIR-III, pp. iii–iv, 1–10, 135–48, 227–60; National Research Council Press Release, July 29, 1980, NRC Records; Jacob I. Fabrikant, "The BEIR Controversy," Edward P. Radford, "Human Health Effects of Low Doses of Ionizing Radiation," and Harald H. Rossi, "Comments on the Somatic Effects Section of the BEIR III Report," *Radiation Research* 84 (1980): 361–406; Joseph Rotblat, "Hazards of Low-Level Radiation—Less Argument, More Confusion," *Bulletin of the Atomic Scientists* 37 (June–July 1981): 31–36; *Philadelphia Inquirer*, June 30, 1980; Marshall, "NAS Study on Radiation," pp. 711–14; O'Neill, "Low-Level Radiation," pp. 3–6.
16. "Growing Debate over Dangers of Radiation," *U.S. News and World Report*, May 14, 1979, pp. 25–26; *New York Times*, May 3, 1979, July 2, 1980.

a source of public concern and debate. EPA acted under the authority it had acquired when it took over the duties of the Federal Radiation Council, which, among other functions, had issued nonbinding guidance to federal agencies on radiation protection. EPA administrator Train invited agencies with an interest in occupational radiation exposure to participate in "the updating of the current basic Federal guidance" and noted that the existing recommendations had been issued by the FRC more than fourteen years earlier.[17]

A review of occupational radiation standards seemed appropriate, because in the years since the FRC had issued its guidelines new information had become available and recent studies of radiation hazards, including the 1972 BEIR report, had been published. In addition, new problems that had surfaced after the FRC's recommendations of 1960 required careful consideration. Two of the most troubling and perplexing questions that had received little attention from the FRC were protecting "fertile women" from excessive exposure and limiting the doses that "transient workers" received.

The protection of fertile women raised difficult and sensitive questions. On the one hand, embryos and fetuses were, from all existing experimental evidence, especially vulnerable to injury from radiation exposure. Therefore, reducing the occupational exposure of women who might be pregnant was a logical means to reduce risks to their unborn children. On the other hand, lowering permissible doses for women working in jobs where they were exposed to radiation could make it more difficult for them to find employment or to receive promotions. A regulation that required lower limits for fertile women could, in other words, lead to job discrimination against those women. In addition, such a requirement would present delicate questions of privacy regarding whether a women was fertile.

Regulatory requirements, if imposed, had to consider exposure by all fertile women; if applied only to women after they knew of their pregnancy, the embryo or fetus could already have been subjected to excessive exposure. In 1965 the ICRP had advised special precautions for "women of reproductive capacity," and in 1971 the NCRP had recommended that permissible occupational exposure for pregnant women be reduced from 5 rems per year to 0.5 rem for the entire gestation period.

17. Russell E. Train to Dixy Lee Ray, September 6, 1974, Atomic Energy Commission Records, Public Document Room, Nuclear Regulatory Commission, Washington, D.C. (hereafter cited as AEC/NRC).

The NCRP's action forced EPA, the AEC, and other agencies to examine fully and weigh carefully all sides of the issue.[18]

The regulation of radiation exposure by transient workers also involved complex issues. By the early 1970s a trend toward hiring an increasing number of temporary workers was apparent in the nuclear industry; approximately 30 percent of the workers who left government or private nuclear plants between February 1969 and December 1972 had been employed for less than three months. The major reason for the high percentage of transients was that the nuclear industry often hired them to perform simple maintenance, repair, and other tasks in areas of high radiation. Plant owners would, for example, pay a worker for several hours to do a job that might only take a few minutes to complete. In that time the worker could receive close to a maximum permissible dose of radiation. Although the exposure was within legal limits, it was usually greater than full-time employees received over a much longer period.

The benefit of using transient workers for a nuclear facility was that it reduced exposure of the permanent staff, who did not exhaust their permissible doses performing the routine tasks that temporary employees carried out. But the practice generated increasing concern among radiation protection professionals. In part, they were worried by evidence that transient workers were poorly informed about the risks of radiation and the hazards of the jobs they undertook. This was particularly troubling if the same workers were hired repeatedly as temporaries and received high doses each time. In addition, the exposure of growing numbers of individuals increased the possibility of genetic consequences for the entire population. The problem was not acute, but it was prominent enough that the NCRP in 1971 urged that permissible doses for temporary workers be reduced to those of the general population, or one-tenth of the occupational level. Those who objected to the use of transient workers suggested that plant owners should strive to reduce exposure to all workers rather than lower the doses that permanent employees received by hiring transients.[19]

In consultation with an interagency committee, EPA began its reevaluation of occupational radiation standards in October 1974. As delibera-

18. SECY-R-75-162 (November 25, 1974), H. D. Bruner to Dr. Ray, August 26, 1974, AEC/NRC; *Science Trends,* July 15, 1974, p.1; Lauriston S. Taylor, *Radiation Protection Standards* (Cleveland: CRC Press, 1971), p. 86.

19. Robert Gillette, "'Transient' Nuclear Workers: A Special Case for Standards," *Science* 186 (October 11, 1974): 125–29; Roger E. Kasperson and John Lundblad, "Setting Health Standards for Nuclear Power Workers," *Environment* 24 (December 1982): 14–20.

tions continued, its efforts received additional impetus from an appeal by the Natural Resources Defense Council (NRDC) for substantial reductions in the existing limits. The NRDC submitted petitions to both EPA and the NRC in September 1975 and presented its case in a statement written by two of its staff experts, Thomas B. Cochran and Arthur Tamplin (who had left Livermore laboratory by that time). Cochran and Tamplin, frequently citing the 1972 BEIR report, insisted that radiation hazards were greater than previously recognized. They also suggested that the linear hypothesis might understate the risks of exposure. Therefore, they urged that occupational standards be reduced by a factor of ten for workers under the age of forty-five and by lesser amounts for workers forty-five and older. Cochran and Tamplin concluded that this revision would substantially lower both the somatic and the genetic risks of radiation exposure as well as provide greater protection for fertile women.[20]

In August 1976, nearly a year after the NRDC submitted its analysis, EPA denied the petition. It found Cochran and Tamplin's arguments that the risks of low-level exposure were greater than the existing regulations recognized to be unproven and unpersuasive. It also pointed out that the practice of keeping occupational exposures "as low as practicable" meant that most radiation workers did not approach the permissible limit of 5 rems per year; the average annual dose of those monitored was about 0.2 rem per year. EPA rejected the NRDC's specific recommendations but promised to be mindful of its concerns as the reassessment of occupational exposure progressed.

The staff of the NRC reached the same conclusions as EPA on the NRDC petition and recommended in September 1977 that the Commission deny it. By that time radiation hazards had begun to emerge as a prominent public issue and the Mancuso, Bross, and Najarian reports had received considerable attention. The Commission, to the consternation of the nuclear industry, elected to postpone a decision on the NRDC petition and on revised occupational limits until after the update of the 1972 BEIR report, then in process, was completed and until after EPA took action on new exposure guidelines.[21]

After consultation with other agencies and further consideration of the issue, EPA issued draft guidelines on occupational exposure for public comment in January 1981. The draft proposed recommended exposure levels

20. SECY-75-585 (October 8, 1975), NRC Records.

21. SECY-77-515 (September 28, 1977), D. E. Vandenburgh to Joseph E. Hendrie, April 3, 1978, Carl Walske to Hendrie, April 5, 1978, NRC Records.

that included modest, though important, changes from the existing guidelines. As the FRC had done, the EPA draft urged that occupational exposure to radiation be reduced to a minimum. In keeping with recently adopted terminology in the field, it called for exposure levels to be "as low as reasonably achievable" rather than the older "as low as practicable." EPA further proposed that permissible limits be reduced to a maximum of 5 rems per year from the sum of external and internal exposure. Under existing guidelines a worker could receive up to 5 rems per year from internal exposure and another 5 rems from external exposure, and up to 12 rems in a year as long as his or her average whole-body exposure did not exceed 5 rems annually. EPA also suggested a total lifetime limit of 100 rems. The draft addressed the issue of exposure by fertile women but did not make a recommendation. Instead, it cited four possible alternatives for protecting unborn children and asked for public comments on them.[22]

The most controversial item in the EPA's draft involved the complex issue of exposure of individual body organs to internal radiation. In 1977 the ICRP had published revised recommendations that advanced a new approach to occupational doses from radionuclides that entered the body by being breathed or swallowed. In its older recommendations it had used a "critical organ" concept, which set limits for the organ most likely to be affected by internal emitters but did not account for damage to other organs. With more knowledge to work with, the ICRP refined its approach by proposing new limits for individual organs according to the risk of injury. This meant that permissible exposures for some organs were higher and for some organs lower than previously. The ICRP specified that the total internal exposure to all affected organs plus external exposure must not exceed the equivalent of a whole-body dose of 5 rems. The new approach would allow doses up to 50 rems for some individual organs as long as the basic 5-rem whole-body limit was met. The ICRP's recommendations on this issue elicited complaints from environmentalists, who claimed that they relaxed existing standards and, therefore, increased risks to radiation workers. Former ICRP member Karl Z. Morgan called the 50-rem organ limit an "extremely bad" proposal.[23]

The EPA draft guidelines accepted the ICRP's concept for internal ex-

22. U.S. Environmental Protection Agency, *Proposed Federal Radiation Protection Guidance for Occupational Exposure (EPA 520/4-81-003)*, January 16, 1981, NRC Records; *Federal Register* 46 (January 23, 1981): 7836–44.

23. SECY-79-1B (September 18, 1979), SECY-80-46 (January 24, 1980), Robert B. Minogue to Commissioner Ahearne, October 26, 1979, NRC Records; *Recommendations of the International Commission on Radiological Protection (ICRP Publication 26)* (Oxford: Pergamon Press, 1977); *Nucleonics Week*, March 15, 1979.

posure but restricted the dose to any single organ to 30 rems. EPA's proposals, if adopted, would apply to federal regulation of workers exposed to radiation in medical, industrial, defense, research, and educational activities. But the agency whose programs would be most affected was the NRC, and it harbored some reservations. Some NRC staff members agreed with the environmentalists, who opposed any "relaxation" of radiation limits. One unnamed NRC source declared in September 1980, "The federal government ought not to relax radiation protection standards for workers. We don't feel there's any reason for this." This was a minority view, however. The staff and eventually the Commission, recognizing that the ICRP's proposals were a redistribution of exposure limits for individual organs rather than a relaxation, endorsed the new approach. The NRC informed EPA that it supported the ICRP's system of dose calculation as "based on the best scientific information available." Therefore, a 50-rem upper limit for certain individual organs seemed more appropriate than a 30-rem level. In addition, the NRC opposed EPA's proposed lifetime dose of 100 rems because it threatened "a person's employability, job continuity, and ability to plan and pursue a career" without commensurate benefits.[24]

After further consideration, EPA issued its revised guidelines on January 27, 1987. The final version was similar to the draft and maintained the basic occupational external and internal exposure limit of 5 rems per year. One change from the earlier proposal was that EPA accepted the ICRP's (and the NRC's) position on internal doses to individual organs and used the upper level of 50 rems, while pointing out that a worker's exposure still must stay within the 5-rem whole-body limit. Another change was that the final version eliminated the earlier proposal's lifetime occupational dose limit. EPA's final guidelines included recommendations on exposure of unborn children. They specified that "exposure of an unborn child should be less than that of adult workers." They further urged that workers be kept informed of the special sensitivity of embryos and fetuses and that, once a women declared her pregnancy, her exposure not exceed 0.5 rem for the "entire gestation period." EPA addressed the job discrimination issue by stating that measures to protect the unborn did "not create a basis for discrimination" and that employers were responsible for obeying the provisions of the Civil Rights Act of 1964.[25]

24. SECY-81–232 (April 10, 1981), Nunzio Palladino to Ann McGill Gorsuch, July 24, 1981, NRC Records; *Nucleonics Week,* March 15, 1979; *Inside N.R.C.,* June 1, 1981, August 10, 1981; *Inside E.P.A.,* September 26, 1980.

25. *Federal Register* 52 (January 27, 1987): 2822–34.

The NRC's Revised Part 20 Regulations

While EPA was deliberating over its guidelines for occupational exposure of all radiation workers, a process that took more than twelve years, the NRC was considering changes in its regulations on the safety of employees of its licensees. The NRC's exposure limits were spelled out in Part 20 of Title 10 of the *Code of Federal Regulations,* commonly referred to simply as "Part 20." (The design objectives for releases from nuclear power plants that the NRC adopted in 1975 were included in Part 50 of Title 10, which governed the licensing of reactors.) The NRC decided to review its regulations for the same reasons that EPA had undertaken revisions of its recommendations on occupational exposure. The AEC had issued the original Part 20 rules in 1957 and a revised version in 1960. By the early 1970s they were in need of a thorough reassessment. The NRC sought to make certain that its regulations remained compatible not only with EPA's guidelines on occupational exposure but also with the positions of the ICRP and the NCRP and with the latest research findings on radiation hazards. Those goals led to a protracted rulemaking process that pointed up the complexities of the process.

Although the NRC conducted preliminary reviews of Part 20 during the latter part of the 1970s, especially in response to the NRDC petition for reductions in occupational exposure, it did not undertake a major effort until summer 1979. By that time EPA was working on its revised standards, the report of the Libassi task force and the contention within the BEIR committee had received considerable attention, and public concern over radiation hazards had intensified in the wake of Three Mile Island. William J. Dircks, director of the Office of Nuclear Material Safety and Safeguards, launched the NRC's reappraisal of its radiation protection regulations with a widely circulated memorandum that argued that Part 20 was badly outdated. He suggested that the regulation "often inhibits rather than enhances good radiation safety practice" and "does not have a suitable framework for incorporating present and future requirements."

In response to Dircks's recommendations, the NRC established a task force to consider a major overhaul of Part 20. The task force developed a list of improvements in the regulation that needed to be considered. They included making a clear statement of the agency's principles for radiation protection, strengthening "as low as reasonably achievable" requirements for both occupational and population exposure, reducing permissible doses for radiation workers and the public, placing better controls on exposures for fertile women and transient workers, and, in general, apply-ing the recommendations of the ICRP, the NCRP, and other experts as well as recent research findings to the regulations. After approval by the Commission, the agency published an "advanced notice of proposed rule-making" in March 1980 that announced its plans and sought public com-ment. It expressed the NRC's expectation that "this rulemaking will be complex and controversial."[26]

One goal of revising Part 20 that received particular attention was en-suring that licensees kept the exposures of their employees to a level that was "as low as reasonably achievable." Although the design objectives that the NRC adopted in 1975 made ALARA a requirement for off-site releases, the basis for applying it to occupational exposure was less clear. An NRC staff paper reported in February 1977, "Current regulations do not sup-ply specific requirements and guidance for operational policies and de-sign approaches to ALARA that are enforceable." The problem had reached worrisome proportions because system and equipment mainte-nance was causing higher than anticipated exposures to nuclear plant workers. Among the causes of the elevated levels were unexpectedly heavy radioactive deposits on reactor components and unexpectedly low relia-bility of equipment as well as routine maintenance procedures. One re-sult of the relatively high occupational exposures was that plant owners had hired more transient workers. The NRC wanted to force them to find ways to decrease occupational doses by making plant improvements rather than by using transients.[27]

Occupational doses received by the overwhelming majority of indi-vidual plant workers were well within the NRC's regulatory limits. Be-tween 1969 and 1980 the average annual doses per worker ranged between 0.60 and 1.02 rems; in 1980, 99.5 percent of those workers received less than the regulatory limit of 5 rems and 76 percent received less than 1 rem. Nevertheless, the problem of collective occupational exposure had become more serious in the same period; the number of workers exposed increased eight times, and the collective dose per reactor increased by four times. Although substantial increases in collective exposure had appeared ear-lier, the plant improvements that the NRC demanded of licensees after the Three Mile Island accident exacerbated the problem. The NRC was committed to arresting the trend toward higher collective exposures, and

26. SECY-79-528 (September 14, 1979), SECY-79-636 (November 28, 1979), NRC Records; *Federal Register* 45 (March 20, 1980): 18023–26.
27. SECY-77-54 (February 4, 1977), NRC Records.

Figure 9. A worker at the National Reactor Testing Station walks through entrance portal monitors to be checked for radiation, ca. 1974. (National Archives 434–SF–17–28)

its efforts to do so were carefully monitored by its congressional over-seers and some of its nongovernmental critics.[28]

The NRC received seventy-one comments on the advanced notice of proposed rulemaking that it published in March 1980. Those comments and views expressed in public meetings, in conferences with representatives of the nuclear industry, environmental groups, radiation protection

28. Robert B. Minogue to John W. Gofman, September 11, 1978, Joseph M. Hendrie to John D. Dingell, September 22, 1978, Henry A. Waxman to Hendrie, April 13, 1979, SECY-81–517 (August 28, 1981), NRC Records; U.S. General Accounting Office, *Actions Being Taken to Help Reduce Occupational Radiation Exposure at Commercial Nuclear Powerplants (GAO/EMD 82–91),* August 24, 1982.

professionals, and other experts, and in the BEIR-III report of 1980 formed the bases for the NRC's draft revisions to Part 20. The proposal that the staff sent to the Commission in April 1985 for approval to publish for public comment was similar but not identical to the guidelines on occupational exposure that EPA was considering. Like EPA, the NRC staff's draft called for reducing the basic occupational whole-body exposure limit to a maximum of 5 rems per year. For the first time, the 5-rem limit would be calculated as the sum of external and internal exposure. Further, the new proposal would eliminate the provision in Part 20 that allowed up to 12 rems in a single year if a worker's average exposure did not exceed 5 rems annually. In accordance with the recommendations of the ICRP, the NRC staff's draft would permit "planned special exposures" of 10 rems at a time, up to 25 rems for a lifetime. The staff's recommendation on internal radiation also followed the latest recommendations of the ICRP by setting limits for individual organs, which were lower in some cases and higher in others up to a limit per organ of 50 rems. The draft explicitly required that licensees follow "as low as reasonably achievable" principles in their radiation protection programs.

On the issue of exposure levels for fertile women, the NRC staff's position anticipated what EPA later adopted — 0.5 rem during the gestation period for women who had declared their pregnancy and efforts to ensure that all radiation workers were well informed about the special sensitivity of embryos and fetuses to radiation. In other ways the staff's proposal included items that were not a part of EPA's deliberations on occupational exposure. One of the most important of these was that the staff retained the permissible whole-body level for population exposure as 0.5 rem, which was one-tenth of the occupational limit. The population limit stirred questions from Commissioner James K. Asselstine, who wondered why the NRC's standard of 0.5 rem (or 500 millirems) was twenty times higher than the 25-millirem level that EPA used for whole-body exposure by a member of the public from a uranium fuel cycle facility. The staff responded that EPA's ALARA level applied to emissions from nuclear facilities while the Part 20 limits applied to exposures from all sources except natural background and medical doses; a licensee would comply with this provision by demonstrating that a member of the public was unlikely to receive more than 0.1 rem (or 100 millirems) from "sources under the licensee's control." Thus the effective exposure limit for members of the public from NRC licensees was reduced to 0.1 rem. This was still higher than EPA's 25-millirem level, but the NRC staff told Asselstine that the regulations were "relatively compatible" because EPA's limit was not an absolute standard. Although EPA officials disagreed with this interpretation, the NRC did not take further action to reconcile the differences in population limits.[29]

The NRC staff's proposed revisions in Part 20 did not include lower exposure standards for transient radiation workers. The problem of relatively high doses received by temporary employees had not been solved by the time the draft was completed, but the industry had made progress in protecting workers. The average exposure for nuclear power plant workers in 1984 was 0.56 rem, the lowest level in the fifteen years for which the NRC had data, and collective doses had declined slightly. The NRC entered into an agreement with the Institute of Nuclear Power Operations (INPO), an industry group formed after Three Mile Island to push for improved industry performance, to develop and implement programs "to minimize individual and collective occupational exposure." The industry was committed to reducing occupational doses as much as possible not only to carry out ALARA rules and safeguard the health of its employees but also because of its growing concern over the "burgeoning problem" of lawsuits claiming compensation for radiation injuries. Although the NRC staff's Part 20 draft did not call for lower exposure limits for temporary workers, it strengthened requirements for determining their exposure histories to make certain that they did not exceed permissible levels.[30]

The Commission approved publishing the recommendations for changes in the radiation protection regulations in November 1985 after the staff addressed Asselstine's questions on the distinction between EPA and proposed NRC population limits and other matters. The revisions elicited a mixed response. Nuclear industry representatives supported some of the proposals but expressed reservations about others. They agreed that the new regulations, if adopted, would be clearer and more consistent in some ways than the old ones, but they were not certain that the benefits justified the costs. The NRC estimated that implementing the revised rules would cost all of its licensees a total of about $33 million ini-

29. SECY-82-168 (April 21, 1982), SECY-85-147 (April 22, 1985), Robert B. Minogue to Commissioner Asselstine, August 26, 1985, NRC Records; *Inside N.R.C.*, September 2, 1985.

30. SECY-85-147, SECY-83-130 (April 7, 1983), NRC Records; Teresa A. Nichols, "Occupational Radiation Risk: The Politics of Uncertainty, Proliferation of Litigation," *Nuclear Industry* 31 (November 1984): 8–13; J. R. Wargo, "Radiation Claims Seen Increasing," *Nuclear Industry* 32 (March 1985): 11–13; *Inside N.R.C.*, September 2, 1985; U.S. Congress, House, Committee on Education and Labor, Subcommittee on Health and Safety, *Hearings on OSHA Oversight: Worker Health and Safety at Operating Nuclear Powerplants*, 99th Cong., 1st sess., 1985, pp. 30–37.

tially and $8 million per year subsequently, chiefly for computer software, dosimetry improvements, training programs, and compliance with ALARA requirements. A committee of the Atomic Industrial Forum, a leading industry group, commented, "There is no conclusive evidence that use of current regulations has resulted in inadequate worker protection. Therefore, the proposed revisions should not be implemented until such time that it can be demonstrated that this is the most beneficial expenditure of resources in terms of radiological protection."

Other industry officials regarded the revisions more favorably. Eugene Reimer, a health physicist for Baltimore Gas and Electric, suggested that the costs of implementing the NRC's proposals would not be great and that the improvements would be well worth the investment. He even went so far as to say that the NRC had prepared the revisions "in such a way so that people can understand them without misinterpretation." He was overly sanguine on the issue of public understanding; some of the reactions to the NRC's proposals showed a high level of misinterpretation and led to harsh criticism of the agency. The principal cause of denunciation was the NRC's plan to follow the ICRP's recommendations on internal exposures to body organs. Some of them had been tightened and some of them had been loosened according to research findings on the risk of damage from radiation; the permissible whole-body level of exposure still could not exceed 5 rems. But critics of the NRC interpreted the proposed changes as evidence that the agency was relaxing its standards.[31]

Articles in popular magazines advanced the same views. A piece in the *Nation* written by Brian Jacobs cited Mancuso, Bross, Najarian, and others on the hazards of low-level exposure and condemned the NRC for planning to "permit a more than tenfold increase in the allowable exposure of many of the most dangerous types of radiation." When Ralph E. Lapp, a radiation expert and author of several books on the subject, questioned the accuracy of the article, Jacobs responded that Lapp was "clearly aligned with industry." He reiterated his point that the "N.R.C. is planning to permit a significant increase in both occupational and public exposures to radioisotopes which the commission considers to be dangerous." An article in *Redbook* accused the NRC of preparing to relax its standards to protect the nuclear industry. Those articles and others like

31. Sara Cherner, "Radiation Protection: Changes in 10CFR20," *Nuclear Industry* 33 (April 1986): 13–17; Nuclear Information and Resource Service Press Release, "Radiation Alert," April 1986, Box 340 (NRC–Correspondence/Udall 1982–85), Papers of Morris K. Udall, University of Arizona, Tucson.

them prompted a series of letters from Congress and members of the public protesting the NRC's alleged softening of its Part 20 requirements. Public concern about radiation safety had been heightened by the disaster at the Chernobyl nuclear power station in the Soviet Union, which occurred less than four months after the NRC published its proposed revisions. The fear of widespread radiation injury from the massive release of radiation from Chernobyl made the revisions in Part 20 that the NRC was considering seem ill advised and irresponsible, at least in the misconstructions of their effect that some critics advanced.[32]

Many of the 813 comments that the NRC received on its proposals came from members of the public who objected to them on the erroneous grounds that they allowed higher exposures that threatened public health. In fact, the draft rules lowered whole-body permissible doses delivered to the public by NRC licensees to 0.1 rem from the previous 0.5 rem. The 0.1 rem was even more of a reduction than it appeared on the surface, because it was a sum of both external and internal exposure. In addition to considering the comments it received, some of which were based on a better understanding of the revised provisions, the NRC weighed the influence of several new expert studies of radiation hazards that had appeared after it first published the proposed changes to Part 20 in January 1986. They included recent reports by the ICRP, the NCRP, the United Nations Scientific Committee on the Effects of Atomic Radiation, and the BEIR committee.

The most influential of those evaluations was the new BEIR report, published in 1990 as BEIR-V. It updated the BEIR-III study of 1980 and incorporated important new information on the doses of radiation that Japanese survivors of the atomic bombs had received. Based on revised estimates of the levels of gamma radiation in Hiroshima and Nagasaki, BEIR-V concluded that risks of cancer and leukemia were three to four times higher than BEIR-III had suggested. As a result, the ICRP announced in 1990 that it intended to reduce its recommended occupational exposure limit from 5 rems to 2 rems. The NRC staff considered the conclusions of the BEIR-V committee and the ICRP but decided not to reduce the exposure limits it had originally proposed. It retained the 5-rem whole-body limit but noted that, in accordance with ALARA principles, most workers received far less than the permissible dose and, indeed, less

32. Brian Jacobs, "Increasing Our Radiation Dose," *Nation* 243 (September 6, 1986): 169–74; "Letters: Not-So-Risky Business," ibid., 243 (November 15, 1986): 506; Anne Conover Heller, "Radiation: How Much Is Too Much?" *Redbook* 167 (October 1986): 30–32.

than the 2-rem dose that the ICRP had indicated it would recommend. The BEIR-V findings were still inconclusive, and the NRC staff did not support further reductions in the permissible exposures. It pledged to follow new developments and adjust the regulations if additional scientific evidence or expert analysis made revisions advisable.[33]

The Commission approved the revisions to Part 20 by a unanimous vote on December 13, 1990. It gave licensees until January 1, 1993, to implement the new regulations, and later extended the deadline to January 1, 1994. The Commission's action culminated a process that had begun in earnest more than eleven years before. It did not, however, end the controversy over the NRC's approach to radiation protection. Several antinuclear groups criticized the new rules. The Nuclear Information and Resource Service commented that the NRC was "straining its credibility by adopting an obsolete standard" and showing "a callous disregard for the health risks posed by low-level radiation exposure."[34]

Below Regulatory Concern

At the same time that the NRC was making changes in Part 20 it was deliberating over a related issue—defining a level of radiation exposure so low that it need not be closely regulated. The NRC's attempts to fix this level, which became known as "below regulatory concern" (BRC), generated even more controversy than the Part 20 revisions and triggered so much criticism that the agency eventually withdrew its BRC policy. It discovered that the level of radiation that it deemed below regulatory concern did not fall below public concern.

The concept "below regulatory concern" was not new when the NRC set out to revise its radiation protection regulations in the early 1980s. Over the years the AEC and the NRC had granted thirty-nine exemptions for uses of low-level radioactive materials that they had concluded posed negligible public health risks; the uses that were exempted from Part 20 requirements included watches and clocks, lock illuminators, glassware, and smoke detectors. On a case-by-case basis, then, the AEC and the NRC

33. SECY-90–387 (November 26, 1990), NRC Records.
34. Samuel J. Chilk to James M. Taylor, December 19, 1990, NRC Records; *Philadelphia Inquirer,* December 14, 1990; *Baltimore Sun,* December 14, 1990; *Inside N.R.C.,* August 24, 1992.

had long followed a policy of granting regulatory exemptions for certain uses of radiation sources without raising objections or public fears. When the NRC staff drew up its first draft revisions of Part 20 in 1981–82, it proposed a "de minimis" level for public exposure of 0.1 millirem. The staff suggested that the chances of injury from exposure below that level were so small that regulatory attention and resources should not be invested in them. In effect, it proposed for the first time a threshold below which exposure to radiation would be considered harmless. This was a departure from the existing adherence to a linear hypothesis that assumed that any amount of radiation caused injury in proportion to the dose received.[35]

In proposing the inclusion of a de minimis level in the Part 20 revisions, the NRC staff told the Commission in April 1985 that the "lack of these levels in radiation protection standards has resulted in unwarranted expenditures of resources for incremental risks which are considered trifles in comparison to the risks which individuals are subjected to daily as part of normal living habits and activities." It also pointed out that other federal agencies had decided that such an approach was a sound way to focus resources on serious risks without compromising public health. The Food and Drug Administration, for example, had recently issued a proposal for determining an acceptable level of carcinogens in food additives.[36]

While the staff and the Commission were still considering the inclusion of de minimis levels in the revised Part 20 regulation, the concept of defining a boundary for regulatory concern received further impetus from Congress. In December 1985 it passed the Low Level Radioactive Waste Policy Amendments Act, which established federal policies for the disposal of low-level waste materials in regulated landfills. The law contained a provision that instructed the NRC to determine which radioactive waste materials posed enough of a risk to public health to be sent to specially constructed landfills and which posed so little risk that they could be disposed of in ordinary landfills.

As a result of the low-level waste amendments act, the NRC began work on a separate policy statement on levels of radiation that, in the terminology of the new law, were "below regulatory concern." This replaced the consideration of de minimis levels of radiation that had been included in the early drafts of the Part 20 revisions. "Below regulatory concern" was not precisely the same as "de minimis"; it was not intended to imply

35. SECY-82–168 (April 21, 1982), NRC Records; *Inside N.R.C.*, October 18, 1982; "Outlook on BRC," attachment to *Nucleonics Week*, September 26, 1991, pp. 1, 4.
36. SECY-85–147 (April 22, 1985), NRC Records.

that BRC levels were absolutely safe or certifiably harmless. A BRC level, unlike a de minimis level, was not a threshold below which a risk of radiation injury was, by definition, absent. BRC levels were those that were low enough not to require full-scale regulatory control, even if they did pose a very slight risk to exposed individuals or populations. The NRC staff defined them as levels "that warrant limited government attention taking into account the cost of further regulation and the likelihood that such regulation would alter the resulting dose."[37]

The key issue that the NRC had to resolve was the level of exposure that it judged to be below regulatory concern. This caused a great deal of controversy within the staff and the Commission. Robert Bernero, director of the Office of Nuclear Material Safety and Safeguards, argued for a BRC level of 1 millirem per year for individual members of the public, but Victor Stello, the director of the NRC staff, insisted on a level of 10 millirems. This stirred protests from Bernero and members of his staff, who finally agreed to support Stello's limit if it were supplemented with a collective dose limit of 100 person-rems per year (a "person-rem" was the same unit that formerly had been called a "man-rem"). The contention was heightened by the figures advanced by experts in other organizations. The NRC's Advisory Committee on Reactor Safeguards concluded that a level for individuals of 1 millirem was too low and recommended 3 to 5 millirems instead. The Environmental Protection Agency, which was also working to comply with the low-level radioactive waste amendments act of 1985, arrived at a similar figure of 4 millirems for individuals. The NRC staff objected that at such low levels the distinction between 3 millirems and 5 millirems was meaningless and that only orders of magnitude, such as between 1 millirem and 10 millirems, should be debated.

The conflicting views of the NRC staff were replayed when the commissioners took up the issue. Eventually, they compromised on the individual limit by deciding on a level of 10 millirems but using a 1-millirem limit on an interim basis until the agency gained more experience with the policy. One important consideration in the development of BRC that weighed heavily with the Commission was that members of the public routinely, if unknowingly, accepted similar or greater doses of radiation in the conduct of their daily lives. A person who moved from Washington, D.C., to Denver, for example, was exposed to an additional 60 to 70 millirems per year because of Denver's elevation, and a traveler flying across the coun-

37. Ibid., SECY-88-69 (March 8, 1988), NRC Records; *Inside N.R.C.,* August 5, 1985; "Outlook on BRC," p. 6.

try from New York to Los Angeles received about 5 millirems from cosmic rays. With that in mind, the Commission favored a collective dose of 1,000 person-rems per year rather than the 100 person-rems the staff proposed. This was the equivalent of one million persons receiving 1 millirem per year. The NRC calculated that the BRC policy would cause one hypothetical death every other year, but it expected fewer in practice.[38]

The guiding force behind the Commission's consideration of BRC was its chairman, Kenneth M. Carr. Carr was committed to settling on a policy in part because of the requirements of the low-level waste amendments act and in part because he was convinced that it was the right thing to do. Carr, a retired admiral whose positions on some key issues had provoked the hostility of the nuclear industry, made BRC a priority. The pressure for a BRC policy came from Congress and from within the NRC. It was not a result of lobbying from the nuclear industry, which was wary of the impact of BRC on public perceptions of nuclear power. The industry, in the words of one trade publication, sensed "an impending public relations disaster."[39]

In June 1990, after holding meetings, receiving public comments, and considering various options, the NRC issued its policy statement on BRC. Four members of the Commission voted in favor, and one, recently appointed James R. Curtiss, approved it in part and disapproved it in part. Curtiss took issue with the BRC levels cited in the policy statement; he supported a 1 millirem individual dose as a final rather than an interim limit and he objected to a collective dose of 1,000 person-rems rather than the 100 person-rems that the staff had recommended. The policy statement sought to make clear that the agency adopted its BRC criteria to avoid unnecessary regulation of materials that posed little hazard to the public and that could divert attention from sources of greater risk. The BRC policy was especially important with regard to the use of consumer products, the disposal of slightly radioactive waste materials, the cleanup of sites where nuclear fuel cycle plants had caused contamination, and the decommissioning of closed nuclear facilities. The policy statement pointed out that exemptions under the BRC policy would be granted only after full case-by-case consideration and only if the NRC was convinced that an applicant would maintain radiation levels within BRC limits.[40]

38. SECY-89-360 (December 1, 1989), Margaret V. Federline to Maria Lopez-Otin and others, February 28, 1990, NRC Records; "Outlook on BRC," pp. 5–8.

39. "Outlook on BRC," pp. 9–10.

40. "Below Regulatory Concern: Policy Statement," July 3, 1990, NRC Records.

The BRC policy was a carefully considered articulation of a controversial issue. Despite differing views within the staff and the Commission about the proper radiation levels for BRC, the need to define a policy for exemptions from full-scale regulatory control was accepted without dissent. From the NRC's perspective, the policy statement spelled out a way to accomplish important objectives without undermining public health. The NRC (and the AEC before it) had long been committed to avoiding excessive regulation, and this goal was even more pressing in the 1980s because of diminishing agency resources. The issues to which BRC was applicable, especially low-level waste, decommissioning, and decontamination of sites, were taking on increasing visibility, and it seemed sensible to agency officials to formulate a policy for allocating resources and regulatory attention to the problems that presented the greatest hazards to public health.

The NRC's purposes and the reasoning behind its approach to BRC were obscured by the outcries of protest that followed publication of the policy statement. Although the agency had anticipated opposition to its action, it was not prepared for the intensity and scope of the criticism. As the debate within the NRC had demonstrated, the BRC levels cited in the policy statement were hardly sacrosanct; their soundness could be, and had been, subjected to probing questions. But the objections to the BRC policy statement that greeted its publication were seldom grounded in studious analysis; in most cases they were accusations that the NRC was providing a conscienceless giveaway to the nuclear industry at a high cost in human lives. When Carr held a press conference after the announcement of BRC, reporters peppered him with questions about whether the policy favored the economic welfare of the industry over the health of the public. Antinuclear groups focused on the same issue. Public Citizen, for example, called BRC "a trade-off of people's lives in favor of the financial interests of the nuclear industry." It claimed that the policy could cause 12,412 cancer deaths per year in the population of the United States.[41]

A series of public meetings that the NRC held to explain the BRC policy were attended by audiences that ranged from 75 to 350 persons. Most of the attendees denounced the agency in sessions that lasted from five to seven hours; many called for the resignation of the commissioners or their indictment on criminal charges. The "very widely and strongly held" public misperception that came through at the meetings, according to an NRC

41. *Nucleonics Week*, July 5, 1990; "Outlook on BRC," p. 8.

observer, was that the BRC policy would allow a large number of cancer deaths. Members of Congress, perhaps unaware that the BRC policy was in significant measure a response to the mandate in the low-level waste amendments act of 1985, joined in attacking the NRC's policy statement and introduced legislation to void it. Within a short time, four states took action to prohibit BRC practices or to announce opposition to the policy; the number later grew to twelve states and more than one hundred local governments. Whatever the merits or demerits of the NRC's BRC policy statement, the reaction to it made vividly clear the difficulty of attempting to sponsor a calm and reasoned discussion of radiation hazards.[42]

Faced with a firestorm, the NRC retreated. It first tried to establish foundations and win support for a BRC policy, albeit a modified version, through a "consensus-building" process that involved the nuclear industry, states, antinuclear groups, EPA, and others. While it attempted to persuade interested parties to join in searching for a consensus, the NRC declared a moratorium on implementing the BRC policy statement. When the consensus-building effort failed, the Commission indefinitely extended the moratorium in December 1991. In the Energy Policy Act of 1992, Congress formally revoked the BRC policy statement; the Commission officially withdrew the policy and terminated staff action to carry it out in June 1993.[43]

The Clean Air Act Amendments

At the same time that the NRC and EPA were revising occupational radiation standards and considering BRC levels, they were engaged in an increasingly acrimonious debate over fulfilling the mandate for radiation protection in amendments to the Clean Air Act of 1970 that Congress enacted in 1977. This was a prolonged process that produced frustration and ill will in both agencies; it also proved to be a textbook case in which policies were driven in directions that were beyond the control of and sometimes inconsistent with the wishes of policy makers. In this instance, the differences between EPA and the NRC were triggered

42. SECY-90–339 (October 3, 1990), NRC Records; "Nuclear Waste Dumpsites," *Bulletin of the Atomic Scientists* 46 (September 1990): 6; "Outlook on BRC," pp. 8–9, 19–20.

43. SECY-93–106 (April 23, 1993), Samuel J. Chilk to William C. Parler and James M. Taylor, June 24, 1993, NRC Records; "Outlook on BRC," pp. 21–22.

primarily by statutory requirements and court rulings rather than juris-dictional issues, though jurisdictional matters, as always, were a part of the dispute.

The Clean Air Act amendments required EPA to develop new ambi-ent air standards for radiation if it determined that radioactive pollutants could "reasonably be anticipated to endanger public health." This provi-sion was a late addition to the legislation that caught the nuclear indus-try and the affected federal agencies off-guard. Since EPA was very likely to find that radiation from nuclear plants and other sources could "en-danger public health," the law had potentially far-reaching implications. As expected, EPA made that determination in December 1979, which meant that it was obligated to issue standards for radioactive pollutants, including those regulated by the NRC, by June 1980. Neither EPA nor the NRC viewed the requirements of the Clear Air Act as useful or nec-essary in protecting public health. Instead, the law's provisions embod-ied a step backward from the approach that both agencies were taking. The radiation exposure standards that EPA issued in January 1977 as well as the design objectives that the NRC issued in May 1975 and the Part 20 revisions on which it had begun to work were based on the dose received rather than on an ambient air standard. Both agencies were convinced that a dose limit provided greater protection than an emission standard. "Dose is really what counts, and from a scientific standpoint is logical," an EPA official commented. "There is really nothing to be accomplished by setting emissions standards."[44]

As a result, EPA delayed taking any action to issue emissions standards. Its technical staff argued that the existing dose limits and application of the "as low as reasonably achievable" principle fulfilled the requirements of the Clean Air Act. Others, however, took a different view. In June 1981 the Sierra Club filed suit in U.S. District Court for the Northern District of California. It argued that under the Clean Air Act EPA was obliged to publish emissions standards for radionuclides. The court agreed; on Sep-tember 30, 1982, it ordered EPA to issue standards within 180 days. On April 6, 1983, EPA published for public comment air quality standards for radioactive emissions. Although it had told the court that it did not know

44. David G. Hawkins to Douglas M. Costle, August 4, 1977, Edward F. Tuerk to Cos-tle, August 19, 1977, Box 4 (Air and Waste Management), Jodie Bernstein to the Adminis-trator, September 9, 1977, Box 5 (General Counsel), Intra-Agency Memorandums 1977–1983, Office of the Administrator, EPA Records; *Nucleonics Week,* December 28, 1978; John O'Neill, "Clean Air Act: The '77 Amendments Could Mean Big Trouble," *Nuclear Industry* 28 (Sep-tember 1981): 22–24.

how to prepare air standards that corresponded to doses received by individuals, it now proposed an "indirect standard" for dose limitations. The standards for Department of Energy facilities, for example, specified that emissions would be restricted to a level that would cause no more than a whole-body dose of 10 millirems or a single-organ dose of 30 millirems. NRC licensees were subject to an emissions limit that would cause no more than a dose of 10 millirems to any individual; this level did not apply to fuel cycle facilities because they were still covered by the 25-millirem standard that EPA had issued in 1977.[45]

EPA used the same assumptions and background information to arrive at its air quality standards that it and other agencies had always employed in preparing radiation control limits. It reaffirmed that exposure to radiation should be kept "as low as practicable" and it accepted a linear hypothesis for radiation risks. "The risk of cancer from exposure to radiation," EPA reiterated, "has not been shown to have a threshold level." With this in mind, it proposed standards that reflected what was possible with available technology to provide "an ample margin of safety." A number of categories of NRC licensees that released radiation to the air would be subjected to the new regulations, including hospitals, operators of research and test reactors, shipyards, manufacturers that produced radioactive devices, and the radiopharmaceutical industry. EPA based its dose limits on its conclusion that airborne emissions from most of those facilities rarely caused doses of more than 1 millirem per year, and therefore, a standard of 10 millirems per year was reasonable.[46]

EPA's proposed standards for radioactive air pollutants elicited a storm of protests from other agencies, radiation protection experts, and professional societies. They complained that the limits were unnecessarily strict (EPA's regulatory limits for NRC licensees were the same as the NRC cited a few years later as "below regulatory concern"). The NRC suggested that EPA's proposed regulations would place "significant economic and administrative burdens on many thousands of licensees" without providing a "significant reduction in any health risk." The Society of Nuclear Medicine and the American College of Nuclear Physicians echoed the same argument and criticized EPA for failing to show the need for "unreasonably stringent and unnecessary standards." The Health

45. *Energy Daily,* April 1, 1983; U.S. Congress, House, Committee on Armed Services, Subcommittee on Procurement and Military Nuclear Systems, *Hearings on EPA Radon and Radionuclide Standards,* 98th Cong., 1st sess., 1983, 49, 403; O'Neill, "Clean Air Act," p. 23.
46. *Federal Register* 48 (April 6, 1983): 15076–88.

Physics Society pointed out that EPA's proposed limits were so low that they would be "difficult to measure" and wondered why the agency offered new standards "when existing standards have not been proven to provide inadequate protection to the public and the environment." Several members of Congress and the Office of Management and Budget also questioned EPA's approach to restricting air pollution by radioactive materials.[47]

EPA received a similar appraisal of its radionuclide standards from an advisory group of outside experts it used to evaluate scientific issues, the Science Advisory Board. In December 1983, William D. Ruckelshaus, who had returned to the post of EPA administrator earlier in the year to try to restore the credibility the agency had lost in the early Reagan years, asked the board to review the scientific bases for the proposed limits. Ruckelshaus was committed to improving EPA capabilities for risk assessment and to setting standards that had a "sound scientific base." The criticisms of the proposed standards for airborne radioactivity persuaded him to evaluate them carefully before taking any further action. In response to Ruckelshaus's request, the Science Advisory Board reported in August 1984 that the proposed standards were overly conservative because they relied exclusively on a linear model for calculating risks from radiation exposure. The board contended that the use of "only one model, which is generally considered conservative, in the risk assessment phase is scientifically inappropriate." It suggested that in preparing the regulation, EPA's Office of Radiation Programs had employed the BEIR-III report of 1980 "in an excessively selective manner."[48]

The Science Advisory Board's position further fueled the controversy over EPA's radionuclide standards. Supporters of the proposed limits claimed that the board's findings were biased by the fact that some of its members had received funding from the Department of Energy. The Natural Resources Defense Council told Ruckelshaus that the board's comments failed to reveal "any basic flaw in the agency's approach." But Ruckelshaus found the conclusions of the board and other critics of the proposed standards more convincing. Faced with a deadline imposed by the U.S. District Court for the Northern District of California to take final action on the limit for radionuclides, EPA announced on October 23, 1984,

47. House Subcommittee on Procurement and Military Nuclear Systems, *Hearings on EPA Radon and Radionuclide Emission Standards*, pp. 2–6, 88–98, 111–16; *Inside E.P.A.*, December 16, 1983.
48. William D. Ruckelshaus, "Science, Risk, and Public Policy," *Science* 221 (September 9, 1983): 1026–28; *Inside E.P.A.*, December 16, 1983, August 24, 1984.

that it had decided to withdraw the proposed regulations. It further indicated that it was prepared to remove radionuclides from the list of air pollutants if it were found in contempt of court; the term it used for this was "de-list." Environmental groups denounced the decision; they alleged that "EPA's refusal to regulate these emissions will force thousands of Americans to risk their lives and health." The Sierra Club immediately went back to court to challenge EPA's action, where it received a sympathetic hearing. Judge William Orrick called Ruckelshaus a "scofflaw" and on December 11, 1984, found him and EPA in contempt of court.[49]

Although EPA's Office of General Counsel had advised Ruckelshaus that he could deal with a contempt citation by de-listing radioactive materials as toxic air pollutants, it later concluded that the agency lacked a statutory basis for doing so. Therefore, the only option was to issue air quality standards for radionuclides. Faced with a court order to take action and persuaded that the levels originally proposed were unnecessarily strict, Ruckelshaus opted to issue new standards that were considerably less stringent. As a result, EPA established whole-body exposure levels of 25 millirems and single-organ exposures of 75 millirems for NRC and Department of Energy facilities. It explained that "emissions [from sources covered by the Clean Air Act] are presently controlled at levels that provide an ample margin of safety in protecting public health from the hazards associated with exposure to airborne radionuclides." EPA's position triggered immediate and vocal complaints from environmental groups. The Environmental Defense Fund, the Natural Resources Defense Council, and the Sierra Club challenged EPA's standards in federal court.[50]

EPA marshaled its defense for its approach to regulating radionuclides under the Clean Air Act. Before the case was decided, however, another case involving the regulation of vinyl chloride under the act provided EPA the opportunity, and, in its analysis, the necessity, to reconsider its arguments. As a result of both the vinyl chloride decision, *Natural Resources Defense Council v. EPA* (1987), and new scientific findings on radiation hazards, EPA changed its position dramatically.

In the vinyl chloride decision, the U.S. Court of Appeals for the District of Columbia Circuit ruled that EPA could consider only the health effects of air pollutants in deciding on a level of risk for air pollutants.

49. *Inside E.P.A.,* August 17, September 28, October 12, October 26, November 9, December 14, 1984; *Federal Register* 50 (February 6, 1985): 5190–5200.

50. *Inside E.P.A.,* December 14, 1984, January 11, January 18, March 8, October 18, 1985; *Federal Register* 50 (February 6, 1985): 5191.

Other factors, such as costs and technological capabilities, could be weighed only in determining a margin of safety. EPA interpreted the ruling as a mandate to reassess its position on regulating radionuclides under the Clean Air Act. At about the same time, new scientific evidence from Hiroshima and Nagasaki suggested that radiation might present greater risks than experts had previously believed. Revised estimates of gamma radiation released by the atomic bombs, which were later incorporated into the BEIR-V report of 1990, convinced EPA officials that the Clean Air Act requirements for radionuclides should be tightened.[51]

In March 1989 EPA issued for public comment a new proposal for regulating radionuclides under the Clean Air Act. Rather than offer a single standard for various sources of airborne emissions, it provided a range of levels that might be included in the final rule. In the case of NRC licensees, EPA proposed possible standards that ranged from 10 millirems per year effective whole-body dose to 0.3 millirem per year. Those limits were far lower than the NRC's existing regulations and its proposed Part 20 revisions. They were also potentially much lower or, at most, no higher than the "below regulatory concern" limit of 10 millirems that the NRC was considering. Further, in contrast to its 1983 proposal for radionuclide standards, EPA suggested that as a result of ongoing litigation its new limits might apply to nuclear power plants and other fuel cycle facilities.[52]

EPA's proposed regulations were deeply troubling to the NRC. The staff told the Commission that the potential consequences for the agency and its licensees were "far-reaching." The staff suggested that the rule, if issued in final form, "represents the entry of EPA into a field of regulation that it has heretofore declined to enter. It raises the possibility that there could be, in addition to NRC regulation of licensed facilities, an overlay of more stringent EPA regulation and perhaps a further overlay of still more stringent regulation by states." The NRC was particularly disturbed by the likelihood that EPA's approach would lead to costly and unnecessary dual regulation. NRC chairman Lando W. Zech, Jr., told EPA administrator William K. Reilly, "The EPA proposed Clean Air Act regulations will add a considerable duplicative regulatory burden and additional costs on NRC licensees . . . with no attendant significant improvement in public safety."[53]

51. Natural Resources Defense Council v. EPA, 824 F.2d 1146 (1987); *Inside E.P.A.*, February 26, 1988.

52. *Federal Register* 54 (March 7, 1989): 9612–54; *Inside E.P.A.*, December 16, 1988.

53. SECY-89-150 (May 8, 1989), Lando W. Zech, Jr., to William K. Reilly, May 15, 1989, NRC Records.

The nuclear industry was equally distressed. Byron Lee, Jr., president of the Nuclear Management and Resources Council, an industry lobbying group, told Reilly that a "risk to the public which would warrant additional EPA regulation of radionuclides for the nuclear industry does not exist." He insisted that the "proposed regulation . . . would result in an ineffective expenditure of regulatory resources, with the possible result that other significant risks would be less well controlled."[54]

The NRC and EPA struggled to find a mutually satisfactory approach to regulating radionuclides under the Clean Air Act. It was not an easy or harmonious process. The trade journal *Inside E.P.A.* reported in April 1990 that differences between the two agencies had produced an "acrimonious feud." The fundamental issue was the NRC's contention that EPA's proposed regulations were unnecessary and potentially counterproductive versus EPA's argument that they were legally and scientifically sound. The NRC was concerned, for example, that EPA's proposed standards would curtail use of radioactive iodine 131 by medical licensees to treat thyroid cancer and other conditions. As Peter Crane, an NRC attorney who was himself taking iodine 131 treatment for a thyroid condition, put it, "The central risk issue involved is not the risk to some hypothetical members of the public with a minuscule chance of developing a thyroid problem as a result of emissions from a hospital. Rather, the central risk relates to some thousands of real people with a present thyroid problem requiring treatment with radioiodine in the here and now."[55]

EPA insisted, however, that its proposals conformed with the requirements imposed on it by the courts and with the latest scientific findings about radiation risks. When the BEIR-V report appeared in 1990 with its conclusion that radiation hazards had been underestimated, one EPA staff member commented, "Some of the pot shots [the NRC] has taken will now have to cease." Officials in EPA's Office of Radiation Programs went so far as to discuss the idea of requesting that the NRC's environmental responsibilities be transferred to EPA or even that the entire agency be made a division of EPA.[56]

Gradually, despite the ill will created by the debate over establishing standards for radionuclides under the Clean Air Act, the NRC and EPA worked out their differences. Faced with protests from the NRC, the National Institutes of Health, the Department of Energy, radiation protec-

54. Byron Lee, Jr., to William K. Reilly, June 9, 1989, NRC Records.

55. Peter Crane to Hugh Thompson, February 15, 1990, NRC Records; *Inside E.P.A.,* April 13, 1990.

56. *Inside E.P.A.,* January 5, May 18, 1990.

tion professionals, nuclear physicians, the nuclear industry, and others, EPA formally asked Congress to amend the Clean Air Act "to eliminate unnecessary and duplicative authority to regulate radionuclide emissions from NRC-licensed facilities." In October 1990, as a part of a major rewrite of the act, Congress allowed EPA discretion to refrain from regulating NRC licensees if it found that the NRC's exposure limits provided an "ample margin of safety." Within a short time EPA placed stays on its regulation of NRC licensees, including power reactors, until it could decide whether it wanted to rescind the standards it had proposed.[57]

After lengthy consideration of the best means to avoid dual regulation of airborne emissions of radionuclides, EPA and the NRC signed a memorandum of agreement in August 1992. It dealt with the regulation of NRC licensees other than nuclear power reactors, which was the source of the divergent positions of the two agencies. The memorandum of agreement provided that EPA would rescind its standards under the Clean Air Act once the NRC took certain steps to ensure that its regulations allowed an ample margin of safety from the hazards of radionuclides. The agreement stipulated that the NRC would issue a regulatory guide that set a goal for public exposure to radiation from licensees other than power reactors of 10 millirems per year. It also specified that the NRC would work with its "agreement states," which exercised responsibility for regulating many applications of nuclear materials, to promote adoption of compatible standards.[58]

The memorandum of understanding did not immediately resolve the differing positions of EPA and the NRC. A survey by EPA showed that of more than 360 facilities licensed by the NRC or agreement states that were reviewed, all had emissions of less than 10 millirems and 95 percent had less than 1 millirem. Still, EPA was not completely satisfied; its officials were concerned that NRC regulations did not require with sufficient clarity that emissions from its own licensees and those of agreement states conform with the dose limit of 10 millirems. Finally, after the NRC adopted language that was more binding on its licensees, EPA agreed to rescind its Clean Air Act radionuclide standards for various categories of NRC licensees, including power reactors.[59]

The contention between the NRC and EPA over the Clean Air Act

57. William G. Rosenberg and James O. Mason to Quentin N. Burdick, November 15, 1989, NRC Records; *Inside N.R.C.*, November 5, 1990.

58. James M. Taylor to the Commission, September 22, 1992, NRC Records.

59. James L. Blaha to Commissioner Assistants, May 24, 1993, Mary Nichols to Ivan Selin, July 6, 1994, Selin to Carol M. Browner, December 21, 1994, Browner to Selin, March 31, 1995, NRC Records.

amendments was symptomatic of the debate over low-level radiation effects between the late 1970s and the early 1990s. Whether the issues were highly visible, such as the BEIR-III report or the Mancuso affair, or largely matters of concern only to those directly affected, such as the application of the Clean Air Act amendments, they were sources of controversy, uncertainty, and, frequently, acrimony. They were always complex, often convoluted, and usually incomprehensible to casual observers. The questions that stirred discord tended to obscure the broad areas of consensus on the subject of radiation protection. Although Rossi and Radford disagreed sharply and publicly over methodological aspects of the BEIR-III study, the panel members who worked on the report generally concurred on most of its major findings and on the exaggerated public fears of low-level radiation. And although the NRC and EPA took divergent positions on exposure limits, the effective differences were very small. Moreover, they used the same assumptions and basic approach when developing radiation safety programs, including adherence to the linear hypothesis, commitment to the "as low as reasonably achievable" objective, and advocacy of avoiding the risks of radiation exposure without compensating benefits.

Nevertheless, the differences among authorities and agencies over radiation hazards received the most attention. They were destined to continue as long as many key questions about radiation effects and uncertainties about radiation hazards remained to be answered. A series of remarkable research findings and notable new reports attempted to shed light on outstanding issues during the 1980s and early 1990s. They provided important information and fresh perspectives on old issues, but, perhaps inevitably, they also stirred controversy.

CHAPTER FIVE

The Ambiguities
of Radiation Effects

As debates continued over exposure limits that would protect public health from radiation hazards, new studies on the nature and
severity of those hazards appeared. A series of reports published in the
1980s and 1990s prompted a reexamination of prevailing views but
yielded no definitive conclusions. They provided a confusing and sometimes contradictory variety of assessments of the risks of exposure to low-
level radiation. While researchers presented new information on radiation, the subject remained a source of prominent media attention. It also,
from all evidence, remained a cause of acute public fears that exceeded
those raised by other environmental or industrial hazards that threatened
public health and individual well-being.

Studies of Radiation Effects
on Atomic Bomb Survivors

The most important source for evaluating the dangers of
radiation to large population groups was the study of survivors of the
atomic bombings of Hiroshima and Nagasaki. It supplied the best available epidemiological data on the effects of radiation on humans, and scientific knowledge about radiation hazards drew in significant measure
from the work of the Atomic Bomb Casualty Commission, a collabora-
tive effort by American and Japanese scientists that got under way in fall
1945. But those studies, despite the heroic efforts of the scientists who

carried them out, offered only imperfect information about low-level radiation effects.

It was impossible to calibrate with precision the doses that individuals received from the atomic blasts, though scientists were able to provide rough estimates of the exposures received by many survivors. Of more than 82,000 people who were in Hiroshima or Nagasaki when the atomic attacks occurred and whose health histories were traced, more than half received less than 10 rems of exposure, and less then 10 percent received more than 100 rems. One of the principal investigators of the effects of radiation on atomic bomb survivors, William J. Schull, reported in 1995 that the "average survivor" of the attacks on Hiroshima and Nagasaki received an "intermediate dose" of about 25 rads, and some individuals received "high doses" of as much as 600 rads. The population of the two cities received relatively heavy doses immediately after the bombs exploded. Extrapolating the results of prompt exposure to radiation at Hiroshima and Nagasaki to exposure by radiation workers or members of the public over a long period was, therefore, a problematic process that produced unavoidably uncertain conclusions.[1]

Nevertheless, in the late 1970s the studies of atomic bomb survivors remained the best available source for estimating low-level radiation hazards. Epidemiological studies of persons exposed to radiation in their jobs or in medical treatments were even more inconclusive, as the controversies over the Mancuso, Bross, and Najarian reports had demonstrated. The U.S. General Accounting Office observed in early 1981 that "there do not appear to be very many definite conclusions that can be drawn about the cancer risks of low-level ionizing radiation exposure." It added: "Considering all this uncertainty, it is not surprising that scientific and political issues have become intertwined in the public debate on radiation protection regulation."[2]

The scientific debate over radiation that had emerged in sharp relief during the preparation of the BEIR-III report in 1979–80 continued with increased intensity when new research results suggested that hazards from nuclear power and other sources of gamma radiation might be more se-

1. M. Susan Lindee, *Suffering Made Real: American Science and the Survivors at Hiroshima* (Chicago: University of Chicago Press, 1994); William J. Schull, *Effects of Atomic Radiation: A Half-Century of Studies from Hiroshima and Nagasaki* (New York: Wiley-Liss, 1995), p. 320 n. 2; SECY-85-147B (June 25, 1985), Nuclear Regulatory Commission Records, Public Document Room, Washington, D.C.

2. U.S. General Accounting Office, *Problems in Assessing the Cancer Risks of Low-Level Ionizing Radiation Exposure (EMD-81-1),* January 2, 1981.

rious than BEIR-III had indicated. The new study, published in 1981, was conducted by William E. Loewe and Edgar Mendelsohn of Lawrence Livermore National Laboratory, who used computer technology to reconstruct the atomic bomb explosions at Hiroshima and Nagasaki. They concluded that data about the radiation released by the bombs had been misinterpreted. Specifically, they found that much of the radiation at Hiroshima was in the form of gamma rays and that earlier studies had greatly overestimated the presence of neutrons, a rare form of radiation.

The new study undermined the arguments of scientists who had insisted that a linear hypothesis for estimating radiation risks exaggerated the dangers. The most outspoken proponent of this view, Harald H. Rossi, had based his position in large part on the theory that neutron radiation had caused many of the cancer cases in Hiroshima (earlier studies had recognized the predominance of gamma radiation in Nagasaki). But the Livermore study indicated that gamma radiation rather than uncommon neutron radiation was primarily responsible for the radiation deaths and injuries in Hiroshima. This suggested that the effects of gamma radiation could be more dangerous than experts had previously believed.[3]

The Livermore study renewed the controversy over radiation effects that had erupted during the preparation of the BEIR-III report. Rossi's chief rival, Edward Radford, commented that the new findings meant that the basis for the BEIR-III conclusions on radiation hazards "had collapsed." He estimated that the risks of dying from cancer after exposure to gamma radiation would be doubled. Although Radford's view received support from some experts, others took issue with his conclusions. A number of scientists expressed doubts that the Loewe-Mendelsohn findings were as definitive as Radford claimed or that they showed that low-level radiation was necessarily more dangerous than earlier estimates had suggested. Loewe and Mendelsohn themselves declared, "We take exception to statements that our results show gamma radiation is much more hazardous than previously assumed."[4]

Despite the disagreements over the meaning of the new data, scientific authorities concurred on the need for a thorough reappraisal of the Hiroshima data and its implications for low-level radiation hazards. Seymour Jablon of the National Academy of Sciences spoke for many of

---

3. Eliot Marshall, "New A-Bomb Studies Alter Radiation Estimates," *Science* 212 (May 22, 1981): 900–903; W. E. Loewe and E. Mendelsohn, "Revised Dose Estimates at Hiroshima and Nagasaki," *Health Physics* 41 (October 1981): 663–66.

4. "Letters," *Science* 213 (July 3, July 24, August 7, 1981): 6–8, 392–94, 602–4; *New York Times*, May 16, 1981.

his colleagues when he commented, "It really is urgent that we get on with this job. . . . Given the unique experience at Hiroshima and Nagasaki and the tens of millions of dollars which have been spent trying to accumulate the human biological data, it really is appalling to think that we stand here, 36 years later, debating orders of magnitude in the doses."[5]

As a result of the new information and the controversy it stirred, American and Japanese scientists undertook a series of experiments to learn more about radiation doses in Hiroshima and Nagasaki. Their work was sponsored by the Radiation Effects Research Foundation, which had replaced the Atomic Bomb Casualty Commission in 1975. At Los Alamos National Laboratory, researchers went so far as to build a replica of the bomb that had destroyed Hiroshima, which was fueled with uranium 235. Because a uranium 235 design had been used only once, in the bombing of Hiroshima, less was known about its yield and the radiation it emitted than bombs fueled with plutonium. The plutonium design had been used in the experimental explosion of the first atomic bomb in the New Mexico desert, in the bomb dropped on Nagasaki, and in postwar atomic tests. Researchers conducted experiments with the replica of the uranium 235 bomb in which they allowed the fuel to fission but not to reach the point of explosion. In this way they learned a great deal about the radiation that the Hiroshima bomb released.

The results of the new experiments on radiation from the uranium 235 bomb, which were reported in 1987, supported the findings of Loewe and Mendelsohn. They showed that very little neutron radiation was emitted in Hiroshima; at the same time they confirmed the previous estimates of radiation in Nagasaki. This indicated that most of the cancer cases in Hiroshima as well as in Nagasaki were attributable to gamma radiation. In 1985 the number of cancer and leukemia deaths in the two cities that exceeded normal rates of incidence between 1950 and 1978 was estimated to be 525. Although the cause of the "excess" cancer deaths could not be pinpointed, scientists assumed that radiation from the bombs was responsible, and the new evidence suggested that gamma radiation was primarily to blame. The new studies also concluded that many of the survivors of the atomic bombs received lower doses than previously believed. The revised estimates of radiation at Hiroshima made a reassessment of the risks of radiation exposure axiomatic, but the im-

5. Eliot Marshall, "New A-Bomb Data Shown to Radiation Experts," *Science* 212 (June 19, 1981): 1364–65.

plications of the data remained uncertain. "What this all means in terms of radiation risks," observed an article in *Science* in 1987, "is already being hotly debated."[6]

The 1990 BEIR-V Report

Once again the source of much of the debate over radiation risks was whether they conformed to a linear model. To address that question and others that the new atomic bomb studies raised, a new BEIR committee undertook a reevaluation of the BEIR-III report of 1980. In December 1989 the committee published its conclusions as BEIR-V, and it departed sharply from the earlier findings. It estimated that the risk of fatal cancer from exposure to low levels of radiation was three to four times as great as BEIR-III had projected. On the issue that had caused so much contention in the preparation of BEIR-III—the best model for predicting the consequences of exposure—the BEIR-V report reached a mixed judgment. It accepted the linear hypothesis for the induction of solid tumors but found that a linear-quadratic pattern applied to leukemia. In light of the new evidence from the atomic bomb survivors, the BEIR-V committee concluded that a linear, no-threshold model of cancer risk (other than leukemia) was most consistent with the data. But it also noted that "its risk estimates become more uncertain when applied to very low doses."[7]

In contrast to the well-publicized internal disputes that preceded the BEIR-III report, the BEIR-V committee presented its findings without dissent. Despite the estimates of substantially elevated cancer risks, Arthur C. Upton, chairman of the committee, emphasized that the BEIR-V conclusions should not cause undue alarm because they did not represent a "revolutionary change." He pointed out that BEIR-V reaffirmed the need for practices that radiation protection professionals had carried out for

6. *New York Times,* August 5, 1985; *Washington Post,* August 5, 1985; James V. Neel, Gilbert W. Beebe, and Robert W. Miller, "Delayed Biomedical Effects of the Bombs," *Bulletin of the Atomic Scientists* 41 (August 1985): 72–75; Leslie Roberts, "Atomic Bomb Doses Reassessed," *Science* 238 (December 18, 1987): 1649–51.

7. Committee on the Biological Effects of Ionizing Radiation, *Health Effects of Exposure to Low Levels of Ionizing Radiation—BEIR V* (Washington, D.C.: National Academy Press, 1990), quotation on p. 6; Eliot Marshall, "Academy Panel Raises Radiation Risk Estimate," *Science* 247 (January 5, 1990): 22–23. BEIR-IV was a study published in 1988 that focused on the hazards of radon.

years, including the assumption that no threshold for radiation injury existed, that no exposure should occur without providing a benefit, and that all doses should be kept to a level that was "as low as reasonably achievable." Upton further suggested that since most individuals received very little radiation exposure, the "average citizen should not view [BEIR-V] as a source of great concern."[8]

Despite Upton's reassurances, it was clear that the BEIR-V report provided ample reason to reevaluate existing radiation standards. In November 1990 the ICRP announced a reduction in its recommendations for occupational exposure from 5 rems to 2 rems per year for a whole-body dose. The Environmental Protection Agency and the Nuclear Regulatory Commission weighed the new risk estimates in carrying out their mandates for radiation protection. Both agencies had conducted lengthy rulemaking proceedings on radiation standards before BEIR-V appeared, and both had already taken major steps to tighten their regulations. Although EPA did not propose to revise the occupational standards it had published in 1987, the BEIR-V report played an influential role in its position on regulating radionuclides under the Clean Air Act amendments. The NRC's Part 20 revisions were not completed at the time of the publication of BEIR-V and the change in the ICRP's recommendations. The NRC carefully considered whether to reduce permissible doses further in response to the findings of the new reports. It decided against doing so, because most exposures of its licensees were well below the ICRP's new limits and the BEIR report, though based on more data than were available earlier, still was not a final verdict on low-level radiation risks.[9]

In the years following the publication of BEIR-V, some research findings supported and others raised questions about its conclusions. In 1996 the Radiation Effects Research Foundation provided new information on Japanese atomic bomb survivors that seemed to substantiate BEIR-V's estimates. It reported that cancer mortality rates followed a linear model for solid tumors at doses as low as 5 rems. Although uncertainties remained, particularly with regard to how the results from Hiroshima and Nagasaki applied to even smaller doses of radiation, the new data offered support for a linear hypothesis for levels as low as the

8. Arthur C. Upton, "Health Effects of Low-Level Ionizing Radiation," *Physics Today* 44 (August 1991): 34–39; Tim Beardsley, "Fallout," *Scientific American* 262 (March 1990): 35–36; *Washington Post*, December 20, 1989.

9. *1990 Recommendations of the International Commission on Radiological Protection (ICRP Publication 60)* (Oxford: Pergamon Press, 1991); *New York Times*, June 23, 1990.

5-rem regulatory limit for occupational exposure that was in effect in most countries.[10]

While the results of the foundation's work conformed with BEIR-V's conclusions, other research did not. In 1992 new questions arose about the radiation that the uranium 235 bomb emitted in Hiroshima. Continuing research at Livermore laboratory suggested that, contrary to the findings of the 1980s, the bomb had released a great deal of neutron radiation. Tore Straume, a biophysicist at Livermore, devised a new method for measuring neutrons, and with a team of American and Japanese scientists collected and analyzed samples of concrete from Hiroshima. Their findings suggested that a high level of neutrons was present in Hiroshima after the bomb exploded. If this were so, it indicated that survivors in Hiroshima received higher levels of radiation, especially neutron radiation, than BEIR-V had calculated. This, in turn, meant that radiation from the bomb had been less effective in causing cancer than BEIR-V had concluded, because the cancers that had occurred resulted from higher doses than BEIR-V postulated. The new findings were not definitive, but if they proved to be correct, the reassessment of radiation risks would itself need to be reassessed. As William Loewe, whose work had inspired the reevaluation that culminated in BEIR-V, commented, Straume's results could mean that the older BEIR-III estimates were "almost right by accident." Thus the evidence of radiation risks offered by the study of the survivors of the atomic bombs remained an extremely valuable but perpetually inconclusive source of information.[11]

Studies of Radiation Effects from Nuclear Power

If the conclusions of studies of the effects of exposure to radiation from the atomic bombs in Hiroshima and Nagasaki were frustratingly ambiguous, those from studies of low-level exposure to radiation from other sources were even less definitive. A series of investigations in areas near Three Mile Island, Chernobyl, and other nuclear plants and a variety of other epidemiological analyses of radiation hazards did

10. *Inside N.R.C.,* November 11, 1996.

11. Eliot Marshall, "Study Casts Doubt on Hiroshima Data," *Science* 258 (October 16, 1992): 394; *New York Times,* October 13, 1992.

not produce clear results. However, they did command a great deal of attention and, inevitably, generate controversy.

The Three Mile Island accident created enormous public fear that it would cause a heavy toll in cancer deaths in the areas around the plant. In response to allegations that the accident had sharply increased cancer mortality, the Pennsylvania Department of Health undertook a preliminary study of cancer deaths in a twenty-mile radius of the plant between 1974 and 1983. The survey, published in 1985, showed that cancer deaths were no higher than normal rates in the five years after the accident (indeed, the total number was slightly lower than expected). The Department of Health cautioned that its findings were not a final assessment because of the latent period of most cancers. The department later conducted another study of cancer rates between 1982 and 1989 among people who lived within five miles of the plant and again found no increase in cancer.[12]

The Department of Health's conclusions were corroborated in a study sponsored by the Three Mile Island Public Health Fund, which was created by a court order to study public health in the area of the plant. Three researchers from Columbia University, Maureen C. Hatch, Jeri W. Nieves, and Mervyn Susser, and one from the National Audubon Society, Jan Beyea, determined that cancer rates between 1975 and 1985 did "not provide convincing evidence that radiation releases from the Three Mile Island nuclear facility influenced cancer risk." They found that a "small wave" of excess cancers had occurred in 1982 among people living within three and one-half miles of the plant, but they observed no correlation between the incidence of cancer and radiation exposure. The research team suggested that the slightly higher cancer rates might be attributable to stress caused by the accident.[13]

In January 1997 researchers from the University of North Carolina—Steve Wing, David Richardson, Donna Armstrong, and Douglas Crawford-Brown—published an article that contested those findings. Using the same data, they contended that radiation levels from the accident were greater than Hatch and her colleagues had assumed and that the releases had caused an elevated rate of cancer, particularly lung cancer and

12. J. R. Wargo, "State Study of TMI Effects Finds No Evidence of Cancer," *Nuclear Industry* 32 (October 1985): 15–17; *Philadelphia Inquirer,* June 19, 1991.

13. Maureen C. Hatch, Jan Beyea, Jeri W. Nieves, and Marvyn Susser, "Cancer near the Three Mile Island Nuclear Plant: Radiation Emissions," *American Journal of Epidemiology* 132 (September 1990): 397–412; *Washington Post,* May 27, 1991; *Philadelphia Inquirer,* May 29, 1991.

leukemia. The arguments of the North Carolina team elicited a sharp re-buttal from Hatch, Susser, and Beyea. Complaining that Wing and his colleagues had misrepresented their methodology and conclusions, they called the article "tendentious and unbalanced." The only point on which the researchers agreed was that more study and evaluation of epidemio-logical trends around Three Mile Island were essential. In 1999 prelimi-nary findings of a new study supported the conclusion that the accident did not cause an increase in cancer. Evelyn Talbot of the University of Pitts-burgh and colleagues traced the health histories of thirty-five thousand people who lived within five miles of the plant over a period of eighteen years. They found that cancer rates were no higher than "would have been expected if the area had no nuclear power plant." Reactions to Talbot's study suggested that it would not end the uncertainties or the contro-versy over the effects of Three Mile Island on the local population.[14]

The disagreements over the impact of Three Mile Island were minor compared to the competing views that emerged over the consequences of the Chernobyl disaster of April 1986. The radiation released by the Chernobyl accident—an estimated 100 million curies—was far greater than that released at Three Mile Island—an estimated 15 curies. Therefore, it seemed apparent that the consequences for the exposed population would also be far greater. But scientists offered widely divergent estimates on how many cancer deaths Chernobyl would cause over a period of a few decades. They ranged from a few thousand to more than one hun-dred thousand; the lower end of the range would be too small to detect among cancer deaths from other causes.[15]

In the decade after Chernobyl, epidemiological data did not provide clear testimony on the likely long-term effects of the radiation released by the accident. By 1992 there was unmistakable evidence that cases of thyroid cancer among children in areas that received the heaviest doses had sharply increased. In the Gomel region of Belarus, for example, where the norm had been one or two cases of thyroid cancer among children per year, thirty-eight cases were detected in 1991. A disturbingly high num-

14. Steve Wing, David Richardson, Donna Armstrong, and Douglas Crawford-Brown, "A Reevaluation of Cancer Incidence Near the Three Mile Island Nuclear Plant: The Col-lision of Evidence and Assumptions," *Environmental Health Perspectives* 105 (January 1997): 52–57; *Washington Post,* February 24, 1997; *Philadelphia Inquirer,* February 24, 1997, March 23, 1999; *Boston Globe,* March 28, 1999.

15. Colin Norman and David Dickson, "The Aftermath of Chernobyl," *Science* 233 (Sep-tember 12, 1986): 1141–43; Lynn R. Anspaugh, Robert J. Catlin, and Marvin Goldman, "The Global Impact of the Chernobyl Reactor Accident," ibid., 242 (December 16, 1988): 1513–19.

ber of cases occurred in other sections of Belarus, located just north of the reactor site. The thyroid cancers led the World Health Organization to report that "the carcinogenic effect of radioactive fallout is much greater than previously thought."[16]

Although the incidence of thyroid cancer among children was ominous, other evidence of radiation effects was more favorable. The World Health Organization found no increase in leukemia in the populations hit hardest by fallout from Chernobyl by 1993. This was surprising, because a rise in the incidence of leukemia was the earliest sign of long-term radiation effects in Hiroshima and Nagasaki. Experts had expected that excess cases would appear among victims of Chernobyl between 1991 and 1993.[17]

The uncertain and sometimes puzzling data on the consequences of Chernobyl helped to provoke continuing controversy over the effects of the accident. In April 1996 Yuri M. Shcherbak, a physician, founder of the Ukrainian Green party, and the Ukraine's ambassador to the United States, published an article in *Scientific American* that described Chernobyl as an example of "the ever growing threat of technology run amok." He conceded that early estimates of more than one hundred thousand cancer cases from the accident appeared too high, but he suggested that "the prospects for the long-term health of children in the high-radiation regions are, sadly, poor." Shcherbak's views brought a rejoinder from Zbigniew Jaworowski of the Central Laboratory for Radiological Protection in Poland. He insisted that although Chernobyl "qualifies as an enormous industrial catastrophe . . . in terms of human fatalities, it cannot be regarded as a major one." He argued that the increase in thyroid cancer might have resulted from agents other than radiation from Chernobyl and pointed out that leukemia and other cancer rates had not risen since the accident. Shcherbak responded by inviting Jaworowski "to find a nice-looking home within the area contaminated by strontium, cesium, and plutonium where he could settle down with his family."[18]

Despite the contention over the severity of the hazards from Chernobyl's fallout, experts agreed on the importance of the data for understanding the effects of low-level radiation. Indeed, it appeared likely to replace the atomic bomb survivor studies as the best source for epidemiological information on the risks of exposure to low-level radiation. An

16. *New York Times,* September 3, 1992; *Wall Street Journal,* September 3, 1992; *Nucleonics Week,* November 18, 1993.

17. *Nucleonics Week,* April 22, 1993.

18. Yuri M. Shcherbak, "Ten Years of the Chornobyl Era," *Scientific American* 274 (April 1996): 32–37; "Damage Assessment," ibid., 275 (October 1996): 10, 12.

article in *Science* reported in 1986 that delegates to a meeting of the International Atomic Energy Agency concurred that "the Chernobyl disaster offers a unique opportunity to gain a better understanding of the effects of radiation on a large population." One expert told his colleagues that "the accident has provided conditions for a vast human experiment."[19]

While some researchers debated the effects of radiation from Three Mile Island and Chernobyl, others conducted studies of cancer rates around nuclear plants that had not suffered accidents. The most extensive survey was sponsored by the National Cancer Institute (NCI), a part of the National Institutes of Health of the U.S. Department of Health and Human Services. The NCI investigators—Seymour Jablon, Zdenek Hrubec, John D. Boice, Jr., and B. J. Stone—studied cancer deaths in 107 counties with nuclear facilities within or adjacent to their boundaries. Each county was compared to three similar "control counties." The facilities in the survey included fifty-two commercial nuclear power stations and ten Department of Energy plants. The NCI report, published in 1990, found "no evidence to suggest that the occurrence of leukemia or any other form of cancer was generally higher in the study counties than in the control counties." The authors of the study acknowledged its limitations, notably that it only examined cancer mortality, not incidence, and that it focused on entire counties rather than smaller populations within counties. Nevertheless, it was the most comprehensive and authoritative analysis of cancer risks from the normal operation of nuclear power plants.[20]

In keeping with the controversy over radiation safety, the NCI report received a mixed greeting. Michael T. Rossler of the Edison Electric Institute commented, "The study . . . shows there is not a problem to individuals, that there is not a danger from radiation." Daryl Kimball of the Physicians for Social Responsibility, by contrast, declared that the NCI survey "raises more questions than it answers" and "does not dispel the doubts and concerns that the medical community has had about the nuclear industry." Studies of nuclear hazards done in other countries generally supported the NCI's findings. A survey in France showed no increased rates of leukemia among young people who lived near nuclear plants, and a study in Canada produced similar results. But a few investigations took issue with the favorable conclusions about the effects of

19. Norman and Dickson, "Aftermath of Chernobyl," p. 1141.

20. Seymour Jablon, Zdenek Hrubec, John D. Boice, Jr., and B. J. Stone, *Cancer in Populations Living Near Nuclear Facilities (NIH Publication No. 90–874)* (Washington, D.C.: National Cancer Institute, 1990), quotation on p. 1.

low-level radiation by claiming increased risks in the area of nuclear facilities. The Massachusetts Department of Health, for example, concluded
in 1990 that leukemia rates around the Pilgrim nuclear plant were four
times higher than normal. A panel of six scientists rejected that finding
after reviewing the evidence but called for more research on the risks of
exposure to low-level radiation.[21]

Other Studies of Radiation Effects

The most controversial of the epidemiological studies of
the effects of exposure to low-level radiation was conducted in Great
Britain. Indeed, it was the British study that prompted the investigations
in the United States, France, and Canada, and it continued to generate
debate after the other studies were completed. In 1983 a British television
journalist, James Cutler, noticed a cluster of excess leukemia cases among
children in the town of Seascale. Five cases of leukemia had occurred in
children less than ten years old between 1954 and 1983; statistically, less
than one case was expected. The town is located three miles from a reprocessing plant and other nuclear facilities at Sellafield, the site of a nuclear accident that released radiation to the environment in 1957. After Cutler broadcast his findings, the British government established a committee
to investigate, and it recommended further study of the Seascale cluster.
In response, the epidemiologist Martin J. Gardner and several colleagues
set out to determine if the Sellafield complex could be linked to the cases
of leukemia in Seascale.

The results of Gardner's research, published in 1990, were both star-
tling and unsettling. After considering various possibilities, he and his colleagues suggested that there was a connection to Sellafield. In four of the
five cases of childhood leukemia in Seascale, the fathers of the victims had
worked at Sellafield and received fairly high doses (though well within
permissible limits). Their cumulative doses were about 10 rems over a period of six or seven years and about 1 rem in the six months before the
children were conceived. Gardner acknowledged that his sample was too
small to be conclusive, but even those who were skeptical of his findings

21. Tim Beardsley, "Nuclear Numbers," *Scientific American* 264 (February 1991): 30; *Nucleonics Week*, July 11, 1991; *Energy Daily*, July 5, 1991; *New York Times*, September 20, 1990,
October 25, 1990; *Patriot Ledger* (Quincy, Mass.), December 1, 1992.

agreed that his study was very well executed. If he were right, the implications for radiation protection were potentially enormous. Gardner's work seemed to indicate a genetic hazard from radiation exposure that experts had not previously recognized. Indeed, the results of forty years of genetic studies on atomic bomb survivors had shown no discernible effects among children in Hiroshima and Nagasaki conceived after the atomic attacks, even though their parents had received much heavier doses than the fathers of the Seascale leukemia victims.[22]

Gardner's findings, not surprisingly, triggered a great deal of debate (though *Science* probably exaggerated in a headline that read: "British Radiation Study Throws Experts into Tizzy"). His research also inspired new inquiries into what came to be called the "Gardner phenomenon." A study in Canada tested Gardner's theory by examining 112 cases of childhood leukemia in the vicinity of five nuclear plants. It found no correlation between the occurrence of leukemia and the occupational radiation exposure of the victims' fathers. Although the work of the Canadian researchers undermined Gardner's thesis, other investigators thought that there might be something to the Gardner phenomenon. Their view was supported by a continuing trend of excess childhood cancer in Seascale. In 1993 a new report by the British Health and Safety Executive, which monitored industrial health and safety, found that the rate of childhood leukemia in Seascale was fourteen times the national average. In other locations, however, it saw only "fragile evidence" of a connection between a father's occupational radiation exposure and childhood cancer.[23]

While researchers scrambled to identify unique characteristics of Seascale that might explain the susceptibility of its children to leukemia, Sir Richard Doll, an Oxford University epidemiologist, zeroed in on Gard-

22. Martin J. Gardner, Michael P. Snee, Andrew J. Hall, Caroline A. Powell, Susan Downes, and John D. Terrell, "Results of Case-Control Study of Leukaemia and Lymphoma among Young People Near Sellafield Nuclear Plant in West Cumbria," *British Medical Journal* 300 (February 17, 1990): 423–29; Jean L. Marx, "Lower Radiation Effect Found," *Science* 241 (September 9, 1988): 241; Leslie Roberts, "British Radiation Study Throws Experts into Tizzy," *Science* 248 (April 6, 1990): 24–25; "Radiation Risks Revisited," *Scientific American* 262 (May 1990): 36; Malcolm Grimston, "Leukaemia's Alleged Links with Nuclear Power Establishments," *Atom* 409 (January 1991): 6–10; Schull, *Effects of Atomic Radiation*, pp. 250–52, 273.

23. Richard Stone, "Can a Father's Exposure Lead to Illness in his Children?" *Science* 258 (October 2, 1992): 31; Sharon Kingman, "New Sellafield Study Poses a Puzzle," ibid., 262 (October 29, 1993): 648–49; Roberts, "British Radiation Study," ibid., 24; *Nucleonics Week*, February 27, 1992, September 24, 1992, January 21, 1993.

While the debate over the "Gardner phenomenon" proceeded, Gardner himself died of lung cancer (*Nucleonics Week*, February 4, 1993).

ner's theory. He contended that if Gardner were right, many more cases of childhood leukemia should have shown up among children of Sellafield workers in other nearby areas. Because childhood cancer rates in other locations were not higher than expected, he maintained that the Gardner thesis was seriously deficient. Those conclusions did not go unchallenged. A representative for the environmental group Greenpeace acknowledged "problems with the Gardner hypothesis" but questioned Doll's findings on the basis that he accepted official reports of radiation exposures for Sellafield employees.[24]

The uncertainties and controversies that surrounded reports on the effects of radiation from Three Mile Island, Chernobyl, Sellafield, and other nuclear plants were also apparent in surveys of the risks of occupational radiation exposure. Some of the occupational investigations showed little or no correlation between low-level exposure and elevated cancer risks. A thirteen-year study conducted by researchers from Johns Hopkins University of the health effects of radiation among workers at eight naval shipyards, begun shortly after Najarian had reported elevated rates of leukemia at the Portsmouth naval shipyard in 1978, found no increased risk of cancer. A study of nuclear plant workers in the United States, Great Britain, and Canada performed by the International Agency for Research on Cancer produced similar results. In a report published in 1994, it concluded that existing radiation protection standards and practices, based on evidence from the atomic bomb survivors, were sound. And in 1996 a panel sponsored by the National Academy of Sciences discovered that U.S. sailors who participated in the Bikini atomic bomb tests of 1946 had not suffered elevated cancer rates from their exposure to radiation.[25]

Balanced against those encouraging findings were others that were considerably gloomier. Steve Wing of the University of North Carolina, who later published an analysis of higher than normal cancer risks from the Three Mile Island accident, concluded in a 1991 article that workers at Oak Ridge National Laboratory had a clearly elevated risk of cancer from radiation, even when their exposure did not exceed permissible limits. "I think it's disturbing," commented Wing. "We have seen an association between cancer mortality and radiation doses at a very low level." The following year, Alice Stewart, who during the 1950s had first identified a cor-

24. "Paternal Dose Disputed as Cause of Child Cancer," *Nuclear News* 36 (November 1993): 80; Sara Downs, "Hiroshima's Shadow over Sellafield," *New Scientist* 140 (November 13, 1993): 25–29; *New York Times,* March 8, 1994.

25. "Best Estimates of Low-Level Radiation Risk," *Nuclear News* 37 (December 1994): 48; *New York Times,* November 3, 1991; *Washington Post,* October 30, 1996.

relation between in utero x-ray exposure and leukemia in children and who had worked with Thomas Mancuso in the final stages of his controversial study, reported similar results at Hanford. She and her colleague, George W. Kneale, who had also collaborated with Mancuso, found that 3 percent of Hanford employees who worked between 1944 and 1978 had died from occupational radiation exposure that was within permissible levels. The findings of the Wing and Stewart surveys were contested by other researchers, who suggested that their results used a sample that was too small to be conclusive and that they did not adequately account for other possible causes of the higher cancer rates they detected.[26]

The Wing and Stewart studies offered support for the claim that radiation standards were too lax. Stewart commented in 1992, "It is increasingly clear that BEIR V and other similar bodies relied upon to establish radiation safety standards substantially underestimated the cancer risk of occupational exposure."[27] As the debate continued over the studies that indicated that exposure to low-level radiation carried more serious risks than authorities had recognized, some researchers took a dramatically conflicting position. The linear hypothesis held that even the energy in very low doses of radiation could damage DNA strands in cells and that eventually mutations that occurred in this way could lead to cancer. In their radiation protection regulations, the NRC, EPA, and other agencies had always assumed that any amount of radiation that an individual received could cause cancer, though, of course, the chances were greater at higher doses. Their regulations were based on the linear model's assumption that no threshold dose of radiation safety existed.

By the mid-1990s some experts were insisting that the linear hypothesis vastly overstated the dangers of low-level radiation exposure and that radiation protection regulations were unnecessarily restrictive. Their conclusions were grounded in part on the results of epidemiological studies that showed little or no harm from exposure to low-level radiation among atomic plant workers, medical patients, and Japanese atomic bomb survivors whose exposures had been relatively light (they rejected the statistical analysis of the Radiation Effects Research Foundation that supported a linear model for cancer mortality rates in Hiroshima and Nagasaki at doses as low as 5 rems). Those who dissented from the linear hypothesis

26. *Washington Post,* March 20, 1991; *Wall Street Journal,* March 20, 1991; *Washington Times,* March 20, 1991; *New York Times,* December 8, 1992; Len Ackland, "Radiation Risks Revisited," *Technology Review* 96 (February–March 1993): 56–61.

27. *Energy Daily,* December 9, 1992.

also based their claims on research that demonstrated that cells had "amazingly sophisticated" repair mechanisms that made the induction of cancer from low-level radiation highly improbable. The new findings indicated that only if the cell repair mechanisms were overwhelmed by heavy doses of radiation was the likelihood of cancer appreciably increased.[28]

Critics of the linear hypothesis argued that it was a seriously flawed basis for radiation protection and called for a complete overhaul of existing regulations. Myron Pollycove, an emeritus professor of laboratory medicine and radiology at the University of California–San Francisco and a consultant to the Nuclear Regulatory Commission, contended that the result of adherence to a linear model was to "impair health care, research, and other benefits of nuclear technology, and waste many billions of dollars annually for protection against theoretical risks." He and other authorities suggested that small doses of radiation, far from being a threat to health, were beneficial to individuals. The argument that the risks of low-level radiation exposure had been greatly overestimated and that regulations should be revised, not surprisingly, aroused spirited opposition. The battle between those who believed that the linear hypothesis was too permissive and those who considered it overly strict was, in the words of a Department of Energy official, "like a religious dispute. . . . It's very, very intense."[29]

The controversy over the effects of low-level radiation continued, even after decades of research that produced new data and exemplary scientific analyses of its meaning. On balance, the studies were encouraging; with the exception of those members of the populations in Hiroshima and Nagasaki and areas around Chernobyl who received relatively heavy doses, most studies of low-level radiation showed few, if any, consequences, or at least no obvious health impact, in exposed populations. But those reports, as their authors readily acknowledged, were not definitive judgments. The difficulty of sorting out the effects of radiation ruled out conclusive findings; it was impossible to distinguish in an unassailable way

28. *Nucleonics Week,* October 28, 1993; Jim Muckerheide, "The Health Effects of Low-Level Radiation: Science, Data, and Corrective Action," *Nuclear News* 38 (September 1995): 26–34; "HPS: Low-Dose Effects May Be Nonexistent," *Nuclear News* 39 (April 1996): 18–19; Theodore Rockwell, "What's Wrong with Being Cautious?" *Nuclear News* 40 (June 1997): 28–32; Marvin Goldman, "Cancer Risk of Low-Level Exposure," *Science* 271 (March 29, 1996): 1821–22; *Energy Daily,* April 19, 1996.

29. "Threshold Argument Continues at Annual Symposium," *Nuclear News* 39 (November 1996): 39–40; Myron Pollycove, "The Rise and Fall of the Linear No-Threshold Theory of Radiation Carcinogenesis," ibid., 40 (June 1997): 34–37; *Nucleonics Week,* November 20, 1997, November 27, 1997; *Washington Post,* April 14, 1997.

cancer cases or birth defects caused by radiation from those caused by other agents. Further, in most cases it was still too early for firm determinations about radiation effects. Even fifty years of studying Japanese atomic bomb survivors did not yield results that could be regarded as final. The uncertainties inherent in the data about low-level radiation and the conclusions that experts drew from them both prompted and sustained controversy.

Public Fear of Radiation

Amid ambiguities about the effects of exposure to low-level radiation, one aspect of radiation protection stood out with remarkable clarity—the deep-seated fear that radiation generated among a large segment of the public. One example was a public opinion sampling of college students and members of the League of Women Voters that was taken in Oregon in 1978. It showed greater fear of nuclear power than of activities that caused tens of thousands of deaths every year. Asked to rank thirty sources of risk "according to the present risk of death from each," both groups rated nuclear power as number one, ahead of smoking, motor vehicles, motorcycles, handguns, and alcoholic beverages. This response probably reflected in part the widely held misconception that a nuclear plant could explode like an atomic bomb. A Harris poll conducted in 1975, for example, showed that 39 percent of those surveyed believed that a failure in a nuclear power plant could produce a "massive nuclear explosion" (24 percent thought this could not occur, and 37 percent were not sure). But the results of the Oregon poll that ranked nuclear power as the number one risk, it seems safe to assume, also testified to acute public fear of radiation.[30]

Radiation stood in a class by itself among environmental toxins and hazardous manufactured products in its ability to incite public dread. Robert L. DuPont, a practicing psychiatrist who specialized in studying "phobia," which he defined as "fear based on an exaggerated, unrealistic danger," argued in 1980 that low-level radiation from nuclear power was

30. Paul Slovic, Baruch Fischhoff, and Sarah Lichtenstein, "Rating the Risks," *Environment* 21 (April 1979): 14–21, 36–39; Stanley M. Nealy, Barbara D. Melber, and William L. Rankin, *Public Opinion and Nuclear Energy* (Lexington, Mass.: Lexington Books, 1983), p. 83.

uniquely capable of inspiring anxieties that were out of proportion to risk. "Nothing else," he declared, "is so apt to produce phobic fear." As early as 1949 C. F. Behrens, the head of the U.S. Navy's recently established atomic medicine division, had arrived at a similar conclusion about public attitudes toward radiation. "There are some peculiar ideas relative to radiation that are related to primitive concepts of hysteria and things in that category," he observed. "There is such a unique element in it; for some it begins to border on the mystical."[31]

Researchers offered a variety of explanations for the intensity of public fear of radiation and the concomitant antipathy toward nuclear power. One of the earliest and most prevalent theories held that radiation is especially terrifying because it is undetectable to human senses. A report sponsored by the World Health Organization in 1957, for example, suggested that because radiation "cannot be seen, heard, smelt, tasted, or felt, it easily provokes irrational phantasies." Without denying the importance of the imperceptibility of radiation in arousing anxieties, other analysts have cited additional considerations that fuel public fear. One is the involuntary imposition of risk from radiation released by nuclear power facilities. Individuals view the technology as something beyond their control; large outside forces, such as the nuclear industry, utilities, and the federal government, determine the level of risk, weigh the hazards against the benefits, and set standards of safety. This contrasts with statistically more dangerous activities that individuals assume voluntarily, such as smoking or driving.

Another consideration in risk perception is whether or not a risk is immediate and dramatic. The impact of a major catastrophe that kills or injures many people at once is greater than a series of less visible or disastrous tragedies, even if the toll of many isolated events far exceeds that of a single event. In the case of radiation from nuclear power, the specter of a catastrophic accident dominated public attitudes toward the safety of the technology. To make matters more frightening, Kai Erikson argued, a radiological accident has no definite end; uncertainty about the long-term effects of exposure continues. "Invisible contaminants remain a part of the surroundings," he wrote. "An 'all clear' is never sounded." Public views of risk are also dependent on the degree of familiarity with a hazard. In a book on the Three Mile Island accident, the historians Philip L.

31. *Nuclear Phobia—Phobic Thinking about Nuclear Power* (Washington, D.C.: Media Institute, 1980), pp. 2–7; Advisory Committee on Human Radiation Experiments, *Final Report* (Washington, D.C.: Government Printing Office, 1995), pp. 21, 42.

Cantelon and Robert C. Williams emphasized this element in public apprehension by comparing modern-day fears of radiation with fourteenth-century fears of the bubonic plague. Both, they maintained, derived in significant measure from a dread of unknown and seemingly unfathomable hazards.[32]

Those considerations, taken alone or in combination, are helpful in understanding the bases of public fears about radiation and nuclear power. But they do not in themselves fully explain attitudes toward radiation because they do not clearly distinguish it from hazards with similar characteristics. Other potential dangers to health, such as chemicals, electrical shocks, or ultraviolet rays, cannot be detected by human senses, at least until they cause injury or disease. Many industrial practices impose involuntary risks over which individuals have little or no control, such as producing electricity from fossil fuels, placing additives in food, and engineering genetic materials. A number of industries and activities have a demonstrated capacity for causing "big event" catastrophes, such as toxic chemical releases, airplane crashes, or dam failures. In many of those cases, especially the dangers inherent in the production of noxious chemicals, the effects of long-term exposure can be as uncertain, unending, and unfamiliar as those from radiation.

It seems apparent, therefore, that additional considerations help to account for the singularly acute public fear of radiation. The major ingredient that seldom receives sufficient attention is the historical context of efforts to ensure adequate radiation protection. Indeed, public attitudes toward radiation cannot be fully understood in the absence of historical explanation. The historical axiom that distinguishes radiation from other hazards of a similar nature is that after the end of World War II radiation hazards were perpetually in the news. They were much more visible than other hazards and usually depicted in a way that fueled public fears. As a result of its history, radiation achieved its unique standing among a plethora of agents that posed a threat to public health.

Public fear of radiation predated the scientific achievement of nuclear fission in the 1930s and 1940s. Publicity about the hazards of x-rays and radium, especially the afflictions of the radium dial painters, attracted

32. *Nuclear Phobia*, pp. 11, 24–29; H. W. Lewis, *Technological Risk* (New York: W. W. Norton, 1990), pp. 26–41; Kai T. Erikson, "Radiation's Lingering Dread," *Bulletin of the Atomic Scientists* 47 (March 1991): 34–39; Robert L. DuPont, "The Nuclear Power Phobia," *Business Week*, September 7, 1981, pp. 14–16; Philip L. Cantelon and Robert C. Williams, *Crisis Contained: The Department of Energy at Three Mile Island* (Carbondale: Southern Illinois University Press, 1981), pp. 9–10.

sporadic public attention in the decades before World War II. Books, articles, films, and other sources depicted radioactive elements both as life-giving and life-enhancing rays and as malevolent death rays. Neither image prevailed, and public apprehension about radiation remained subdued. Nevertheless, by the late 1930s, as the historian Spencer R. Weart has concluded, "there was already a special anxiety connected with radioactive life-forces."[33]

Those anxieties were substantially magnified by the development and use of atomic bombs. Although the initial public reactions to the bombings of Hiroshima and Nagasaki focused on the force of the blasts, within a short time accounts of the effects of radiation, embellished in a wide variety of science fiction books and articles, comics, and films, combined to accentuate public fears about the hazards of radiation for living and future generations. Those fears were given greater intensity and perhaps greater legitimacy by the fallout controversy of the late 1950s and early 1960s. The fallout debate called sustained attention to the risks of exposure to low-level radiation for the general population more than any previous treatment of the subject. It made radiation safety a bitterly contested political issue for the first time, and it fueled already growing public apprehension of exposure. It also seriously undermined the credibility of the AEC, which received a great deal of criticism for placing the most benign interpretation on the radioactive consequences of nuclear testing. In 1981, when the governor of Nevada, Robert List, was asked about why the people of his state were so strongly opposed to a radioactive waste disposal site within their state, he responded, "It goes back to the atmospheric testing in the 1950s. The AEC misled the public and [now] people don't trust the authorities."[34]

The Limited Test Ban Treaty of 1963, which prohibited atmospheric testing by its signatories, effectively ended the fallout debate, at least as a prominent public issue. But it did not halt the increasing public concern about low-level radiation that the fallout controversy had fostered. This was evident in public protests against the construction of nuclear power plants in the early 1960s. Critics of the proposed Ravenswood plant in New York City and the Bodega Bay and Malibu plants in California cited their concern about radiological contamination if the reactors were built.

33. Spencer R. Weart, *Nuclear Fear: A History of Images* (Cambridge, Mass.: Harvard University Press, 1988), p. 54.

34. Luther J. Carter, *Nuclear Imperatives and Public Trust: Dealing with Radioactive Wastes* (Washington, D.C.: Resources for the Future, 1987), p. 79.

As utilities ordered increasing numbers of nuclear plants in the late 1960s, fear of radiation played a major role in spawning criticism of and opposition to nuclear power. By the early 1970s the arguments of Gofman and Tamplin and others who claimed that nuclear power plants would cause thousands of cancer deaths every year were making national headlines.[35]

Even when the controversy over the allegations of Gofman and Tamplin diminished, growing antinuclear activism kept the dangers, or alleged dangers, of radiation from nuclear power highly visible among the public. A cover story on the nuclear power debate in *Newsweek* in April 1976, for example, featured a photograph of a mother holding two young children and a poster that asked, "What Do You Do in Case of a Nuclear Accident?" It gave a hauntingly apocalyptic answer: "Kiss Your Children Goodbye."[36]

In other cases, a message about the dangers of radiation was delivered in a lighter vein that perhaps was equally effective in influencing public attitudes. In May 1977, for example, Johnny Carson, host of "The Tonight Show," posed as the confused and illogical "Floyd R. Turbo" for his approximately ten million viewers. "Floyd" explained his reasons for supporting nuclear power and took issue with nuclear critics: "They say if there is a leak in a nuclear power plant the radiation can kill you. Nix! Radiation cannot kill you because it contains absolutely no cholesterol." "Floyd" also countered the argument that radiation could "hurt your reproductive organs" by commenting: "My answer is, so can a hockey stick. But we don't stop building them."[37]

The revival of controversy over radiation effects returned the subject to national headlines. The claims of atomic veterans, the concerns that citizens who lived downwind from the Nevada test site had suffered abnormally high rates of cancer, the Mancuso, Najarian, and Bross studies of radiation effects, the BEIR-III report, and other issues won a great deal of media and public attention in the late 1970s and early 1980s. A series of lawsuits in which atomic veterans, downwinders, and others pressed claims for compensation and charged the government with willful negligence in its nuclear testing programs attracted considerable media coverage. The trials highlighted in sharp relief not only the uncertainties about the effects of low-level radiation but also the hostility between radiation

35. J. Samuel Walker, *Containing the Atom: Nuclear Regulation in a Changing Environment, 1963–1971* (Berkeley and Los Angeles: University of California Press, 1992), pp. 64, 91, 349–51.

36. "How Safe Is Nuclear Power?" *Newsweek,* April 12, 1976, p. 70.

37. "Johnny Carson Sets Us Straight," *Nation* 224 (June 18, 1977): 745.

protection professionals who took opposing positions in their testimony. The attention that the debate over the effects of low-level radiation received during the 1980s, while substantial, was small compared to that commanded by the Three Mile Island accident in 1979 and the Chernobyl disaster of 1986. Each generated enormous publicity that focused in significant measure on the hazards of radiation and the projected consequences of the releases from the damaged plants.[38]

At the same time that the effects of radioactive fallout from nuclear bomb testing and from Three Mile Island and Chernobyl were triggering new concerns, another radiation issue rose to prominence. In the mid-1980s high concentrations of radon, a naturally occurring radioactive gas that is a decay product of radium, were discovered in populated sections of Pennsylvania, New Jersey, New York, and other parts of the country. Radon gas is a potentially serious cause of lung cancer, though the precise magnitude of its threat is, like all estimates of radiation effects, uncertain. The Environmental Protection Agency, drawing on projections of lung cancer deaths based on the experiences of uranium miners who received doses much heavier than residential levels, undertook a massive campaign to convince Americans to test their homes for radon gas and to take corrective action if hazardous levels were found. EPA's actions, which received generous coverage in the press, included the publication of booklets and television advertisements about the threat of lung cancer from radon. Critics complained that EPA vastly overstated the risks of radon to public health while downplaying the scientific debate over the severity of the hazards. In the case of radon, unlike that of radiation from other sources, the public seemed largely indifferent, or at least insufficiently concerned to test their homes for radon levels.[39]

The public seemed more concerned, however, about reports of public exposure to radiation from government activities. In the late 1980s and early 1990s a series of articles about radiation releases, some intentional and some inadvertent, from nuclear weapons production plants generated a flurry of excitement and condemnation of the Atomic Energy Commission and its successor, the Department of Energy. In perhaps the most notorious case, the Hanford weapons facility secretly discharged large amounts of iodine 131 and other radioactive elements into the atmosphere

38. Barton C. Hacker, *Elements of Controversy: The Atomic Energy Commission and Radiation Safety in Nuclear Weapons Testing, 1947–1974* (Berkeley and Los Angeles: University of California Press, 1994), pp. 266–72.

39. Leonard A. Cole, *Element of Risk: The Politics of Radon* (New York: Oxford University Press, 1993); *New York Times,* February 20, 1998.

in December 1949 to test environmental monitoring methods and learn more about the nature of radioactive fallout. The releases of radiation to the environment of the areas surrounding the plants that occurred in the early cold war era fed fears of increased rates of cancer and other diseases. At about the same time that the radiation releases from weapons plants were making headlines, the NRC's "below regulatory concern" policy statement attracted considerable media attention and an outburst of public denunciation.[40]

In late 1993 and early 1994 media coverage, and from all indications, public outrage, reached new heights over reports of experiments on radiation effects conducted on human subjects between 1945 and 1974. This story, as Charles C. Mann put it in *Science,* sent the nation's press into "one of its classic feeding frenzies." The stories that appeared brought renewed focus on radiation and placed the government in a distinctly unfavorable light. They also helped to persuade President William J. Clinton to launch an investigation of the radiation experiments. The presidential commission he appointed determined that some ethical abuses had taken place in the conduct of research on human subjects, particularly the injection of plutonium in patients without informed consent or expectation of therapeutic benefits and in the tracer studies conducted at the Fernald school and elsewhere. But the commission also pointed out that much of the work performed between 1945 and 1974 provided valuable data and that government researchers had demonstrated more sensitivity to ethical issues than many press accounts of the experiments indicated.[41]

In summer 1997 a familiar subject — radioactive fallout from atmospheric bomb testing during the 1950s and early 1960s — returned to the headlines. The National Cancer Institute reported that tests in Nevada had spread high levels of iodine 131 to areas far from the site of the ex-

40. William Lanouette, "Reporting on Risk: Who Decides What's News?" *Risk: Health, Safety and Environment* 5 (Summer 1994): 223–32; Terrence R. Feyner and F. G. Gosling, "Coming In from the Cold: Regulating U.S. Department of Energy Nuclear Facilities, 1942–96," *Environmental History* 1 (April 1996): 4–33; Michele Stenehjem Gerber, *On the Home Front: The Cold War Legacy of the Hanford Nuclear Site* (Lincoln: University of Nebraska Press, 1992), pp. 79–112; U.S. General Accounting Office, *Nuclear Health and Safety: Examples of Post World War II Radiation Releases at U.S. Nuclear Sites (GAO/RCED-94-51FS),* November 24, 1993; Advisory Committee on Human Radiation Experiments, *Final Report,* pp. 506–38.

41. Advisory Committee on Human Radiation Experiments, *Final Report,* pp. 758–75; Charles C. Mann, "Radiation: Balancing the Record," *Science* 263 (January 28, 1994): 470–73; Roger M. Anders, "Writing Cold War History: The DOE Human Radiation Experiments Experience," *Society for History in the Federal Government Occasional Papers,* No. 2 (1999): 29–44.

plosions, including "hot spots" in New England, the Midwest, and Idaho, Montana, and the Dakotas. It emphasized that no clear link had been established between iodine 131 in fallout and thyroid cancer, but it also estimated that contaminated milk from the tests could cause between 10,000 and 75,000 cases of thyroid cancer in the United States. The anger and alarm that the report produced was compounded by the revelation that although the AEC did not warn milk producers about possible contamination, it did alert the Eastman Kodak Company and other firms that fallout could damage the film they manufactured. "It really is odd," commented Senator Tom Harkin of Iowa in September 1997, "that the Government would warn Kodak about its film but it wouldn't warn the general public about the milk it was drinking."[42]

Early in 1999 a study conducted by the Fred Hutchinson Cancer Research Center of Seattle provided a more encouraging evaluation of the effects of iodine 131 fallout. It showed no increase in thyroid cancer among more than three thousand people who had been exposed to radiation releases from Hanford as children. This was welcome news, but it did not resolve the uncertainty about radiation exposure or visibly mitigate suspicion of the federal government. The Hutchinson Center's report was greeted skeptically by downwinders and other critics. As Susan Nielsen, a columnist for the *Seattle Times,* wrote, "Even if every scientist in America blessed the study, Hanford's downwinders still would not believe." And, she added, in light of the historical record, especially the human radiation experiments and the government's lack of candor about fallout hazards, "who could blame them?"[43]

For a period of more than fifty years, radiation hazards were a source of an abundance of sustained publicity and, as a result, of uniquely intense public fears. Reports of the threat of radiation to public health tended to emphasize bad news. Lauriston S. Taylor, who held very strong views on the subject after five decades of leadership in the field of radiation protection, complained bitterly in 1978, "Of the many dozens of [popular] articles that I have read over the years, I do not recall any that have not contained gross errors of fact as well as what can only be regarded as deliberate distortions designed to alarm the reader." An article published in

42. *USA Today,* July 25, 1997; *Washington Post,* July 26, 1997, August 2, 1997, October 2, 1997; *New York Times,* July 29, 1997, August 13, 1997, September 30, 1997, October 2, 1997; Pat Ortmeyer and Arjun Makhijani, "Worse Than We Knew," *Bulletin of the Atomic Scientists* 53 (November–December 1997): 46–50.

43. *New York Times,* January 28, 1999; *Seattle Times,* January 14, 1999, March 15, 1999; *Portland Oregonian,* February 1, 1999.

the *Journal of the American Medical Association* in 1991 reached similar, if less strident, conclusions. It compared newspaper coverage of two articles published earlier in the journal, one by Steven Wing and colleagues on a higher incidence of leukemia at Oak Ridge and one by National Cancer Institute researchers on the lack of evidence for increased cancer rates in areas around nuclear power plants. The study found that the disturbing conclusions of Wing's article received more attention than the encouraging conclusions of the National Cancer Institute.[44]

Nevertheless, the content of media reports on radiation effects did not clearly distinguish it from other environmental and industrial dangers, which were also often treated in inflammatory or ill-informed ways.[45] Even when news reports on radiation were balanced and accurate, the information they offered was frequently unsettling. The distinction between accounts of radiation effects and those of other technological hazards was more quantitative than qualitative; radiation was unique in remaining a regular source of headlines for five decades. After Hiroshima, the many ramifications of atomic energy were big news, and the effects of radiation were a major part of the story. The nature of radiation risks generated public apprehension, but the prevalent anxieties were greatly enhanced by the visibility that radiation issues commanded. Although most experts agreed that public fears of low-level radiation far exceeded the risks of exposure, those fears were hardly unreasonable based on the information or impressions that the public gleaned from the popular media.

Conclusion

Radiation safety organizations and federal agencies that followed their recommendations acted responsibly and judiciously to protect radiation workers and the public from the risks of low-level exposure from industrial, medical, and other civilian applications. From the early 1930s, when the first tolerance doses were issued, the ICRP, the NCRP,

---

44. Gideon Koren and Naomi Klein, "Bias against Negative Studies in Newspaper Reports of Medical Research," *JAMA: The Journal of the American Medical Association* 266 (October 2, 1991): 1824–26; Lauriston S. Taylor, "Radiation Safety: Pitfalls and Some Solutions," draft, [1978], Box 51 (Sense of Humor in Radiation Protection), Lauriston S. Taylor Papers, Francis A. Countway Library, Boston, Massachusetts; *Los Angeles Times,* September 13, 1994.

45. See, for example, Allan Mazur, *A Hazardous Inquiry: The Rashomon Effect at Love Canal* (Cambridge, Mass.: Harvard University Press, 1998), pp. 121–41, 210.

and other groups drew on the best available scientific information to arrive at their recommendations on permissible levels of exposure. They applied existing knowledge in conservative ways in an effort to provide a wide margin of safety for both occupational and population exposure. As new research findings were published, they reconsidered and often revised their recommendations. Critics cited the fact that the ICRP and the NCRP called for lower permissible doses and that the AEC, the NRC, and other agencies tightened their regulations over the years as evidence that the older standards had been too lax. But the revisions were reasonable in light of new scientific information and the likelihood of increasing public exposure to radiation; adhering to obsolete standards surely would not have been a desirable alternative. Radiation protection professionals denied that earlier permissible levels had proven to be dangerous and insisted that newer standards extended the margin of safety.

Radiation experts and government agencies did not claim that the permissible doses they adopted were unerringly safe. As a matter of policy, they did not apply a threshold theory to the practice of radiation protection. They acted on the premise that, in the absence of findings to the contrary, exposure in any amount presented a risk of injury. Their objective was to establish standards and regulations that provided ample, if not absolute, safety and still allowed the use of radiation sources. Although the term "as low as reasonably achievable" was not adopted until the 1970s, radiation protection organizations and government agencies had followed the principles it embodied for decades. They sought to develop recommendations, in the cases of the ICRP and the NCRP, and regulations, in the cases of government agencies, that offered exposure limits that were generally safe and at the same time technologically and economically feasible.

The difficulty of striking such a balance created a great deal of controversy. There was much disagreement over the levels that seemed "safe enough" and the extent to which they provided a reasonable trade-off for the benefits of radiation sources. Although the permissible doses that radiation professionals published were based on careful and thoughtful analysis of available information, they were not unassailable. The most common complaint was that the standards are overly lax and exposed the population, at least in theory, to levels of radiation that could cause serious harm. This kind of criticism first became prominent during the fallout controversy of the 1950s and early 1960s. The AEC was deeply concerned that public anxieties about low-level radiation would impair its nuclear weapons testing programs and, as a result, played down the potential threat to public health that fallout conceivably represented. The AEC forfeited its own credibility during the fallout debate and never recovered it.

During the late 1960s and early 1970s the lack of trust in the AEC's priorities and performance on radiation safety issues contributed to the bitterness of the allegations against the agency's programs. Even as the AEC took important steps to make its regulations more stringent, it was accused of indifference to the hazards of low-level exposure. The connection between the AEC's rules for radiation releases from commercial nuclear plants and the bomb testing activities that stirred public apprehensions was indirect; the Part 20 regulations first adopted in 1957 did not apply to fallout. One sign of the separation of functions within the AEC was that it followed the lead of the NCRP by tightening its regulations for commercial applications in the midst of the fallout controversy. But the fact that the AEC was responsible for both weapons testing and the regulation of commercial nuclear power obscured the distinctions between its programs and undermined the credibility of its judgment on all radiation safety issues.

In the decades after the controversy over fallout from atmospheric weapons testing declined in prominence, the AEC, the NRC, and other agencies were criticized most frequently for using radiation standards that were insufficiently rigorous. By the mid-1990s, however, existing radiation standards were also under attack for being too strict. Grounding their arguments on the lack of epidemiological or empirical evidence that showed a clear link between low-level exposure and harmful health effects, some radiation professionals claimed that a reassessment of the prevailing assumptions used in radiation protection was long overdue. They denied that the linear no-threshold model was a valid basis for policy and cited the high costs that it imposed. One of the leading advocates of this position, Theodore Rockwell, a veteran of the U.S. Navy's nuclear programs and a founding director of a group called Radiation, Science, and Health, Inc., complained that his colleagues in the field of radiation protection failed to recognize the costs of excessive caution. He suggested that the assumption that exposure to any amount of radiation might cause injury produced "five different kinds of harm: billions of dollars wasted, ridiculous regulations imposed that degrade the credibility of science and government, destructive fear generated, detrimental health effects created, and environmental degradation accelerated."[46]

46. Rockwell, "What's Wrong with Being Cautious?" p. 28.

In the absence of definitive evidence about the effects of low-level exposure, disputes over radiation hazards seemed destined to resist a widely acceptable resolution. Reporting on the differing views aired at an international conference in Seville, Spain, in November 1997, the trade journal *Nucleonics Week* observed, "The controversy promises to continue for decades as more information is amassed on the way radiation affects the human organism."[47] More than a century after Roentgen discovered x-rays, scientists had learned a great deal about the effects of radiation but not enough to reach firm conclusions about the hazards that low doses present. The debates among experts on the risks of low-level radiation were a testimony to the complexity and ambiguity of the subject and to the difficulty of making policy decisions that would satisfy those who took conflicting positions.

Radiation protection was controversial not only because of scientific uncertainties but also because of political sensitivities. Deciding on a level of radiation exposure that seemed appropriate for workers and the public necessarily involved a bewildering array of public health, energy, environmental, and national defense issues that inevitably aroused differing views. The questions that required consideration were not strictly scientific matters. They included, for example, whether the need for testing atomic weapons in the atmosphere outweighed the possible public health effects of radioactive fallout, whether the benefits of nuclear power plants were a fair return for the radiation they emitted, and whether the anxieties of the public about radiation should take precedence over the judgment of experts who were much less concerned about low-level effects. The politics of radiation protection made the seemingly timeless question of what constituted an acceptable level of exposure a divisive, emotional, and highly visible issue after the mid-1950s.

47. *Nucleonics Week,* November 27, 1997.

Essay on Sources

This book draws heavily on the records of federal agencies involved in radiation protection. The records of the Nuclear Regulatory Commission (NRC) were the basic source; they include an abundant variety of documents relating to radiation standards designed to protect workers and the public from radioactivity produced by nuclear fission. The records of the NRC also include regulatory materials from its predecessor agency, the Atomic Energy Commission (AEC). The NRC records cited in the notes are available to the public for research at the agency's Public Document Room, 2120 "L" Street NW, Washington, D.C. Other AEC records are housed by another of its successor agencies, the Department of Energy (DOE). To consult documents in the custody of DOE that are cited in this volume (as AEC/DOE), researchers should contact the department's History Division. The "Records Relating to the Study of Health and Mortality among Atomic Energy Workers—Mancuso Study" are available as a part of Record Group 434 (General Records of the Department of Energy) at the National Archives in College Park, Maryland.

A substantial body of Environmental Protection Agency (EPA) records (Record Group 412) from the Office of the Administrator for the period 1970–82 is open at the National Archives in College Park. Although it does not include specific files on EPA's radiation programs, it contains a few materials of value on the subject. The records of EPA also include the files that it inherited from the Federal Radiation Council. The records of the Joint Committee on Atomic Energy, part of Record Group 128 (Records of the Joint Committees of Congress), have some useful items on radiation protection. They are housed at the National Archives in Washington, D.C. The U.S. Public Health Service has microfilmed a large number of records relating to its role in radiation safety that are maintained by the library of its Division of Radiological Health in Rockville, Maryland. The archives of the National Academy of Sciences in Washington, D.C., contain files on the BEIR report of 1972, mostly of an administrative nature.

In addition to agency records, the personal papers of key individuals contain important documents on the history of radiation protection. The papers of Lauriston S. Taylor at the Francis A. Countway Library, Harvard University School of Public Health, Boston, Massachusetts, are voluminous and essential. They include a rich variety of published and unpublished materials from the many facets of Taylor's long career in the field of radiation protection. The papers of Herbert M. Parker, another leader in the field for many years, contain useful materials on a wide range of subjects. They are housed in the university archives at the University of Washington in Seattle. The papers of Presidents Richard M. Nixon, Gerald R. Ford, and Jimmy Carter include some unique and valuable documents on radiation issues that reached the White House. The Nixon papers are in the Richard M. Nixon Presidential Materials Project at the National Archives in College Park; the Ford papers, in the Gerald R. Ford Library in Ann Arbor, Michigan; and the Carter papers, in the Jimmy Carter Library in Atlanta, Georgia. There are a few items of interest in the papers of Chet Holifield and Craig Hosmer at the University of Southern California, Los Angeles; the Chesapeake Bay Foundation at the University of Maryland, College Park; the Union of Concerned Scientists at the Institute Archives of the Massachusetts Institute of Technology, Cambridge; Morris K. Udall at the University of Arizona, Tucson; and Barry Commoner at the Library of Congress, Washington, D.C.

In addition to archives and manuscripts, published sources provided very useful information for this study. Lauriston S. Taylor compiled a massive collection of documents on the history of the National Committee on Radiation Protection and the International Commission on Radiological Protection that was published as *Organization for Radiation Protection: The Operations of the ICRP and NCRP, 1928–1974* (Springfield, Va.: National Technical Information Service, 1979). Trade publications offer valuable news and insights that often are not available elsewhere, especially for recent events. I have benefited greatly from reports in *Nucleonics Week, Inside N.R.C., Inside E.P.A., Energy Daily, Nuclear News,* and *Nuclear Industry.* Congressional hearings, scientific journals, and newspapers and popular magazines informed this study on debates among scientists over radiation issues, public views of radiation hazards, and other important matters.

The secondary literature on the history of radiation protection is not large, but it has recently been greatly enriched by several excellent scholarly accounts. Barton C. Hacker draws on a staggering array of sources to provide an evaluation of radiation safety in nuclear weapons testing programs in two books, *The Dragon's Tail: Radiation Safety in the Manhattan Project, 1942–1946* (Berkeley and Los Angeles: University of California Press, 1987), and *Elements of Controversy: The Atomic Energy Commission and Radiation Safety in Nuclear Weapons Testing, 1947–1974* (Berkeley and Los Angeles: University of California Press, 1994). M. Susan Lindee traces the history of the Atomic Bomb Casualty Commission and the problems it faced in *Suffering Made Real: American Science and the Survivors at Hiroshima* (Chicago: University of Chicago Press, 1994). William Schull, a leading scientist for the Atomic Bomb Casualty Commission, offers a wealth of information in terms accessible to a layperson in *Effects of Atomic Radiation: A Half-Century of Studies from Hiroshima and Nagasaki* (New York: Wiley-Liss, 1995). Bettyann Holtzman Kevles, *Naked to the Bone: Medical Imaging in the Twentieth Century* (New Brunswick: Rutgers University Press, 1997), is an engaging analysis of the scientific, medical, and cultural impact of x-rays and later technologies used to see inside the body.

The *Final Report* of the Advisory Committee on Human Radiation Experiments (Washington, D.C.: Government Printing Office, 1995) is a balanced and informative assessment of a sensitive and highly publicized subject. Leonard A. Cole surveys the debate over radon policies in *Element of Risk: The Politics of Radon* (New York: Oxford University Press, 1993). Spencer R. Weart, *Nuclear Fear: A History of Images* (Cambridge, Mass.: Harvard University Press, 1988), is the definitive work on public fears of all things related to nuclear energy. Claudia Clark, *Radium Girls: Women and Industrial Health Reform, 1910–1935* (Chapel Hill: University of North Carolina Press, 1997), is a detailed account of the tragedies that befell the radium dial painters. She emphasizes the role of the Consumers' League in calling attention to the plight of the dial painters and condemns the scientific community for failing to make clear the hazards of radium, but she overstates the level of scientific understanding of the effects of internal emitters. Catherine Caufield, *Multiple Exposures: Chronicles of the Radiation Age* (New York: Harper and Row, 1989), is a readable overview that contains some valuable information on the history of radiation protection. But it must be used with caution. It draws on few primary sources and, perhaps as a result, is flawed by inaccuracies and oversimplifications.

A few older studies remain useful to anyone with an interest in the history of radiation protection. Lawrence Badash, *Radioactivity in America: Growth and Decay of a Science* (Baltimore: Johns Hopkins University Press, 1979), is indispensable for understanding what scientists knew about radiation in the early twentieth century. Jack Schubert and Ralph E. Lapp, *Radiation: What It Is and How It Affects You* (New York: Viking Press, 1957), is a good introduction to the use and hazards of radiation even forty years after its publication. Gilbert F. Whittemore, "The National Committee on Radiation Protection, 1928–1960: From Professional Guidelines to Government Regulation" (Ph.D. diss., Harvard University, 1986), promises to become the standard work on the NCRP when it is published in book form.

Other works that I have published offer more details on the AEC's radiation protection regulations than are included in this volume. See George T. Mazuzan and J. Samuel Walker, *Controlling the Atom: The Beginnings of Nuclear Regulation, 1946–1962* (Berkeley and Los Angeles: University of California Press, 1984); J. Samuel Walker, *Containing the Atom: Nuclear Regulation in a Changing Environment, 1963–1971* (Berkeley and Los Angeles: University of California Press, 1992); and J. Samuel Walker, "The Atomic Energy Commission and the Politics of Radiation Protection, 1967–1971," *Isis* 85 (March 1994): 57–78. For a brief discussion, see J. Samuel Walker, "The Controversy over Radiation Safety: A Historical Overview," *JAMA: The Journal of the American Medical Association* 262 (August 4, 1989): 664–68.

Other books and articles on topics related but not central to the history of radiation protection that I found to be helpful are cited in the footnotes.

Index

Advisory Committee on the Biological
Effects of Ionizing Radiations (BEIR),
47–51
Advisory Committee on the Medical Uses
of Isotopes (AEC), 84, 88
"ALARA" rule, 57–66, 154; and EPA
emissions standards, 121, 128; and NRC-
revised Part 20 regulations, 108–9, 111, 114
American Association for the Advance-
ment of Science, 41
American Board of Health Physics, 81
American Board of Nuclear Medicine, 81
American College of Nuclear Medicine, 81
American College of Nuclear Physicians,
81, 122
American College of Radiology, 81
American Journal of Medical Sciences, 2
American Medical Association, on use of
x-rays, 6–7
Anders, William A., 59
Anderson, Jack, 95
antinuclear groups, 115, 119
Arab-Israeli War, 75
Argonne National Laboratory, 60–62
Armstrong, Donna, 136
Ash, Roy L., 75–76
Asselstine, James K., 111–12
Atomic Bomb Casualty Commission, 129,
132
Atomic Energy Act of 1946, 13–14
Atomic Energy Act of 1954, 26, 29–30

Atomic Energy Commission (AEC),
13–18; abolished, 29, 60; atmospheric
testing by, 20; attempts to tighten
public exposure standards, 31–35; avoid-
ance of excessive regulation by, 119;
credibility of, 22, 95, 148, 150–52, 154–55;
disagreements with EPA on design
guidelines, 72–73; exemptions for materials with negligible risks, 115–16;
fallout controversy and, 20, 22–23; and
Gofman-Tamplin controversy, 65–66;
human research sponsored by, 16–17;
internal conflict with regulatory staff,
31–35, 41; issues radiation-protection
standards, 26; jurisdictional conflict
with EPA, 68–76, 78–79; medical-
radiation regulation, 84–85; military
orientation of, 13; occupational standards, 108; promotion of nuclear-power
commercial applications by, 26, 30–31;
public-safety areas of responsibility, 14–
15, 29; relationship with EPA, 68–76;
relationship with NCRP, 15–16. *See also*
design guidelines
Atomic Industrial Forum, 113
atomic tests: atmospheric, 18–20, 91–92;
fallout controversy, 18–28, 37

Baltimore Gas and Electric, 113
Barnard Free Skin and Cancer Hospital, 13
Batzel, Roger E., 41